The
ANATOMY

of
NONSENSE

Yvor Winters

NEW DIRECTIONS *Norfolk, Connecticut*

CARL A. RUDISILL LIBRARY
LENOIR RHYNE COLLEGE

810.4
W 73a

69635

April, 1970

CONTENTS

PRELIMINARY
PROBLEMS

First Problem

Is it possible to say that Poem A (one of Donne's *Holy Sonnets,* or one of the poems of Jonson or of Shakespeare) is better than Poem B (Collins' *Ode to Evening*) or vice versa?

If not, is it possible to say that either of these is better than Poem C (*The Cremation of Sam Magee,* or something comparable)?

If the answer is no in both cases, then any poem is as good as any other. If this is true, then all poetry is worthless; but this obviously is not true, for it is contrary to all our experience.

If the answer is yes in both cases, then there follows the question of whether the answer implies merely that one poem is better than another for the speaker, or whether it means that one poem is intrinsically better than another. If the former, then we are impressionists, which is to say relativists; and are either mystics of the type of Emerson, or hedonists of

9

the type of Stevens and Ransom. If the latter, then we assume that constant principles govern the poetic experience, and that the poem (as likewise the judge) must be judged in relationship to those principles. It is important, therefore, to discover the consequences of assuming each of these positions.

If our answer to the first question is no and to the second yes, then we are asserting that we can distinguish between those poems which are of the canon and those which are not, but that within the canon all judgment is impossible. This view, if adopted, will require serious elucidation, for on the face of it, it appears inexplicable. On the other hand, one cannot deny that within the canon judgment will become more difficult, for the nearer two poems may be to the highest degrees of excellence, the harder it will be to choose between them. Two poems, in fact, might be so excellent that there would be small profit in endeavoring to say that one was better, but one could arrive at this conclusion only after a careful examination of both.

Second Problem

If we accept the view that one poem can be regarded as better than another, the question then arises whether this judgment is a matter of inexplicable intuition, or whether it is a question of intuition that can be explained, and consequently guided and improved by rational elucidation.

If we accept the view that the judgment in question is inexplicable, then we are again forced to confess ourselves impressionists and relativists, unless we can show that the intuitions of all men agree at all times, or that the intuitions of one man are invariably right and those of all others wrong whenever they differ. We obviously can demonstrate neither of these propositions.

If we start, then, with the proposition that one poem may be intrinsically superior to another, we are forced to account for differences of opinion regarding it. If two critics differ, it is possible that one is right and the other wrong, more likely that both are partly right and partly wrong, but in different respects: neither the native gifts nor the education of any man have ever been wholly adequate to many of the critical problems he will encounter, and no two men are ever the same in these respects or in any others. On the other hand, although the critic should display reasonable humility and caution, it is only fair to add that few men possess either the talent or the education to justify their being taken very seriously, even of those who are nominally professional students of these matters.

But if it is possible by rational elucidation to give a more or less clear account of what one finds in a poem and why one approves or disapproves, then communication between two critics, though no doubt imperfect, becomes possible, and it becomes possible that they may in some measure correct each other's errors and so come more near to a true judgment of the poem.

Third Problem

If rational communication about poetry is to take place, it is necessary first to determine what we mean by a poem.

A poem is first of all a statement in words.

But it differs from all such statements of a purely philosophical or theoretical nature, in that it has by intention a controlled content of feeling. In this respect, it does not differ from many works written in prose, however.

A poem differs from a work written in prose by virtue of its being composed in verse. The rhythm of verse permits the expression of more powerful feeling than is possible in prose when such feeling is needed, and it permits at all times the expression of finer shades of feeling.

A poem, then, is a statement in words in which special pains are taken with the expression of feeling. This description is merely intended to distinguish the poem from other kinds of writing; it is not offered as a complete description.

Fourth Problem

What, however, are words?

They are audible sounds, or their visual symbols, invented by man to communicate his thoughts and feelings. Each word has a conceptual content, however slight; each word, exclusive, perhaps, of the particles, communicates vague associations of feeling.

The word *fire* communicates a concept; it also connotes very vaguely certain feelings, depending on the context in which we happen to place it—depending, for example, on whether we happen to think of a fire on a hearth, in a furnace, or in a forest. These feelings may be rendered more and more precise as we render the context more and more precise; as we come more and more near to completing and perfecting our poem.

Fifth Problem

But if the poem, as compared to prose, pays especial attention to feeling, are we to assume that the rational content of the poem is unimportant to its success?

The rational content cannot be eliminated from words; consequently the rational content cannot be eliminated from poetry. It is there. If it is unsatisfactory in itself, a part of the poem is unsatisfactory; the poem is thus damaged beyond argument. If we deny this, we must surely explain ourselves very fully.

If we admit this, we are faced with another problem: is it conceivable that rational content and feeling-content may both be perfect, and yet that they may be unrelated to each other, or imperfectly related? To me this is inconceivable, because the emotional content of words is generated by our experience with the conceptual content, so that a relationship is necessary.

This fact of the necessity of such relationship may fairly return us for a moment to the original question: whether imperfection of rational content damages the entire poem. If there is a necessary relationship between concept and feeling, and concept is unsatisfactory, then feeling must be damaged by way of the relationship.

Sixth Problem

If there is a relationship between concept and feeling, what is the nature of that relationship?

To answer this, let us return to the basic unit, the word. The concept represented by the word, motivates the feeling which the word communicates. It is the concept of fire which generates the feelings communicated by the word, though the sound of the word may modify these feelings very subtly, as may other accidental qualities, especially if the word be used skillfully in a given context. The accidental qualities of a word, however, such as its literary history, for example, can only modify, cannot essentially change, for these will be governed ultimately by the concept; that is, *fire* will seldom be used to signify *plum-blossom,* and so will have few opportunities to gather connotations from the concept, *plum-blossom.* The relationship, in the poem, between rational statement and feeling, is thus seen to be that of motive to emotion.

Seventh Problem

But has not this reasoning brought us back to the proposition that all poems are equally good? For if each word motivates its own feeling, because of its intrinsic nature, will not any rational statement, since it is composed of words, motivate the feeling exactly proper to it?

This is not true, for a good many reasons, of which I shall enumerate only a few of the more obvious. In making a rational statement, in purely theoretical prose, we find that our statement may be loose or exact, depending upon the relationships of the words to each other. The precision of a word depends to some extent upon its surroundings. This is true likewise with respect to the connotations of words. Two words, each of which has several usably close rational synonyms, may reinforce and clarify each other with respect to their connotations or they may not do so.

Let me illustrate with a simple example from Browning's *Serenade at the Villa:*

> So wore night; the East was gray,
>   White the broad-faced hemlock flowers.

The lines are marred by a crowding of long syllables and difficult consonants, but they have great beauty in spite of the fault. What I wish to point out, for the sake of my argument, is the relationship between the words *wore* and *gray*. The verb *wore* means literally that the night passed, but it carries with it connotations of exhaustion and attrition which belong to the condition of the protagonist; and grayness is a color which we associate with such a condition. If we change the phrase to read: "Thus night passed," we shall have the same rational meaning, and a meter quite as respectable, but no trace of the power of the line: the connotation of *wore* will

be lost, and the connotation of *gray* will remain merely in a
state of ineffective potentiality. The protagonist in seeing his
feeling mirrored in the landscape is not guilty of motivating
his feeling falsely, for we know his general motive from the
poem as a whole; he is expressing a portion of the feeling
motivated by the total situation through a more or less common
psychological phenomenon. If the poem were such, however,
that we did not know why the night *wore* instead of *passed,*
we should have just cause for complaint; in fact, most of the
strength of the word would probably be lost. The second line
contains other fine effects, immediately with reference to the
first line, ultimately with reference to the theme; I leave the
reader to analyze them for himself, but he will scarcely succeed without the whole poem before him.

Concepts, as represented by particular words, are affected
by connotations due to various and curious accidents. A word
may gather connotations from its use in folk-poetry, in formal
poetry, in vulgar speech, or in technical prose: a single concept might easily be represented by four words with these distinct histories; and any one of the words might prove to be
proper in a given poetic context. Words gain connotation from
etymological accidents. Something of this may be seen in the
English word *outrage,* in which is commonly felt, in all likelihood, something associated with *rage,* although there is no
rage whatever in the original word. Similarly the word *urchin,*
in modern English, seldom connotes anything related to
hedgehogs, or to the familiars of the witches, by whose intervention the word arrived at its modern meaning and feeling.
Yet the connotation proper to any stage in the history of such
a word might be resuscitated, or a blend of connotations ef-
fected, by skillful use. Further, the connotation of a word may
be modified very strongly by its function in the metrical structure, a matter which I shall discuss at length in connection
with the theories of Ransom.

This is enough to show that exact motivation of feeling by concept is not inherent in any rational statement. Any rational statement will govern the general possibilities of feeling derivable from it, but the task of the poet is to adjust feeling to motive precisely. He has to select words containing not only the right relationships within themselves, but the right relationships to each other. The task is very difficult; and this is no doubt the reason why the great poetry of a great poet is likely to be very small in bulk.

Eighth Problem

Is it not possible, however, to escape from this relationship of motive to emotion by confining ourselves very largely to those words which denote emotion: love, envy, anger, and the like?

This is not possible, for these words, like others, represent concepts. If we should confine ourselves strictly to such a vocabulary, we should merely write didactic poetry: poetry about love in general, or about anger in general. The emotion communicated would result from our apprehension of the ideas in question. Such poetry is perfectly legitimate, but it is only one kind of poetry, and it is scarcely the kind which the Romantic theorist is endeavoring to define.

Such poetry has frequently been rendered particular by the use of allegory. The playful allegorizing of minor amoristic themes which one encounters in the Renaissance and which is possibly descended from certain neo-Platonic elements in medieval poetry may serve as illustration. Let us consider these and the subsequent lines by Thomas Lodge:

> Love in my bosom like a bee
> Doth suck his sweet;
> Now with his wings he plays with me,
> Now with his feet.

Love itself is a very general idea and might include many kinds of experience; the idea is limited by this allegory to the sentimental and sensual, but we still have an idea, the subdivision of the original idea, and the feeling must be appropriate to the concept. The concept is rendered concrete by the image of Cupid, whose actions, in turn, are rendered visible by comparison to the bee: it is these actions which make the poem a kind of anticipatory meditation on more or less sensual love, a meditation which by its mere tone of expression keeps the subject in its proper place as a very minor one. Sometimes the emphasis is on the mere description of the bee, sometimes on the description of Cupid, sometimes on the lover's feeling; but the feeling motivated in any passage is governed by this emphasis. The elements, once they are united in the poem, are never really separated, of course. In so far as the poet departs from his substantial theme in the direction of mere bees and flowers, he will achieve what Ransom calls irrelevance; but if there is much of this the poem will be weakened. Whether he so departs or not, the relation of motive to emotion must remain the same, within each passage. I have discussed this problem in my essay on Ransom.

A common romantic practice is to use words denoting emotions, but to use them loosely and violently, as if the very carelessness expressed emotion. Another is to make a general statement, but seem to refer it to a particular occasion, which, however, is never indicated: the poet thus seems to avoid the didactic, yet he is not forced to understand the particular motive. Both these faults may be seen in these lines from Shelley:

> Out of the day and night
> A joy has taken flight;
>   Fresh spring, and summer, and winter hoar,
> Move my faint heart with grief, but with delight
>   No more—oh, never more.

The poet's intention is so vague, however, that he achieves nothing but stereotypes of a very crude kind.

The Romantics often tried other devices. For example, it would be possible to write a poem on fear in general, but to avoid in some measure the effect of the purely didactic by illustrating the emotion along the way with various experiences which might motivate fear. There is a danger here, though it is merely a danger, that the general idea may not dominate the poem, and that the poem may thus fall apart into a group of poems on particular experiences. There is the alternative danger, that the particular quality of the experiences may be so subordinated to the illustrative function of the experiences, that within each illustration there is merely a stereotyped and not a real relationship of motive to feeling: this occurs in Collins' *Ode to Fear,* though a few lines in the Epode come surprisingly to life. But the methods which I have just described really offer no semblance of an escape from the theory of motivation which I am defending.

Another Romantic device, if it is conscious enough to be called a device, is to offer instead of a defensible motive a false one, usually culled from landscape. This kind of writing represents a tacit admission of the principle of motivation which I am defending, but a bad application of the principle. It results in the kind of writing which I have called pseudo-reference in my volume, *Primitivism and Decadence.* One cannot believe, for example, that Wordsworth's passions were charmed away by a look at the daffodils, or that Shelley's were aroused by the sight of the leaves blown about in the autumn wind. A motive is offered, and the poet wants us to accept it, but we recognize it as inadequate. In such a poem there may be fragments of good description, which motivate a feeling more or less purely appropriate to the objects described, and these fragments may sustain our liking for the poem: this happens in Collins' *Ode to Evening;* but one will find also an account of some kind of emotion essentially irrelevant to the objects described, along with the attempt, more or less explicit, to deduce the emotion from the object.

There remains the method of the Post-Romantics, whether French Symbolists or American Experimentalists: the method of trying to extinguish the rational content of language while retaining the content of association. This method I have discussed in *Primitivism and Decadence,* and I shall discuss it again in this book.

Ninth Problem

The relationship in the poem of rational meaning to feeling we have seen to be that of motive to emotion; and we have seen that this must be a satisfactory relationship. How do we determine whether such a relationship is satisfactory? We determine it by an act of moral judgment. The question then arises whether moral judgments can be made, whether the concept of morality is or is not an illusion.

If morality can be considered real, if a theory of morality can be said to derive from reality, it is because it guides us toward the greatest happiness which the accidents of life permit: that is, toward the fullest realization of our nature, in the Aristotelian or Thomistic sense. But is there such a thing, abstractly considered, as full realization of our nature?

To avoid discussion of too great length, let us consider the opposite question: is there such a thing as obviously unfulfilled human nature? Obviously there is. We need only turn to the feeble-minded, who cannot think and so cannot perceive or feel with any clarity; or to the insane, who sometimes perceive and feel with great intensity, but whose feelings and perceptions are so improperly motivated that they are classed as illusions. At slightly higher levels, the criminal, the dissolute, the unscrupulously selfish, and various types of neurotics are likely to arouse but little disagreement as examples.

Now if we are able to recognize the fact of insanity—if in fact we are forced to recognize it—that is, the fact of the obvious maladjustment of feeling to motive, we are forced to admit the possibility of more accurate adjustment, and, by necessary sequence, of absolutely accurate adjustment, even though we admit the likelihood that most people will attain to a final adjustment but very seldom indeed. We can guide ourselves toward such an adjustment in life, as in art, by means of theory and the critical examination of special instances; but the final act of judgment is in both life and art a unique act—it is a relationship between two elements, the rational understanding and the feeling, of which only one is classificatory and of which the other has infinite possibilities of variation.

Tenth Problem

If the final act of adjustment is a unique act of judgment, can we say that it is more or less right, provided it is demonstrably within the general limits prescribed by the theory of morality which has led to it? The answer to this question is implicit in what has preceded; in fact the answer resembles exactly that reached at the end of the first problem examined. We can say that it is more or less nearly right. If extreme deviation from right judgment is obvious, then there is such a thing as right judgment. The mere fact that life may be conducted in a fairly satisfactory manner, by means of inaccurate judgment within certain limits, and that few people ever bother to refine their judgment beyond the stage which enables them to remain largely within those limits, does not mean that accurate judgment has no reality. Implicit in all that has preceded is the concept that in any moral situation, there is a right judgment as an ultimate possibility; that the human judge, or actor, will approximate it more or less nearly; that the closeness of his approximation will depend upon the accuracy of his rational understanding and of his intuition, and upon the accuracy of their interaction upon each other.

Eleventh Problem

Nothing has thus far been said about human action, yet morality is supposed to guide human action. And if art is moral, there should be a relationship between art and human action.

The moral judgment, whether good, bad, or indifferent, is commonly the prelude and instigation to action. Hastily or carefully, intelligently or otherwise, one arrives at some kind of general idea of a situation calling for action, and one's idea motivates one's feeling: the act results. The part played by will, or the lack of it, between judgment and act, the possibility that action may be frustrated by some constitutional or habitual weakness or tendency, such as cowardice or a tendency to anger, in a person of a fine speculative or poetic judgment, are subjects for a treatise on ethics or psychology; a treatise on poetry stops with the consideration of the speculative judgment, which reaches its best form and expression in poetry. In the situations of daily life, one does not, as a rule, write a poem before acting: one makes a more rapid and simple judgment. But if the poem does not individually lead to a particular act, it does not prevent action. It gives us a better way of judging representative acts than we should otherwise have. It is thus a civilizing influence: it trains our power of judgment, and should, I imagine, affect the quality of daily judgments and actions.

Twelfth Problem

What, then, is the nature of the critical process?

It will consist (1) of the statement of such historical or biographical knowledge as may be necessary in order to understand the mind and method of the writer; (2) of such analysis of his literary theories as we may need to understand and evaluate what he is doing; (3) of a rational critique of the paraphrasable content (roughly, the motive) of the poem; (4) of a rational critique of the feeling motivated—that is, of the details of style, as seen in language and technique; and (5) of the final act of judgment, a unique act, the general nature of which can be indicated, but which cannot be communicated precisely, since it consists in receiving from the poet his own final and unique judgment of his matter and in judging that judgment. It should be noted that the purpose of the first four processes is to limit as narrowly as possible the region in which the final unique act is to occur.

In the actual writing of criticism, a given task may not require all of these processes, or may not require that all be given equal emphasis; or it may be that in connection with a certain writer, whether because of the nature of the writer or because of the way in which other critics have treated him previously, one or two of these processes must be given so much emphasis that others must be neglected for lack of space. These are practical matters to be settled as the occasions arise.

HENRY

ADAMS

OR THE CREATION OF CONFUSION

I. *The Historical Background*

HENRY ADAMS saw modern history as a progress from unified understanding, or the illusion of such, in the century following the year 1150, toward the dispersion of understanding and force in the twentieth century; and he saw himself as the product of an earlier New England. In regard to himself he was correct; and as for modern history, his view of it, though scarcely defensible, provides a clue to certain historical processes of which the history of New England is perhaps the most dramatic single illustration.

The history immediately relevant to an understanding of Adams' mind might be said to begin with the first great theological critics of Aquinas, especially with Ockham. Aquinas endeavored as far as possible to establish a separation between philosophy and theology; philosophy was guided by natural reason, theology was derived from Revelation. But he believed that philosophical knowledge was possible, and in his pursuit of it, he composed the most complete and lucid critique of previous philosophy that had been made, and the most thorough and defensible moral and philosophical system, in all likelihood, that the world has known.

Ockham, the most profound of the medieval nominalists, struck at the very heart of this philosophy by attacking the reality of universals, by endeavoring to show the illusory nature of all ideas whatsoever. Etienne Gilson has described the immediate results as follows: [1]

Thus blended together, Empiricism and theologism made a most explosive combination. At the top of the world, a God whose absolute power knew no limits, not even those of a stable nature endowed with a necessity and an intelligibility of its own. Between His will and the countless individuals that co-exist in space or succeed each other and glide away in time, there was strictly nothing. Having expelled from the mind of God the intelligible world of Plato, Ockham was satisfied that no intelligibility could be found in any one of God's works. How could there be order in nature, when there is no nature? And how could there be a nature when each singular being, thing, or event, can claim no other justification for its existence than that of being one among the elect of an all-powerful God? That was not the God of theology, but of theologism; for though the living God of theology be infinitely more than the "Author of Nature," He is at least that, whereas Ockham's God was not even that. Instead of being an eternal source of that concrete order of intelligibility and beauty, which we call nature, Ockham's God was expressly intended to relieve the world of the necessity of having any meaning of its own. The God of theology always vouches for nature; the jealous God of theologism usually prefers to abolish it.

The universe of Ockham here described bears a precise resemblance, as we shall eventually see, to the universe

[1] *The Unity of Philosophical Experience,* by Etienne Gilson, Scribners, 1937. P. 85.

of Henry Adams, with this exception: that in the universe of Henry Adams there is no God. In the universe of Ockham, all morality and moral knowledge, or what we call such, are independent of nature, and depend directly from the arbitrary will of God; and had that will chanced to be otherwise, they would then have been otherwise. We have no way of obtaining knowledge of man through the study of man: we are the recipients of arbitrary instructions which we disobey at our peril. In the universe of Aquinas, which resembles in many important respects that of his great predecessor, Aristotle, we can learn a great deal by the light of natural reason. The universe was created by God, it is true; but it was so created as to pursue its own laws, and those laws, including many which govern the nature of man, can be discovered with reasonable accuracy after careful examination of the data before us. The risk which Ockham ran is clearly stated by Gilson: [2]

Different as they may be, owing to the various times, places and civilizations in which they were conceived. these doctrines resemble each other at least in this, that all of them are thoroughly intoxicated with a definite religious feeling which I beg leave to call, for simplicity's sake, the feeling of the Glory of God. Needless to say, there is no true religion without that feeling. The deeper it is, the better it is; but it is one thing to experience a certain feeling deeply, and another thing to allow it to dictate, uncontrolled by reason, a completely rounded interpretation of the world. When and where piety is permitted to inundate the philosophical field, the usual outcome is that, the better to extol the Glory of God, pious-minded theologians proceed joyfully to annihilate God's own creation. God is great and high and almighty; what better proof could be given of these truths than that nature and man are essentially insignificant, low and utterly powerless creatures? A very dangerous method indeed, for in the long run it is bound to hurt both philosophy and religion. In such a case the sequence of doctrines too often runs in the following way: with the best intentions in the world, some

[2] Ibid. pp. 37-8.

theologian suggests, as a philosophically established truth, that God
is and does everything, while nature and man are and do nothing;
then comes a philosopher who grants the theologian's success in
proving that nature is powerless, but emphasizes his failure to prove
that there is a God. Hence the logical conclusion that nature is
wholly deprived of reality and intelligibility. This is scepticism, and
it cannot be avoided in such cases. Now one can afford to live on
philosophical scepticism, so long as it is backed by a positive religious faith; yet, even while our faith is there, one still remains a
sceptic in philosophy, and were faith ever to go, what would be left
of us but an absolute sceptic?

Once a more or less Ockhamist position is taken, there are
various ways by which faith may be lost, as one can discover
by examining the history of European thought from the time
of Ockham to the present. Moreover, Ockham was by no
means the inventor of the general religious position which he
took; he was merely the last of its great defenders, and as a
logician the greatest of them. The type of Christianity to place
faith, which results from an act of the will made possible by
Divine Grace, above understanding, has its first great exponent in Augustine, but is older than Augustine. This type of
Christianity, the fideistic, or voluntaristic, derives all knowledge from faith and Revelation, and refuses to take the natural reason seriously; and although some voluntarists are willing to argue rationally from Revelation, their theology leads
commonly and rapidly to a daily dependence upon Grace and
distrust of reason—that is, to extreme mysticism. Aquinas was
a sane enough man to wish to make the most of all his faculties, and a good enough Christian to believe that God had
given him his faculties for use.

The voluntaristic tradition seems to have grown upon Christianity of all kinds since the fifteenth century, but especially
upon the western churches severed from Rome. Voluntarism
is an easy form of Christianity for those who are not vigorous

intellectually but who are slow to give up old habits, and it may for this reason have gained upon the Church of England and upon the Episcopal Church in the United States, churches in which faith seems to have died so slowly and gently that its demise is only half suspected today.[3] It was in Calvinism, however, that voluntarism received its logical expression, and it was in New England that Calvinism was able to work out its own natural development with less interference or outside influence than was possible anywhere in Europe.

The Calvinistic doctrines were all doctrines that should have followed naturally from the position taken by Ockham: the doctrine of predestination, or the arbitrary separation from all eternity of the few to be saved from the many to be damned; the doctrine of God's Decrees, or the predestination from all eternity of every event, to the falling of the last leaf; the doctrine of justification by faith alone; the doctrine, closely allied to the last, of the inefficaciousness of good works; and the doctrine of Grace as an experience essentially mystical and almost melodramatic in its violence.

Yet the Christians of the Reformation, in spite of their anti-moral theology, were extremely moral people; and the Reformation itself was in a large measure a protest against the abuses which had grown up in the Roman Church during a period of decadence. One needed courage, both physical and moral, to go with Luther and Calvin; and of those who believed with the reformers in England, perhaps the most convinced, the most indomitably moral, were those who went into the wilderness rather than compromise their convictions.

But their morality remained fideistic. Good works were good, not because of their intrinsic worth, but because God

---

[3] One of the many amusing comments which I have heard attributed to the late David Starr Jordan goes somewhat as follows: "The Episcopal Church is so constituted that its members can really believe anything; but of course almost none of them do."

had arbitrarily termed them so; good works were the fruits of faith, but could accomplish nothing in themselves; and faith was the arbitrary gift of God, which only a few would receive. Works apparently good, but performed by those not of the elect, were a delusion. And yet in most Calvinistic systems, and by nearly all Calvinistic preachers, man was held morally responsible to God for his behavior. The Calvinists, in refusing to distinguish, with Aquinas, between the ideas of Divine prescience and Divine predestination, which was purely a philosophical matter, found themselves confronted with the very practical conflict between the ideas of predestination and of man's moral responsibility for his acts. The wiser Calvinistic writers have admitted that the ideas are logically incompatible with each other and have said that the conflict is a mystery understood by God alone; but the New England Calvinists, in the isolation of their new community, endeavored all too often to argue their way free; and the result was the destruction of theology. Since the philosophic understanding of morality was essentially lost in their tradition, the source of it having been renounced, the death of theology, which alone could give authority for moral principles or behavior, was a very serious matter; and it was the more serious because New England Calvinism had generated in its adherents very intense moral habits.

These habits, as I have indicated, must have been very strong in the founders of Massachusetts, and the continuation of them may have been in part merely the biological inheritance of a constitutional tendency; but the situation in Massachusetts must have done much to perpetuate and strengthen them. The New Englanders, as predestinarians, believed that they had been sent into a new land to found a pure church; not only were they the elect of God, but they represented the ultimate and predestined culmination of Christian history, which in turn was the predestined triumph of all preceding

human history: these simple men in a struggle for life against
the wilderness represented the dramatic victory of religion,
toward which God had ordained the progress of the world.
This view was seriously taken, and it was seriously expressed
at the time by many writers; the reader may examine it in
its completeness in Cotton Mather's Introduction to the *Mag-
nalia Christi Americana,* an Introduction of which the opening recalls the opening of the *Aeneid,* and which sets out to
summarize the matter of the Christian epic:

> I write the *Wonders* of the Christian Religion, flying from the
> depravations of *Europe,* to the *American Strand:* and, assisted by
> the Holy Author of that *Religion,* I do, with all conscience of
> *Truth,* required therein by Him, who is the *Truth* itself, report the
> *wonderful displays* of His infinite Power, Wisdom, Goodness, and
> Faithfulness, wherewith His Divine Providence hath *irradiated* an
> *Indian Wilderness.*

The morality of these men may have been in fact merely
habitual, but in theory it was predestined and arbitrary, as I
have said. It did not derive, theoretically, from an understanding of human nature and a desire to improve human nature
by careful and enlightened modification. It derived from the
arbitrary will of God: God had given a few simple commands
for behavior, and they were to be obeyed simply and literally.
The theology employed by the 17th century church in New
England modified original Calvinism in certain important
respects; the most important being with reference to the signs
of election. The importance of the mystical experience was
minimized; in its place was encouraged the belief that a man
might know himself one of the elect when he decided to enter
the church and conform to its principles. The doctrine of
predestination was not altered by this belief, for the decision,
apparently an act of the private will, had been predestined.

Every human act thus became a sign in an allegory, as did
every event in nature. If a man sinned, it was fairly obvious

that he was an evil man and one of the damned, in spite of the
theoretic but negligible possibility that he might be predestined to a later repentance and ultimate salvation. The most
insignificant events were predetermined by God in accord-
ance with his eternal plan: by a cast of the dice one might
discover God's will, for the fall of the dice was predestined;
though it is hard in these later days to understand why con-
firmed predestinarians should ever have required the intervention of the dice, when they had renounced with abhorrence the intervention of the Church of Rome.

Further, until the time of Andros, the church ruled the
state; and it was not until the charter of 1692 that there was
any real relaxation of the theory that the church had a right
to do so, and the relaxation, when it came, was merely the
slow beginning of a long process. The result was the fixing of
certain social and mental habits, stronger, in all probability,
than any others which have ever permeated a society at all its
levels. Morality was strong, simple, and arbitrary; and under
the influence of the doctrine of predestination, it transformed
the human mind into an allegorical machine. One can open
the diary of Cotton Mather almost at random and verify this
assertion: people encountered casually on the street, the vicissitudes of private experience, a dog urinating at a wall, were
signs which Mather read for their divine meaning. And one
can verify the assertion in innumerable minor documents of
the time. This allegorism was not a literary movement or device, such as one meets among the neo-Platonists in various
periods; nor was it the property of an academic class, like the
medieval realism which expressed itself in a somewhat less
allegorical allegory than that of the Puritans, for example in
that of Dante; nor was it a pedagogic device for instructing
the illiterate, such as one meets at the lower levels of medieval
literature, doubtless as a result of the influence of the realists;
it was a form of the mind in daily life, a way of seeing the

universe, which appears to have been common to an entire society, and it persisted well into the nineteenth century, after the ideas which had given rise to it had long since passed away. The works of Hawthorne, Melville, Henry James, and Henry Adams are its belated fruits in literature; in fact the diary of Cotton Mather and the *Education* of Henry Adams offer one of the most curious cases of similar temperaments that one is ever likely to find in two literary periods so far apart.

By the end of the 17th century, New England Calvinism was disintegrating, especially along the Massachusetts seaboard; and about 1733 there began in the parish of Jonathan Edwards a revival of Calvinism, which, under the influence of several powerful, though but vaguely Calvinistical field-preachers, was to sweep New England within the next few years. The excitement of this movement resulted in the breaking off of many small and strangely inspired sects from the main Calvinistic body; but it resulted also in the establishment of a revised and renewed Calvinism, under the guidance of Edwardian theology.

Edwardian theology abandoned the early New England modifications of Calvinism; it taught an undisguised determinism and a purely mystical doctrine of Grace. New England mystical tendencies had by no means been suppressed by the earlier doctrine: there had been doctrinal heretics, and even among the orthodox, such as Increase and Cotton Mather, there had been mystical trances, ecstasies, and visions, Cotton Mather, in fact, having been visited by an angel during one of the sunlit mornings of his youth. But Edwards revived and encouraged this tendency by explicit doctrine; and the New Englander's capacity for mystical belief and feeling was thus carried over to the period when Emerson should redescribe the mystical experience, employing the ideas of Romantic pan-

theism recently imported from the literary movements of
Europe, and as far as might be the language of Edwardian
Calvinism, so that Romantic doctrine was offered in a language carrying most of the emotional implications of the New
England religious tradition in its most intense aspects. Mind
and matter, God and Creation were one; the inundation of
the mind by instinct and emotion was Divine Grace; and surrender to whim was surrender to the Spirit. Whitman restated
this doctrine in a vulgar style, and increased its popularity;
William James did much to give it academic respectability;
and it reached its final and dramatic fulfillment in the life
and work of Hart Crane. The mystical tradition would appear
to have had little influence upon Adams at the beginning, but
as we shall ultimately see, he drew very near to it in the later
years of his life.

But Edwards had little influence along the seaboard: the
churches there continued their process of breaking down the
17th century theology which they had long since begun. The
moral sense proved stronger than the belief in predestination,
and with the disappearance of the doctrine of predestination
went most of what was precise and strong in Calvinistic theology. Certainly the doctrine of predestination was the essential
element in Calvinism; and when that went, theology was gone,
for the ancient and habitual antagonism to Romanism, Angli-
canism and Arminianism remained when the doctrinal justification for it was dead: there were a few apostates to Angli-
canism, such as the American Samuel Johnson, but in general
the New Englander was incapable even of thinking of a Christianity antecedent to Calvin. Whatever the intellectual trou-
bles of the New Englander, he was the creature of the strongest
habits that the world had ever seen.

The result was Unitarianism. Among the Unitarian and

related churches of the early nineteenth century there was a good deal of variation in doctrine, but the tendency was toward a belief in a benevolent God, in place of the angry God of the fathers; in Christ as a moral teacher, and not as the son of God; in freedom of the will; in the complete efficaciousness of good works. And there was an increasing tendency toward disbelief in eternal damnation. Unitarianism placed man's responsibility for his acts and his salvation wholly within himself, but the acts of a well-bred man conformed almost inevitably to the strong customs of the society which had been generated by the earlier ideas; so that between the ease with which one might be moral and the gentlemanly attitude of God, salvation appeared a fairly simple matter. This period produced a type of mind which we may still observe in the poetry of Bryant, and in the prose of Prescott and of the first Charles Francis Adams: able, dignified, and at times distinguished; governed easily by firm convictions; uncritical of accepted principles; and tending to substitute general stereotypes for precise perceptions and ideas. Men of this type adopted easily and turned to their own purposes the literary style produced by English deism, a style composed of somewhat vaguely general ideas, of an easy and well-constructed period, and of the highly generalized statement which tended at its best toward the aphorism, at its weakest toward the cliché. *Thanatopsis* is a sound poem and a serious and moving one; and rhetorically it is a masterpiece. But as compared even to so simple a piece as Herbert's *Church Monuments,* it displays a very simple and generalized grasp of its subject; and the same comments may be made upon Bryant's best work throughout—*To a Waterfowl, The Battlefield, The Grave,* and *The Tides.*

It was the Unitarians who provided the immediate background of Henry Adams, and he described their mentality on many occasions, and always with bewilderment. In the history he writes: [4]

No more was heard of the Westminster doctrine that man had lost all ability of will to any spiritual good accompanying salvation, but was dead in sin. So strong was the reaction against old dogmas that for thirty years society seemed less likely to resume the ancient faith in the Christian Trinity, than to establish a new Trinity in which a deified humanity should have a place. Under the influence of Channing and his friends, human nature was adorned with virtues hardly suspected before, and with hopes of perfection on earth altogether strange to theology. The Church then charmed. The worth of man became under Channing's teachings a source of pride and joy, with such insistence as to cause his hearers at last to recall, almost with a sense of relief, that the Saviour himself had been content to regard them only as of more value than many sparrows.

And a few lines below, he adds of the doctrine of Hosea Ballou:

This new doctrine, which took the name of Universalism, held as an article of faith "that there is one God, whose nature is love, revealed in one Lord Jesus Christ, by one Holy Spirit of Grace, who will finally restore the whole family of mankind to holiness and happiness." In former times anyone who had publicly professed belief in universal salvation would not have been regarded as a Christian. . . . Yet the Universalists steadily grew in numbers and respectability, spreading from State to State under Ballou's guidance. . . .

It is their bland security that most puzzles Adams, as it may well puzzle us today. In the *Education* he writes: [5]

Nothing quieted doubt so completely as the mental calm of the Unitarian clergy. In uniform excellence of life and character, moral

[4] *History of the United States during the Administrations of Jefferson and Madison,* by Henry Adams. Albert and Charles Boni, 1930. Vol. IX, pp. 182-3.

[5] *The Education of Henry Adams,* by Henry Adams, Modern Library Edition, p. 34.

and intellectual, the score of Unitarian clergymen about Boston, who controlled society and Harvard College, were never excelled. They proclaimed as their merit that they insisted on no doctrine, but taught, or tried to teach, the means of leading a virtuous, useful, unselfish life, which they held to be sufficient for salvation. For them difficulties might be ignored; doubts were waste of thought; nothing exacted solution. Boston had solved the universe; or had offered and realized the best solution yet tried. The problem was worked out.

And in the *History* he quotes a passage from Channing which illustrates this view, and comments upon it: [6]

"We lay it down as a great and indisputable opinion, clear as the sun at noon-day, that the great end for which Christian truth is revealed is the sanctification of the soul, the formation of the Christian character; and wherever we see the marks of this character displayed in a professed disciple of Jesus, we hope and rejoice to hope, that he has received all the truth which is necessary to his salvation." The hope might help to soothe anxiety and distress, but it defied conclusions reached by the most anxious and often renewed labors of churchmen for eighteen hundred years. Something more than a hope was necessary as the foundation of a faith.

This was, however, the last step possible to a voluntaristic Christianity which should remain non-mystical. Dogmas were ignored as misleading and vicious; theology was so simplified that one could scarcely identify the God in whom one believed. But belief remained, and one's entire theory of human nature, or rather of human conduct, depended arbitrarily but historically and helplessly from that belief. As long as the belief remained, the spiritual result was a kind of placid security; but the New Englander retained his need for security, and wherever the belief departed and the evidence is still available for examination, we commonly find a kind of willed confusion and religious horror, best represented in literature

6 Op. Cit. Vol. IX, pp. 181-2.

by Melville's *Pierre* and *The Confidence Man* and by the later
work of Henry Adams.

The strength of the voluntaristic tradition may be observed
in a New Englander of our own period, the late Irving Babbitt.
Babbitt found that human nature functioned at three levels,
to use his own figure: the naturalistic, which was the level of
the emotions and instincts, and which had been exploited by
the writers of the Romantic movement; the humanistic, or
critical, at which we are able to examine the lower level, understand it, and control it; and the religious, which is above
criticism. In his most valuable book, *Rousseau and Romanticism*, he devotes himself primarily to the criticism of Romantic
principles from what he calls a humanistic position, and he
refers to himself as an Aristotelian. The book is marred by
his reference to the "Inner Check," or conscience, a feeling
which functions at the religious level; but I believe that this
element can be dissected out with no great damage to the
criticism of the Romantic movement.

In his later work, however, his religious doctrines become
more important, and in the book entitled *On Being Creative*,
he asserts the absolute primacy of the will: man must will to
submit his private will to the higher will, in which he must
believe, and from that act understanding can follow; and the
Inner Check, or Conscience, the feeling superior to reason
and which guides us in emergencies, is identified with Divine
Grace. This is Augustinism without the Christianity: we must
believe in that which is superior to reason and which we therefore cannot define, much less examine critically; and in that
which is divorced from any particular historical tradition such
as that which still, I suppose, supports the belief of the Christian. And we have as our ultimate guide an emotional experience which is above rational criticism: the practical question
therefore arises as to how we shall distinguish between an

experience which is above criticism and one which is fairly subject to it, if we cannot bring criticism properly to bear on the first. Babbitt's final position seems to be little better than a starting point for a short-cut back to Emersonian mysticism.

Babbitt believed the Inner Check to be a psychological fact, observable and therefore a fit beginning for discussion. But the question remains as to the exact nature of the fact. The feeling which is called conscience in Protestant and post-Protestant society is presumably real; but when Aquinas comes to define conscience, he identifies it with reason, and he discusses the moral consequences of the identification at great length. From a Thomistic position, there would always remain the possibility of divine intervention in a particular instance; but the Catholic Christian, whether Thomistic or other, would be protected against error by the supervision of the Church, a supervision which Babbitt did not enjoy: and this supervision is, in theory, the supervision of the disinterested reason.

But Aquinas would be forced, I believe, by his definition of conscience and by his use of the Aristotelian doctrine of habit, to identify Babbitt's Inner Check in most of its individual occurrences as an habitual way of feeling about certain kinds of acts; the habit having been generated by training in a particular kind of society, which in turn had grown up originally in conformity with certain kinds of ideas. There is nothing in Babbitt to make one relinquish this interpretation, or even to make one believe that he suspected the possibility of this interpretation; and if the interpretation is true, it follows, as various critics have suggested, that the Inner Check will become progressively weaker as the generating ideas tend less and less to acceptance and the society in consequence alters its nature. Babbitt's doctrine of the Inner Check appears to be a late expression of the voluntaristic belief that morality is arbitrary and incomprehensible; the exact reverse of the Aristotelian doctrine, by which Babbitt appears to be mainly influenced in his early work, that morality is a fair subject for philosophical and psychological investigation, and that its principles can be discovered in a large measure through the use of the natural reason in the study of nature.

I should like also to cite the instance of Henry James, for his connections with Adams are immediate and important. In my essay on James,[7] I have shown that the character in the Jamesian novel is guided by a moral sense, or habit, which, though very intense, has lost its connections with its origins, so that it is never adequately guided by any critical apparatus, and that a good deal of obscurity results directly from this situation in many of the novels. The interesting thing about James as a critic is that he appears to be in precisely the same predicament as the characters in his novels. He objects to various continental writers for their lack of moral sense, and he criticizes many of his own books for the obscurity of their motivation, an obscurity which, though he realizes the fact imperfectly, results from the confusion of his own moral sense; but when he discusses the general principles of fiction,[8] he derides the idea that morality has anything to do with fiction, yet he insists that fiction "must take itself seriously," is obliged "really to represent life"; he takes it for granted "that some incidents are intrinsically much more important than others," although a few lines further, he is willing to grant the artist any subject and judge him only by what he does with it.

His terms, when he goes behind the terms relating to the technical structure of the novel, are extremely confused; but he insists that the novel shall be interesting. And when we have read a great deal of his criticism, we discover that he means that it must be interesting to Henry James; and to

[7] In *Maule's Curse,* by Yvor Winters, New Directions, 1938.
[8] The references are to *The Art of Fiction,* in *Partial Portraits.* It is early, but characteristic.

discover the meaning of this interest, we must first come to understand Henry James, which we can best do through the study of his novels. Ultimately he demands that the novel display (in a very finished form, naturally) the particular moral sense, or feeling for human motivation, which he himself possesses. This moral sense is the product of New England and of a very special section of history; and it has lost all connection with its intellectual sources, merely existing, more and more precariously, in vacuo; but James assumes it to be, if not universal, at least a standard universally applicable, so that he is in about the same situation as the later Babbitt.

Adams possessed the same moral sense, in a very exasperated form. He knew that he had it, and he knew that it closely resembled that of James; but unlike James, he felt that it needed justification, either philosophical or religious, and he convinced himself that neither was possible. Before proceeding to an examination of Adams' thought and art, I wish to cite a few of his references to James, for they will illuminate a great deal of that which is to follow.

In 1903 Adams wrote to James after reading James's life of Story: [9]

More than ever, after devouring your William Story, I feel how difficult a job was imposed on you. It is a *tour de force,* of course, but that you knew from the first. Whether you have succeeded or not, I cannot say, because it all spreads itself out as though I had written it, and I feel where you are walking on firm ground, and where you are on thin ice, as though I were in your place. Verily I believe I wrote it. Except your specialty of style, it is me.

The painful truth is that all of my New England generation, counting the half-century, 1820-1870, were in actual fact only one mind and nature; the individual was a facet of Boston. We knew

[9] *Letters of Henry Adams 1892-1918,* edited by W. C. Ford. Houghton Mifflin, 1938, p. 414.

each other to the last nervous center, and feared each other's knowledge. We looked through each other like microscopes. There was absolutely nothing in us that we did not understand merely by looking in the eye.[10] There was hardly a difference even in depth, for Harvard College and Unitarianism kept us all shallow. We knew nothing—no! but really nothing! of the world. One cannot exaggerate the profundity of ignorance of Story in becoming a sculptor, or Sumner in becoming a Statesman, or Emerson in becoming a philosopher. Story and Sumner, Emerson and Alcott, Lowell and Longfellow, Hillard, Winthrop, Motley, Prescott, and all the rest, were the same mind,—and so, poor worm!—was I!

Type bourgeois-bostonien! A type quite as good as another, but more uniform. What you say of Story is at bottom exactly what you would say of Lowell, Motley, and Sumner, barring degrees of egotism. You cannot help smiling at them, but you smile at us all equally. God knows that we knew our want of knowledge! the self-distrust became introspection—nervous self-consciousness—irritable dislike of America, and antipathy to Boston. *Auch ich war in Arcadien geboren!*

So you have written not Story's life, but your own and mine—pure autobiography—the more keen for what is beneath, implied, intelligible only to me, and half a dozen other people still living; like Frank Boott: who knew our Boston, London, and Rome in the fifties and sixties. You make me curl up like a trodden-on worm. Improvised Europeans we were, and—Lord God!—how thin! No, but it is too cruel! Long ago,—at least thirty years ago,—I discovered it, and have painfully held my tongue about it. You strip us gently and kindly, like a surgeon, and I feel your knife in my ribs.

[10] It is amusing to compare this statement with the statement of Dallas Archer to his father, near the end of *The Age of Innocence:* "You never did ask each other anything, did you? And you never told each other anything. You just sat and watched each other, and guessed at what was going on underneath. A deaf-and-dumb asylum, in fact! Well, I back your generation for knowing more about each other's thoughts than we ever have time to find out about our own."

In 1901 he had written to Elizabeth Cameron: [11]

Harry James has upset me. John Hay has been greatly troubled by Harry's last volume, *The Sacred Fount.* He cannot resist the suspicion that it is very close on extravagance. His alarm made me read it, and I recognized at once that Harry and I had the same disease, the obsession of *idée fixe.* . . .

In 1908 he wrote to William James of his own *Education:* [12]

As for the volume, it interests me chiefly as a literary experiment, hitherto, as far as I know, never tried or never successful. Your brother Harry tries such experiments in literary art daily, and would know instantly what I mean; but I doubt whether a dozen people in America—except architects or decorators—would know or care.

And in 1916, on learning of the death of this friend and alter-ego, he wrote to Elizabeth Cameron: [13]

Today the death of Harry James makes me feel the need of a let-up; I must speak to some one, and here I have no one Jamesian to talk to, except Wendell Holmes, and I never see him, for he is like me in avoiding contemporaries. Harry's death hits me harder than any stroke since my brother Charles' death a year ago. Not only was he a friend of mine for more than forty years, but he also belonged to the circle of my wife's set long before I knew him or her, and you know how I have clung to all that belonged to my wife. Swallow, sister! sweet sister swallow! indeed and indeed, we were really happy then.

II. *The Theory of History*

Adams' theory of history is really a philosophy and a theory of human nature; it is wholly indefensible and perverse, and we should be hard pressed to understand how a man of genius

[11] *Letters of Henry Adams,* op. cit., p. 333.   [12] Ibid. p. 490.
[13] Ibid. p. 638.

could conceive it if we had not some understanding of the
history which is largely responsible for his state of mind.
Briefly, he possessed the acute moral sense of New England to
which I have already referred and the New Englander's need
to read the significance of every event which he saw. But he
was of the Ockhamist tradition; and as for the Mathers, so
for him, the significance could not reside within the event but
must reside back of it. He would scarcely have put it this way,
and he might have denied the paternity of Ockham; but he
belonged to a moral tradition which had taken its morality
wholly on faith for so long that it had lost the particular kind
of intelligence and perception necessary to read the universe
for what it is; and had developed instead a passion to read the
universe for what it means, as a system of divine shorthand
or hieroglyphic, as a statement of ultimate intentions.

He had no faith, however, and hence he could not believe
that there was anything back of the event: the event was merely
isolated and impenetrable. Yet he possessed the kind of mind
which drove him to read every event with a kind of allegorical
precision; and since every event was isolated and impenetrable,
he read in each new event the meaning that the universe is
meaningless. Meaning had been a function of faith; and faith
had been faith not only in God and his decalogue but in a
complete cosmology and chronology, that is, in all of Revelation; and if any part of this system was injured, every part
was destroyed. The discoveries of geologists and astronomers
caused him indescribable suffering and made it utterly impossible that he should examine dispassionately the moral
nature of man.

I shall deal later with Adams' view of the Middle Ages,
thus reversing his chronology. He saw the twentieth century
as an age of multiplicity or chaos, in which man was forced to
recognize the confusion of his own understanding; the twentieth century was thus a falling away from the late twelfth

century, in which man had enjoyed the illusion of a unified mind, society, and cosmology.

It is simplest, perhaps, to begin with his way of looking at human character; and that particular topic immediately indicates something of his relationship to James. In the *Education* he wrote: [14]

Henry James had not yet taught the world to read a volume for the pleasure of seeing the lights of his burning-glass turned on alternate sides of the same figure.

I have shown in writing of James, how the Jamesian burning-glass thus employed resulted very commonly in the reader's being left with two or more versions of both character and action and with no way of making any selection; how it resulted, briefly, in an ambiguity which might in certain novels amount to a perfect opacity. It is a question, as a rule, to what extent James realized and intended this opacity, to what extent he may have succeeded in mystifying himself as well as his reader, but so far as Adams is concerned, such opacity is a virtue, for it renders the only perceptible truth in experience. Character after character in the *Education* is described as incomprehensible; Adams appears to make the discovery in each instance as if it were cause for astonishment; but eventually one notes that the discovery with regard to nearly every person encountered is inevitable, that it proceeds from a fixed habit of mind and results in a literary mannerism. Of Garibaldi he wrote: [15]

Adams had the chance to look this sphinx in the eyes, and, for five minutes, to watch him like a wild animal, at the moment of his greatest achievement and most splendid action. One saw a quiet-featured, quiet-voiced man in a red flannel shirt; absolutely impervious; a type of which Adams knew nothing. Sympathetic

[14] Op. cit., p. 163.   [15] Ibid., pp. 94-5.

it was, and one felt that it was simple; one suspected even that it might be childlike, but could form no guess of its intelligence. In his own eyes Garibaldi might be a Napoleon or a Spartacus; in the eyes of Cavour he might become a Condottiere; in the eyes of history he might, like the rest of the world, be only the vigorous player in the game he did not understand. The student was none the wiser.

This compound nature of patriot and pirate had illumined Italian history from the beginning, and was no more intelligible to itself than to a young American who had no experience in double natures. In the end, if the "Autobiography" tells truth, Garibaldi saw and said that he did not understand his own acts; that he had been an instrument; that he had served the purposes of the class he least wanted to help; yet in 1860 he thought himself the revolution anarchic, Napoleonic, and his ambition was unbounded. What should a young Bostonian have made of a character like this, internally alive with childlike fancies, and externally, quiet, simple, and almost innocent; uttering with apparent conviction the usual commonplaces of popular politics that all politicians use as the small change of their intercourse with the public; but never betraying a thought?

Precisely this class of mind was to be the toughest problem of Adams's practical life, but he could never make anything of it. The lesson of Garibaldi, as education, seemed to teach the extreme complexity of extreme simplicity; but one could have learned this from a glow-worm. One did not need the recollection of the low-voiced, simple-mannered seafaring captain of Genoese adventurers and Sicilian brigands, supping in the July heat and Sicilian dirt and revolutionary clamor, among the barricaded streets of insurgent Palermo, merely in order to remember that simplicity is complex.

One might at first consideration decide that Garibaldi was incomprehensible to Adams merely because he was an extremely foreign type; but Adams was convinced that Garibaldi could understand nothing of himself; and Adams could do no better with Seward, who was surely a native American product: [16]

A slouching, slender figure; a head like a wise macaw; a beaked nose; shaggy eyebrows; unorderly hair and clothes; hoarse voice; offhand manner; free talk and perpetual cigar, offered a new type —of western New York—to fathom; a type in one way simple because it was only double—political and personal; but complex because the political had become nature, and no one could tell which was the mask and which was the features. At table, among friends, Mr. Seward threw off restraint, or seemed to throw it off, in reality, while in the world he threw it off, like a politician, for effect. In both cases, he chose to appear as a free talker, who loathed pomposity and enjoyed a joke; but how much was nature and how much was mask, he was himself too simple a nature to know.

And if one is to trust the testimony of the chapter entitled *Eccentricity*, he found the entire English nation so impenetrably obscure that they provided him with material for little save satirical bewilderment.

And he found the same obscurity in events, whether major or minor: [17]

That Sumner and Hoare, the two New Englanders in great position who happened to be the two persons most necessary for his success at Washington, should be the first victims of Grant's lax rule, must have had some meaning for Adams's education, if Adams could only have understood what it was. He studied, but failed.

And since he was sure of the impossibility of understanding anything, he was sure above all of the impossibility of understanding his function as a teacher at Harvard: [18]

He never knew whether his colleagues shared his doubts about their own utility. Unlike himself, they knew more or less their

[16] Ibid. p. 104.   [17] Ibid. p. 279.   [18] Ibid. p. 306.

business. He could not tell his scholars that history glowed with
social virtue; the professor of Chemistry cared not a chemical atom
whether society was virtuous or not. Adams could not pretend
that medieval society proved evolution; the Professor of Physics
smiled at evolution. Adams was glad to dwell on the virtues of the
Church and the triumphs of its art: the Professor of Political
Economy had to treat them as a waste of force. They knew what
they had to teach; he did not. They might perhaps be frauds
without knowing it; but he knew certainly nothing else of himself.
He could teach his students nothing; he was only educating himself at their cost.

The mere sequence of these quotations should indicate the
extent to which this state of mind had become a mechanical
affair, habitual and unquestioned. The passages in question
are not quoted from passages of argument which clarify them
in the text; they are essentially as unexplained in the original
text as in that of the present essay. Nowhere does Adams, for
example, so much as look at the reasons traditionally offered
for teaching history, to say nothing of trying to find any new
ones; he merely asserts that it is fraudulent to pretend to teach
history. Nowhere does he examine the validity of the view of
art attributed to the Professor of Economics; he merely op-
poses it to his own interest in art, as if by virtue of its existence
it were indiscutable. One feels that if he had gone to the zoo,
he would have returned in all philosophical seriousness with
the report: "I saw a giraffe: but the farmer beside me denied
the existence of such an animal." His discussion never gets
very far beyond this kind of statement.

He finds the problem of judging works of art equally incomprehensible, and in the chapter of the *Education* entitled
Dilettantism, he tells a story which is supposed to demonstrate
his thesis. He tells of going to an auction and buying a drawing,
which F. T. Palgrave had recommended to him as surely by
Rafael and as having a good deal of intrinsic excellence. After

buying the drawing, he submitted it to various other experts and found them in wide disagreement as to its authenticity and as to its virtues. The moral is, that one cannot form any valid judgments about a work of art.

The story is amusingly told, and makes excellent gossip, but the purpose to which it is put betrays an almost childish mentality. The sketch was, in the first place, a working draft of a fragment of a picture, probably done in a moment and the next day discarded. It was not a finished work of art, and the impossibility of identifying the workmanship to a certainty would be manifest. Further, the question of authorship and the question of excellence are quite distinct from each other. Adams' discovery that two critics can disagree about the value of a work of art—let us assume that we have a finished work— is surely nothing to astonish us. We may assume that a given masterpiece—let us say *Macbeth*—has a certain absolute value and perhaps certain real flaws as well, and that critics will differ in their approximation of a true judgment of the work in proportion to their own imperfections of native ability, education, and capacity for effort; or we may assume that every man's judgment is right for himself, and that all judgments are relative, as Adams repeatedly states. The first theory will account for the persistence of great reputations as well as for difference of opinion; the second will offer an alternative explanation for difference of opinion but for nothing more. Throughout *Mont Saint-Michel and Chartres* he insists that the judgment of art is wholly relative, at the same time that the insistence causes him deep regret. He prefers the older tower of Chartres cathedral to the later, and as far as one can judge from the photographs the preference is certainly sound; but he cannot defend the preference. He apologizes, and says that after all the later tower was better for the people who made it and may be better for his reader: a position which is defensible, needless to say, only if one is willing to push it to its unmistakable conclusion, and assert that the latest road-side horror is better for its builders than either tower and may be better for the reader. There is no defensible compromise in this matter between a thorough relativism and a thorough absolutism.

Adams appears to have felt that modern science had destroyed the last possibility of human understanding, and his later writing is largely the record of an effort to bring scientific ideas to bear upon his problem. He found, first, that modern science made for confusion; and later he tried to find in scientific principles an exact formulation of the reasons why we are moving into greater confusion and of the rate of movement.

He sought in the findings of the 19th century geologists and in the theories of Darwin a new cosmology, to replace the old cosmology which these findings and others had destroyed. His discussion of his geological and evolutionary adventures is as amusing as his account of the investigation of the drawing; but it is incoherent, an assertion and exhibition of confusion, rather than explanation of it; and it is notable mainly for the anguish underlying the wit. In this department of his experience, as in others, his frustrated passion for precise understanding drove him toward the dogmatic certainty, to be achieved at any sacrifice of rationality, that no understanding of any kind was possible: [19]

He was ready to become anything but quiet. As though the world had not been enough upset in his time, he was eager to see it upset more. He had his wish, but he lost his hold on the results by trying to understand them.

His method, in general, is to leap nervously into the midst of a science of which he has no particular knowledge and worry a few details with a kind of irritated persistence: [20]

[19] Ibid., p. 225.　　　　　　　　　　　　　　[20] Ibid., p. 227.

Objections fatal to one mind are futile to another, and as far as concerned the article, the matter ended there, although the glacial epoch remained a misty region in the young man's Darwinism. Had it been the only one, he would not have fretted about it; but uniformity often worked queerly and sometimes did not work as Natural Selection at all. Finding himself at a loss for some single figure to illustrate the Law of Natural Selection, Adams asked Sir Charles for the simplest case of uniformity on record. Much to his surprise Sir Charles told him that certain forms, like Terebratula, appeared to be identical from the beginning to the end of geological time. Since this was altogether too much uniformity and much too little selection, Adams gave up the attempt to begin at the beginning and tried starting at the end—himself. Taking for granted that the vertebrates would serve his purpose, he asked Sir Charles to introduce him to the first vertebrate. Infinitely to his bewilderment, Sir Charles informed him that the first vertebrate was a very respectable fish, among the earliest of all fossils, which had lived, and whose bones were still reposing, under Adams' own favorite Abbey on Wenlock Edge . . . *Pteraspis,* a cousin of the sturgeon, and whose kingdom, according to Sir Roderick Murchison, was called Siluria. Life began and ended there. Behind that horizon lay only the Cambrian, without vertebrates or any other organism except a few shell-fish. On the further verge of the Cambrian rose the crystalline rocks from which every trace of organic existence had been erased.

Now whatever the virtues or defects of the doctrine of Natural Selection, Lyell's statement regarding Terebratula would scarcely damage it; an elementary knowledge of biology is sufficient to give a theoretic explanation of such a phenomenon. And when Adams was in search of his earliest vertebrate ancestor, and was assuming that one would be shown to him, there was no particular justification for his being infinitely bewildered when a particular ancestor was indicated. Nor was there cause for astonishment in the ancestor being a fish; for the fish are the lowest vertebrates. Nor is a cousin to a sturgeon a perfectly respectable fish, for the sturgeon is one of the most primitive fishes surviving. Nor is there cause for astonishment in the fact that the next age preceding, the Cambrian, offered nothing more advanced than shell-fish; for the shell fish, Mollusca and Arthropoda, represent the two phyla most highly developed before the chordates. I know little of the history of geology and biology, but most of this perfectly elementary information was probably available to Adams at the time of his original bewilderment and was unquestionably available to him at the time of his writing the *Education*. His procedure is to be witty rather than intelligent, and, having established a state of confusion for the sake of the wit, to deduce his spiritual suffering from it: that is the literary process; the original psychological process is less simple, as I have shown. The result is a certain iridescence of emotional surface but precisely nothing of sanity. The bewilderment is imposed on the experience, arbitrarily and at every point. What we get is not a philosophical experience, but an emotional experience: a vision of chaos which is cosmological, chronological, and theological.

He draws from this experience the only moral possible to a man in such a condition, the moral that truth is indecipherable: [21]

As he lay on Wenlock Edge, with the sheep nibbling the grass close about him as they or their betters had nibbled the grass—or whatever was there to nibble—in the Silurian kingdom of *Pteraspis*, he seemed to have fallen on an evolution far more wonderful than that of the fishes. He did not like it; he could not account for it; and he determined to stop it. Never since the day of his *Limulus* ancestry had any of his ascendants thought thus. Their modes of thought might be many, but their thought was one. Out of his millions of millions of ancestors, back to the Cambrian mollusks, every one had probably lived and died in the illusion of Truths which did not amuse him, and which had never

[21] Ibid., pp. 231-2.

changed. Henry Adams was the first in an infinite series to discover
and admit to himself that he really did not care whether truth was,
or was not, true. He did not even care that it should be proved
true, unless the process were new and amusing. He was a Darwinian
for fun.

From the beginning of history, this attitude had been branded
as criminal—worse than crime—sacrilege! Society punished it
ferociously and justly, in self-defense. Mr. Adams the father looked
on it as moral weakness; it annoyed him; but it did not annoy
him nearly so much as it annoyed his son, who had no need to
learn from Hamlet the fatal effect of the pale cast of thought on
enterprise great or small.

Adams, in brief, did not care for truth, unless it was amusing; for he was a modern nihilist, and hence a hedonist or
nothing. But his predicament nevertheless annoyed him, for
it frustrated action, just as it did for Melville's *Pierre,* and
Adams was a New Englander, to whom action and the comprehension of his action were constitutionally necessary. The entire perversity, the inconsequence, and the tragedy of Adams'
predicament are indicated in this passage. And the Pteraspis,
elevated in this manner into a symbol, remains one throughout the rest of the book: [22]

History is a tangled skein that one may take up at any point,
and break when one has unravelled enough; but complexity precedes evolution. The pteraspis grins horribly from the closed
entrance.

The Pteraspis appears to Adams to grin horribly precisely
because the entrance is closed, or because Adams thinks it
closed. Adams is not content, even provisionally, to study his
world as it is, in the hope of arriving at a working knowledge
of it; there is no knowledge, for Adams, unless it is a part of
a complete system, deriving from an acceptable definition of
the Absolute: [23]

[22] Ibid., p. 302.   [23] Ibid., p. 226.

Ignorance must always begin at the beginning. Adams must inevitably have begun by asking Sir Isaac for an intelligible reason why the apple fell to the ground. He did not know enough to be satisfied with the fact. The Law of Gravitation was so-and-so, but what was Gravitation? and he would have been thrown quite off his base if Sir Isaac had answered that he did not know.

This neurotic and childish impatience, amounting almost to insolence, is the final fruit of the Christian doctrine in New England; the patience and humility of an Aristotle or a Newton are incomprehensible.

This state of mind grew on him with the years. It is obvious above all in his comments upon his later discovery of twentieth century psychology: [24]

Unfortunately, the pursuit of ignorance in silence had, by this time, led the weary pilgrim into such mountains of ignorance that he could no longer see any path whatever, and could not even understand a signpost . . . He gathered from the books that the psychologists had, in a few cases, distinguished several personalities in the same mind, each conscious and constant, individual and exclusive . . . To his mind, the compound $\Psi\upsilon\chi\acute{\eta}$ took at once the form of a bicycle rider, mechanically balancing himself by inhibiting all his inferior personalities, and sure to fall into the subconscious chaos below, if one of his inferior personalities got on top. The only absolute truth was the sub-conscious chaos below, which everyone could feel when he sought it.

Whether the psychologists admitted it or not, mattered little to the student who, by the law of his profession, was engaged in studying his own mind. On him, the effect was surprising. He woke up with a shudder as though he had himself fallen off his bicycle. If his mind were really this sort of magnet, mechanically dispersing its lines of force when it went to sleep, and mechanically orienting them when it woke up—which was normal, the dispersion or the orientation? The mind, like the body, kept its unity unless it happened to lose its balance, and the professor of physics, who slipped

[24] Ibid., pp. 433-4-5.

on a pavement and hurt himself, knew no more than an idiot what knocked him down, though he did know—what the idiot could hardly do—that his normal condition was idiocy, or want of balance, and that his sanity was unstable artifice. His normal thought was dispersion, sleep, dream, inconsequence; the simultaneous action of different thought centers without central control. His artificial balance was acquired habit. He was an acrobat with a dwarf on his back, crossing a chasm on a slack-rope, and commonly breaking his neck.

By that path of newest science, one saw no unity ahead—nothing but a dissolving mind.

One should note, here, the emotional quality of much of the language; the feeling is that of the romantic tradition. The bicycle rider balances himself "mechanically" (that is, by a base and contemptible trick); his balance is "artificial" (the artificial and the mechanical are roughly equivalent in romantic thought); and the balance is acquired "habit" (habit, in romantic terminology, does not refer to a psychological fact, but to a spiritual vice: habit is mechanical and imperceptive behavior). The balance keeps the rider safe from his inferior personalities and from the chaos, and one might deduce from this that the balance is valuable; but this is not true, for since the balance is artificial, and there is really a chaos, the chaos is the only absolute truth, and, one guesses, one might as well immerse oneself in it as soon as possible.

I do not know how foolish it may seem to many of my readers for me to state my objections to these ideas more explicitly still, but my acquaintance with the minds of my literary contemporaries is extensive, and I am sure that many of them derive an important part of their thought from Adams, though many of them do not know it; and to my great regret I have found that many of the most brilliant of them understand simple matters only with the greatest of difficulty.

I should therefore like to add my belief that a balance which is artificial, or which is, in my terms, a habit formed by willed perseverance deriving from rational understanding of the need for it, and which preserves one from madness, is in its own nature a good; for madness is in its own nature and quite obviously an evil. A morality which preserves one from this loss of balance is defensible beyond argument by virtue simply of the fact that it so preserves one; and a morality such as that of Adams is evil, simply by virtue of the fact that it aims at loss of balance. One does not need Divine Revelation to know this; a single look at a psychopathic ward is sufficient. And once one has admitted the initial advantage of being sane, one will be forced to admit the additional advantages of being as sane, or as intelligent as possible; and a good deal of careful scrutiny may enable us to refine a very little upon the rough scheme of our initial morality. If one is conscious when awake and semiconscious when asleep, it is fair to assume that both conditions are normal at their proper times and to refrain from introducing mysteries into a universe which already contains two or three problems which no human ingenuity has been able to solve.

Adams appears to point ahead to such writers as Pound, Joyce, and Eliot, in this passage; to those who have found the dissolving mind the normal mind, and who have sought to exploit it at the expense of the other. He gives the impression here that he would explore this mind because there is nothing else to do; but in a few other places he indicates a belief, whether temporary or permanent, that the passive mind is the best medium for reaching truth: that is, he approximates a statement of Emersonian or Bergsonian mysticism.

In telling of his early life, he discusses his youthful contemplation of the Concord faith with some amusement: [25]

[25] Ibid., p. 63.

He never reached Concord, and to Concord Church he, like the rest of mankind who accepted a material universe, remained always an insect, or something much lower—a man.

Yet he tells how a little later he came to understand Bee-thoven [26] by listening to him passively and inattentively in a German music hall, and he appears to draw the moral that this was the best way to arrive at an understanding. And in one of the last chapters, in discussing the development of modern science, he writes [27] an extensive passage which is purely Emer-sonian, not only in its irrationality and its mysticism, but in its very vocabulary as well:

Very slowly the accretion of these new forces, chemical and mechanical, grew in volume until they acquired sufficient mass to take the place of the old religious science, substituting their attrac-tion for the attractions of the *Civitas Dei*, but the process remained the same. Nature, not mind, did the work that the sun does on the planets. Man depended more and more absolutely on forces other than his own, and on instruments which superseded his senses. Bacon foretold it: "Neither the naked hand nor the under-standing, left to itself, can effect much. It is by instruments and helps that the work is done." Once done, the mind resumed its illusion, and society forgot its impotence; but no one better than Bacon knew its tricks, and for his true followers science always meant self-restraint, obedience, sensitiveness to impulse from with-out. "Non fingendum aut excogitandum sed inveniendum quid Natura faciat aut ferat."

The success of this method staggers belief, and even today can be treated by history only as a miracle of growth, like the sports of nature. Evidently a new kind of mind had appeared. Certain men merely held out their hands—like Newton, watched an apple; like Franklin, flew a kite; like Watt played with a tea-kettle—and great forces of nature stuck to them as if she were playing ball.

The foolishness of this passage is obvious, but I hesitate to leave it undefined. The actions of Newton, Franklin, and Watt

[26] Ibid., p. 80.   [27] Ibid. p. 485.

bore fruit, I suspect, because of previous thought which illuminated the particular adventures. Franklin, in fact, or so
I seem to remember it, was flying a kite to verify a theory; he
was not merely flying it for fun. The rapid advance of science
in the past two centuries is due to the accumulation of knowledge and the improvement of machinery. The more one knows,
the more rapidly one can learn; and the better one's instruments, the better the instruments one can make. The process
is cumulative and not in itself mysterious. Bacon was scarcely
the prophet of modern science that he is popularly supposed
to have been, and had small comprehension of the best scientific thought of his day; but his two statements are harmless
enough, the first being a recognition of the need of instruments, the second a recognition of the existence of objective
truth.

Explicit statements of this kind are rare and fleeting in the
Education, and it is possible that I over-estimate the importance of this fringe of Adams' thought; for certainly it did
little to mitigate the desolation of spirit of his later years. He
was not an enthusiast, as was Emerson, and he found in this
doctrine no discernible trace of Emersonian beatitude. But in
1909 he wrote in a letter to Margaret Chanler: [28]

I like best Bergson's frank surrender to the superiority of Instinct over Intellect. You know how I have preached that principle,
and how I have studied the facts of it. In fact I once wrote a whole
volume—called my *Education*—which no one ever saw, and which
you must some day look into,—borrow William James's copy, in
hopes that he may have marginally noted his contempt for me,—
in order to recall how Education may be shown to consist in following the intuitions of Instinct. Loeb calls it *Tropism*, I believe;
which means that a mother likes to nurse her own child.

If he came as late as 1909 to feel, however, that in the *Education* he had discovered a way of life, there is small evidence

[28] *Letters of Henry Adams*, op. cit., p. 524.

of such feeling in the book itself, or elsewhere in his writing, before or after. Nothing was comprehensible; each event and fact was unique and impenetrable; the universe was a chaos of meaningless and unrelated data, equivalent to each other in value because there was no way of evaluating anything. Comprehension, judgment, and choice being nullified, there was no reason for action, physical or spiritual, and life was mere stagnation: [29]

The outlook lacked hope. The object of travel had become more and more dim, ever since the gibbering ghost of the Civil Law had been locked in the dark closet as far back as 1860. Noah's dove had not searched the earth for resting-places so carefully, or with so little success. Any spot on land or water satisfies a dove who wants and finds rest; but no perch suits a dove of sixty years old, alone and uneducated, who has lost his taste even for olives. To this, also, the young may be driven, as education, and the lesson fails in humor; but it may be worth knowing to some of them that the planet offers hardly a dozen places where an elderly man can pass a week alone without ennui, and none at all where he can pass a year.

In his old age, he joined his only political party, the Conservative Christian Anarchists, a party of which the only other member was his young friend Bay Lodge. His last letters, in their despair, malice, and frantic triviality are very painful reading.

I have been tracing the disintegration of a mind. Yet the moral sense persisted, strong as ever, but running amuck for lack of guidance. Adams, as I have shown, was as passionate an allegorist as Mather had been; instead of seeing God's meaning in every event, he saw the meaninglessness of a godless universe, but with a Calvinistic intensity of vision. He had, as he confessed in writing of Henry James the "obsession of idée fixe." And not only had he the passion to see his allegori-

[29] *Education,* op. cit., p. 357.

cal vision, but he had the true Calvinist's passion to provide his vision with his own theology. He wrote: [30]

From cradle to grave this problem of running order through chaos, direction through space, discipline through freedom, unity through multiplicity, has always been, and must always be, the task of education.

Yet the problem, though one was bound to endeavor to solve it, could never be solved in fact: the solution must be a delusion: [31]

Chaos was the law of nature; Order was the dream of man.

More than once he thought he saw his solution in permitting himself, as T. S. Eliot would have us do, to be determined by what he took to be his time, by what in fact was casual impulse: [32]

To him, the current of his time was to be his current, lead where it might . . . he insisted on maintaining his absolute standards; on aiming at ultimate Unity.

This Emersonian disguise of his own disintegration, however, was something that he could not consistently maintain: his disintegration was not a voyage, governed by absolute standards, on a supernatural current in the direction of Unity; it was merely disintegration. And the only way to find Order in it, was to discover the reason for the disintegration and chart its rate.

He was too good a determinist and too devoutly sorry for himself to seek any part of the reason in himself, and partly because of these facts, and partly because he was committed to an obscurantistic view of history, he failed to seek it in any segment of history definite and limited enough to imply that the difficulty was due to human error that might in some measure be corrected. Like a true Calvinist and a true determinist,

[30] Ibid., p. 12.   [31] Ibid., p. 451.   [32] Ibid., p. 232.

he turned at once, for his answer, to the Nature of the Universe, and sought to show that the whole universe, as a single mechanism, was running down. The cosmological scope of the doctrine appears most fully in the volume of essays posthumously published as *The Degradation of the Democratic Dogma;* but in *Mont Saint-Michel and Chartres* and in the *Education* he seeks to illustrate the tendency by defining the difference between two extremes of civilization: [33]

Any schoolboy could see that man as a force must be measured by motion, from a fixed point. Psychology helped here by suggesting a unit—the point of history when man held the highest idea of himself in a unified universe. Eight or ten years of study had led Adams to think he might use the century 1150-1250, expressed in Amiens cathedral and the Works of Thomas Aquinas, as the unit from which he might measure motion down to his own time, without assuming anything as true or untrue, except relation. The movement might be studied at once in philosophy and mechanics. Setting himself to the task, he began a volume which he mentally knew as *Mont Saint-Michel and Chartres: A Study of Thirteenth Century Unity.* From that point he proposed to fix a position for himself which he could label: *The Education of Henry Adams: A Study of Twentieth Century Multiplicity.* With the help of these two points of relation, he hoped to project his lines forward and backward indefinitely, subject to correction from anyone who should know better.

We have seen the manner in which Adams demonstrated twentieth century multiplicity; and as I have already said, it seems to me pointless to invent difficulties in a universe in which irreduceable difficulties flourish. The philosophical problem, as I see it, is to define the various possible mysteries, and where choice is possible, to choose those which eliminate the greatest possible number of the remainder; and to keep as scientific, as Aristotelian, an eye as possible upon the condi-

[33] Ibid., p. 435.

tions of our life as we actually find ourselves forced to live it, so that we may not make the mistake of choosing a mystery which shall, in proportion as it influences our actions, violate those conditions and lead to disaster. For example, a strictly deterministic philosophy, whether materialistic or pantheistic, and no matter how enticing the cosmology or theology from which it may derive, can lead only toward automatism in action, and automatism is madness. And similarly, a strictly nominalistic view of the universe can lead only to the confusion and paralysis reached by Adams; whereas a certain amount of understanding, small no doubt in the eye of God and of the philosopher, but very useful in itself, is actually possible. If we find that a theory violates our nature, we have then learned something about our nature; and we have learned that there is something wrong with the theory. When Dr. Johnson demonstrated the real existence of the wall by kicking it, he employed a philosophical argument far from subtle but absolutely unanswerable. The philosopher who needs further convincing may try driving his car against the wall, and at as high a rate of speed as he may feel the ingenuity of his philosophy to require: he may, in this manner, learn something of the nature of absolute truth. Adams quotes Poincaré [34] as saying that it is meaningless to ask whether Euclidean geometry is true, but that it will remain more convenient than its rivals. I am no mathematician and can only guess what this means; but I surmise that it means that a bridge built by Euclidean geometry may conceivably stand, whereas one built by a rival system will certainly fall. If this is true, I should be willing to accept the fact as perhaps a Divine Revelation regarding the nature of the physical universe and as a strong recommendation for the study of Euclidean geometry.

Some such intention as I have just recommended would

[34] Ibid., p. 455.

appear to have motivated Aristotle and even Aquinas. I myself am not a Christian and I fear that I lack permanently the
capacity to become one; but Aquinas's examination of the
nature of man appears to me acute and extremely usable, and
his disposition of theological difficulties perhaps the best disposition possible. Adams, however, is bent on proving the
existence of a unified mind in the 13th century, because he
is bent on proving that man has disintegrated since, and his
discussion of Aquinas centers wholly in the theological difficulties, for he assumes that the philosophy derives from the
theological solutions, whereas in reality the philosophy and the
philosophical method derive very largely from Aristotle, who
was a scientific observer and analyst and neither a Christian nor
a theologian. And since the theological difficulties were real,
and since the answers of Aquinas are less satisfactory to Adams
than they must have been to Aquinas, Adams asserts that the
entire structure, philosophy as well as theology, depends from
faith, and "if Faith fails, Heaven is lost." And as we have seen,
when Adams says that Heaven is lost, he means that everything
is lost.

The unity which Adams finds, therefore, in the 13th century is a unity of faith, which results, he seems to believe, in
a unity of social and artistic purpose. He is aware of the diversity of philosophical views, but he does not take it seriously,
for philosophy is not a serious matter while there is faith, if
indeed it can be shown to be a serious matter at all. Yet the
controversy over universals was essentially a controversy over
the very existence of the rational faculty itself: had there been
no Aquinas to slow the spread of nominalism, to steady the
thought of the period with a little of that rarest form of profundity curiously called common sense, it seems highly im-
probable that the Church as we know it could long have
survived, for the Church rests solidly on a recognition, whether
explicit or implicit, of the reality of ideas; Faith without intel-

lectual unity can scarcely maintain its own unity or any other
for long, as the history of the Reformation seems to indicate.
Within the Church itself there was a diversity of views on
fundamental subjects, a diversity of the most perilous kind;
and the unity of the 13th century Church, in so far as it was
achieved, was due far less to the spirit of the age than to the
mind of Thomas Aquinas.

And to what extent can one fairly say that the Church provided religious unity for Europe as a whole? As one proceeded
downward from the great doctors of the Church, through
various intellectual and social levels, the religion became simpler and simpler, and ultimately more and more pagan. If
even a small part of the conclusions of the folk-lorists of the
past fifty years can be trusted, the Stone Age persisted as a
solid sub-stratum but a little below the surface of Christianity.
The great Church of the thirteenth century, as we know it
in its literary and artistic remains, was the product of a relatively small class, and of a class confined to the centers of culture. Behind the cities lay isolated and small communities,
living on the land, and encountering the outside world for
the most part only as they were devastated by war. The last
great period of the Stone Age, a period of considerable artistic
development and of wide and persistent religious beliefs, had
lasted perhaps twenty thousand years, and had formed the
peasant mind, which is tenacious, whereas Christianity in most
of Europe was a matter of a very few hundred years. One can
learn something of the extent to which most of the population
must have been isolated from the civilization of the time by
reading the first six chapters of Adams' own history, or by
reading the third chapter of Macaulay. The life of the thirteenth century peasant was probably as primitive in every
respect as had been the life of his ancestors in the caves and
about the lakes, and was probably more fraught with peril
and less provided with animal comforts.

Of political unity there was little. Between the death of Charlemagne and the rise of the centralized monarchies of the Renaissance the system was feudal, which is to say chaotic, irresponsible, and brutal. In what sense can the mass of the feudal lords be called Christian? They called themselves Christian, but their Christianity was that neither of Christ nor of any doctor of the Church. Of the entire class perhaps Richard of England is as high a representative as any, and his ideals were not Christian but chivalric; they were vainglorious and merciless, although heroic in their way and impressive in retrospect. The great literary expression of this group of men is the *Song of Roland*, a beautiful poem, which Adams praises because of its strong simplicity and directness, qualities which he associates rightly with the chivalric ideal; but these qualities are the result less of a masterly understanding of human nature than of the exclusion from consideration of most of what is important in human nature. Even George Herbert is a greater poet than Turoldus, as he is a wiser and more civilized man.

And if Richard and Turoldus came close to realizing even this simple ideal, it is wise to remember that few others did so. The medieval baron or prince was in general brutal and unscrupulous; to compare the great industrialists of our own period to these their predecessors is a very harsh judgment, I suspect, in spite of the crimes of our period. Part of our dissatisfaction with our time is due to one of the few really valuable heirlooms left us by the Romantic movement, our sense of social responsibility. We see the injustices and misfortunes suffered by the poor; we feel that much can and should be done to mitigate them; and although we have done a great deal, we feel that we have not done enough, for we see the evils remaining and are embittered. That we have done a good deal, however, anyone may discover by a moderately attentive reading of such writers as Chaucer, Defoe, and

Dickens. Dickens was a reformer, and so may be suspected of over-drawing his picture, but Defoe and Chaucer merely depicted what they saw, with pity, but with no indignation; and if we may trust them, and others like them, the life of most of the lower classes on the land and in the cities equally, and perhaps well into the nineteenth century, beyond all argument in the middle ages and in the Renaissance, was far more terrible than that of any considerable number of persons in North America or in Western Europe during the twentieth century, even at the lowest ebbs of our social and economic life.

I do not ignore the wars of the twentieth century when I say this, and having had no personal experience of them, I may be foolish to speak of them. But if my literary contemporaries would read a few full and leisurely histories, such as those, for example, of Motley, which deal with the wars of the Renaissance or with the wars of the Middle Ages, they might suspect that wars are not much worse than they were: what our ancestors lacked in equipment they made up in thoroughness, and the long protraction of the wars probably caused a suffering greater in proportion to the population of those times than any caused by the wars of our day. In fact the mere figures relating to the increase of population during the past century and a half are proof in themselves that the basic hardships of life have decreased beyond our imagining.

I do not wish to give the impression that I believe our civilization is perfect. We do not enjoy a high degree of civilization, and I believe that probably we never shall; the race is not capable of it. But Adams' view of the Middle Ages, which has been adopted by Eliot and his followers, is merely a version of the Romantic Golden Age; the thirteenth century as they see it never existed, and their conviction that major intellectual and spiritual achievement is possible only in such a Utopia can do nothing but paralyze human effort. Much of the unity and simple strength which Adams so admires in the thirteenth century was merely the result of callous indifference to horrors worse than any the twentieth century has ever known. I have the greatest of respect for the mind of Aquinas, and but little, I fear, for many of the most influential minds of the twentieth century; but I respectfully submit that had Aquinas felt himself determined by the stupidity and confusion of his time, he would probably have accomplished very little. He endeavored to learn as much as possible from the best minds of his time and of the two thousand years, more or less, preceding; and having learned that, he set out to do the best that he could with it. Adams arrived at his view of the middle ages by concentrating on a few great products of literature, thought, and architecture; ignoring everything else, he asserted that these were the thirteenth century. He arrived at his view of the twentieth century by reversing the process. He thus deduced that the world was deteriorating, and so found a justification for his own state of mind.

The Cosmology which expands Adams' view of history to its ultimate generality is to be found in *The Degradation of the Democratic Dogma*. The essays were written during the latter part of Adams' life. In his letters he frequently refers to them as jokes, perpetrated to stir up his slow-witted colleagues; but he also refers to them seriously, and there is every reason to believe that he took them seriously. They merely enlarge upon the theory which we have been examining, and which is stated more briefly in the latter part of the *Education;* and although they are sufficiently astonishing in their irrationality, I do not know that they are much worse in this respect than the two books thus far considered.

The most important of these essays is *A Letter to American Teachers of History*. It begins with the unquestioning acceptance of two theological principles, both the product of the age which he is endeavoring to prove to be one of ultimate confusion: the Law of the Dissipation of Energy, and the assumption that man is governed by physical laws. Whether we regard Adams as the contemner of his own age, or as the apostle of scepticism, this acceptance is sufficiently startling. It can be understood only if we remember that he was the heir of the Puritans and that sooner or later his heritage was certain to overtake him completely. In order to prove the impossibility of absolute truth, he had to start from absolute truth and create what he could believe for the moment to be a comprehensive system.

The Revelation discloses that Energy is being dissipated steadily in a godless universe: the origin of Energy in a godless universe, and the question of how this process, which must end in time, has had no temporal beginning, but has been undergoing a steady process of diminution from all eternity —these difficulties are never met. The end is certain; the beginning does not matter. The principle explains why heat ends in cold, life in death, motion in station. And the principle once established, it follows that each succeeding manifestation of energy is inferior to the last. Man is thus inferior to the early animals, and civilization is a process of decay. The emergence of human reason during this process does not trouble Adams in the least: Reason, as we have seen, leads only to confusion and inaction and is of no help in the attainment of truth; this in spite of the fact that Adams probably believed that he was using his own reason in arriving at the truths which he elucidates. Reason is a degraded form of will: [35]

Reason can be only another phase of the energy earlier known as Instinct or Intuition; and if this be admitted as the stem-history of the Mind as far back as the eocene lemur, it must be admitted for all forms of Vital Energy back to the vegetables and perhaps

[35] *The Degradation of the Democratic Dogma,* by Henry Adams, Macmillan, 1919, pp. 192-5.

even to the crystals. In the absence of any definite break in the
series, all must be endowed with energy equivalent to will. . . . .
Already the anthropologists have admitted man to be specialized
beyond hope of further variation, so that, as an energy, he must
be treated as a weakened Will—an enfeebled vitality—a degraded
potential. He cannot himself deny that his highest Will-power,
whether individual or social, must have proved itself by his highest variation, which was incontrovertibly his act of transforming
himself from a hypothetical eocene lemur,—whatever such a
creature may have been,—into men speaking elaborately inflected
language. This staggering but self-evident certainty requires many
phases of weakening Will-power to intervene in the process of sub-
sidence into the reflective, hesitating, relatively passive stage called
Reason; so that in the end, if the biologists insist on imposing their
law on the anthropologists, while at the same time refusing to
admit a break in the series, the historian will have to define his
profession as the science of human degradation.

We thus see that life has proceeded from the energetic form
of the rock crystal, to the passive and listless form which it
manifests, for example, in the United States in the twentieth
century; and since this process is proven a process of degradation, the emergence of the human mind with its various complex creations, is necessarily a symptom of degeneration.
Human Reason can scarcely go farther, or so one might think
for a moment. But actually there is one further deduction, and
Adams makes it in the course of the essay. Life has deteriorated
from the energetic form of the rock crystal, through all the
forms of vegetation, of animal life, and of civilization, the
highest form of civilization having existed in the thirteenth
century; and the energy of the universe must continue to dissipate itself until life will be reduced again to rock-crystals. This
is an unbroken process of deterioration; and it provides the
cosmological frame for Adams' theory of history.

Man's deterioration thus becomes a matter of cosmology,
of Revealed Truth, and there is no help for the matter. The

best thing man can do is trust his instincts, for they are worth more than his reason, and they will guide him infallibly along the current of his time to progressively more complex degeneracy. Art is a human function, and will be governed by the general law. Art also is deteriorating, but it must deteriorate to express honestly the general deterioration of man; and we thus arrive at one of the central ideas of T. S. Eliot, which has been one of the most influential of the past twenty years, at least among the more scholarly and intellectual of our poets and critics. At the end of *Mont Saint-Michel and Chartres* we find the matter stated in Adams' own words: [36]

Art had to be confused in order to express confusion; but perhaps it was truest so.

If the chaos of the subconscious is the only reality, and if the subject-matter of art determines the form of the work, then we have arrived at *Finnegans Wake* and the poetry of Pound and Eliot as the finest expression of civilization, that is to say, of degeneracy, although in some way which almost eludes me, we have left that other product of degeneracy, the Reason, a little way behind us in arriving at our goal.

III. *The Writing of History*

I have dealt very harshly with the later work of Adams; I have stated my opinion that this work represents the radical disintegration of a mind. The mind, however, had been a great one, though its true greatness is suspected only by professional historians at the present time and is little more than suspected by most of them. Of the early work, the novels and the life of Randolph are trivial; but the life of Gallatin is still regarded by historians as one of the great works in American

[36] *Mont Saint-Michel and Chartres*, by Henry Adams, Houghton Mifflin, p. 375.

biography, and although it is long and heavily documented, and is very different from the birds-eye views of biography which have been so popular during the past ten or fifteen years, it is a massive and distinguished work of literature. It has never gone into a second edition, I believe, and is very hard to obtain.

Lack of space forbids that I write of more than the history. The *History of the United States During the Administrations of Thomas Jefferson and James Madison*,[37] a work in nine volumes, has been reissued only once to my own inexpert knowledge; it is now out of print. All things considered, I suspect that it is the greatest historical work in English, with the probable exception of *The Decline and Fall of the Roman Empire*, although any such judgment by one who is not an expert scholar in a number of historical fields, as well as something of a critic of literature, must be very tentative.

The relationship of literary quality to historical scholarship in a work of this kind perhaps needs to be briefly considered. The historian such as Gibbon or Macaulay, one is inclined to suppose, examines his material to the best of his ability, and on the basis of that examination forms a fairly definite idea of the characters and actions involved. In this stage of his work, he is comparable to the novelist who has long meditated his characters and outlined his plot. The final literary form of the history represents an evaluation, a moral judgment, of the material which he has held in his mind. Such judgment is inevitable, even though the historian refrain completely from any didacticism: it resides in the very act of writing, and no historian, be he a good stylist or a bad, can escape it. The difference in this respect between a good stylist and a bad is merely that the good stylist knows what he is doing, and

---

[37] The latest edition, the one in my possession, and the only one I have seen, was published by Albert and Charles Boni in 1930. It is a great misfortune that the work is not available in some such edition as The Modern Library or The World's Classics.

if he is a conscientious man, both as a scholar and as a stylist, can take every possible precaution to make his judgment sound; whereas the scholar who suffers from the delusion that he can be perfectly impersonal runs the risk at least of being uncritical of his style, that is of the ultimate and definitive boundary of his judgments. Professor Andrews, I believe, has expressed the theory that the historian should have no style; but by the Grace of God, or through God's just retribution, he has achieved the finest historical style with which I am acquainted this side of Adams—the average scholar is likely to be less fortunate unless he is guided by a more admirable doctrine.

The professional research scholar tends to distrust the historian of literary pretensions, such as Motley or Macaulay. The danger, apparently, is that such an historian runs the risk of devoting more attention to the second function which I have mentioned than to the first, and thus of creating something closer to historical fiction than to history. The danger, of course, is real, and the accusation has been levelled repeatedly at Gibbon, Macaulay, Motley, and Parkman, yet all survive; and the amateur such as myself cannot but wonder whether much of the criticism is not due merely to the fact that these writers have survived and have remained so long the objects of careful reading. That they are guilty of many sins I am sure, and that they suffer from the state of scholarship in their respective times or from the vicissitudes of their private lives is more than likely; but that they are guilty of more errors in proportion to their achievement than are many scholars of no great literary pretensions strikes me as much less certain, especially on those occasions when I have just put in a few hours reading what various scholars have written of each other. Certainly there is something to be said for the theory that the history of civilization can best be recounted by a man who is himself a distinguished product of civilization and who is therefore in a position to understand in some measure what civilization really is.

After examining the work of Adams' later years, one might expect him to be the greatest sinner of all in this particular manner, yet I should not be surprised to discover that he is the least; I have at any rate encountered fewer accusations against him than against the others, although this may be merely the result of his being the latest in time and the least subjected to scrutiny. He gives the impression of adhering very closely to his documents, and of judging them carefully and with a watchful attention to the possibility of his being prejudiced. If there is a constant prejudice in his history, in any wise comparable to the political bias of Hume or of Macaulay, it is a distrust of democratic procedure, a distrust which was to reach a state of violent exasperation in his later years. His fascination with confusion is already apparent, although in the history it is restrained; on the other hand, the confusion in the American government during the period which he treats was assuredly real, and it would be hard to convict him of over-emphasis or of drawing unwarranted conclusions.

In order to understand the literary achievement of this work, one needs, I think, to consider a few of the greatest historians in English preceding Adams: Hume, Robertson, Gibbon, Macaulay, Prescott, Motley, and Parkman will suffice.

Modern historiography in English may probably be said to begin with Hume's *History of England*, though it might well begin with Bacon's *Henry VII*, except for the gap in time between that work and the next important efforts. By modern standards, Hume was far from being a careful scholar, but his prose is remarkable both for its virtues and its defects: Hume adapted the style of eighteenth century prose at its best to the purposes of historiography, and he imposed that style so successfully upon historiographical tradition that its influence persisted longer in history than in any other field of literature. The virtues of the prose are its precision, its structure, and its dignity. Hume, in common with the best stylists of his century, possessed a command of the rhetorical possibilities of grammatical structure which diminished notably among the great writers of the century following. Accumulation, climax, antithesis, the ironical by-thrust; the exact identification of causal, temporal and other relations by means of grammatical form; perfect clarity at every moment in the process of difficult stylistic maneuvers; variety and precision of rhythm: such mastery is the norm of his style; he takes it for granted, as a concert pianist takes for granted the athletic proficiency of his fingers. Such a style is necessarily formal, and scarcely lends itself, except in the guise of the mock heroic, to the familiar narrative of the fictionist: it tends naturally toward the expository form and the ironic comment, and, in narrative, toward the heroic.

Hume's very defects as a scholar assisted him in utilizing the possibilities of this style to the utmost.[38] His scholarship was so deficient that he seems to have been largely unaware of geographical, climatic, racial, religious and other influences on history. He saw man as essentially the same in all times and places, and as a perfectly free and unhampered agent, though in certain times and places guilty of incomprehensible stupidity. The history of nations thus became political history purely and simply, and largely a history of individual men; and individual action was to be understood wholly in moral terms. Any man or action who could not be approved by the enlightened standards of the mid-eighteenth century, was judged immediately and without recourse to the study of social

[38] Much of what follows on Hume, Robertson, and Gibbon is based on the essays of J. B. Black, *The Art of History*, Methuen, London, 1926.

or other historical influences, and thus condemned, or more than likely ridiculed. History was seen in two dimensions, and that which appeared out of focus was merely a proper subject for satire. The result is an heroic style greatly tempered with formal irony. It is a style of great beauty, and in dealing with certain subjects probably comes very close to the truth; but in the main it provides a simplification of its material so extreme that its principal value today resides in its impact on later historians.

Hume's style displays another mark of the eighteenth century, more specifically of the literary tradition affected directly or indirectly by deism.[39] The curious self-righteousness, mild but immovable, the security that all problems had been solved and that all were really very simple, which we meet in the thought of Shaftesbury and his followers, and which they seem to have imposed upon the attitudes of most of the writers of the generation or so following, had as one of its most obvious results the kind of stylistic stereotype which we have come to consider as more or less characteristic of eighteenth century style: a stereotype both general and genteel, and commonly sentimental in its tendency, and which is used as a regular substitute for exact rendering of the material under discussion. J. B. Black points out a tendency in the work of Hume's contemporary, Robertson, which may do something to increase the inclination to this vice in Gibbon and in his disciple, Prescott: a concern for the dignity of history, which makes it imperative to eliminate the detail taken from vulgar but vivid reality; to eliminate, for example, the king's dagger left sticking in the body of Rizzio, which Robertson found in his original document.

The effect of these men on the monumental genius of Gibbon was very real, or at least the resemblance is real. The

[39] This subject is discussed a little more fully in my essay on Stevens in the present volume.

style has developed into something that one is tempted to call a prose equivalent of Milton's verse, but it is not that, for it is softer, smoother, and less uncompromising: but it is rich, complex, and massive, and like Milton's verse appears at times to be restricted in its perceptions by its very grandeur: Black quotes Bagehot's complaint that Gibbon cannot say Asia *minor.* Perhaps the following passage will suffice as well as any other to indicate the manner in which Gibbon is frequently constrained by the very nature of his instrument. It is from the portrait of Theodora, and I take the liberty of using my own italics:

> The beauty of Theodora was the subject of *more flattering praise* and the source of more *exquisite delight.* Her features were delicate and regular; her complexion, though somewhat pale, was *tinged with a natural color; every sensation* was instantly expressed by the *vivacity of her eyes; her easy motions displayed the graces* of *a small but elegant figure;* and *either love or adulation* might proclaim that *painting and poetry were incapable of delineating the matchless excellence of her form. But this form was degraded by the facility with which it was exposed to the public eye and prostituted to licentious desire.* Her *venal charms* were abandoned to *a promiscuous crowd of citizens and strangers . . .* The satirical historian has not *blushed to describe the naked scenes* which Theodora was not ashamed to exhibit in the theatre. After exhausting the arts of sensual pleasure, she most *ungratefully murmured* against the *parsimony of Nature;* but her murmurs, her pleasures, and her arts must be veiled in the obscurity of a learned language.

The subject of this passage is a prostitute who became empress. The historian's embarrassment is extreme, but the embarrassment is probably as much as anything stylistic and practical. The normal tone of his prose, the entire state of mind established by it, forbids his dealing with this material with much greater precision.

Prescott, like Gibbon, chose, for his two most famous histories, themes which in themselves possess extraordinary grandeur. They have not the chronological and geographical sweep of the theme of Gibbon, nor are they as important in the development of western civilization; but what they lack in these respects they make up by their strangeness, and the fall of an empire such as that of the Incas, of a civilization such as that of the Mexicans, is sufficiently impressive. The cadence, whether of sentence, of paragraph, or of narrative, is similar to that of Gibbon; the scholarship, within the more limited field, is probably as competent, though on this subject I can merely hazard a guess; the style displays a similar quality of polite imperception, of decadence, and more consistently and obviously, at the same time that it is in spite of this defect beautifully controlled and almost invariably interesting. There may be a greater awareness on the part of Prescott than on that of Gibbon, who in this respect is closer, though not extremely close, to Hume, of the necessity of laboring to understand the minds of people of remote times and cultures. This may account in part for the complete lack of irony in Prescott, although the lack is no doubt more largely due to a lack of perception of another kind, to a kind of provincial caution, placidity, and decorum. Prescott lacks the range and cultivation of Gibbon's mind, and his prose represents a gentle deterioration of that of his master. When in his last history, he endeavored, apparently, to clear his prose of its floridity and magniloquence, he merely retreated, with no appreciable advantage, toward the kind of prose one can find in the average textbook, as a comparison with parallel passages in Motley will easily show.

If style were a more or less independent organism, living, maturing and dying according to its own principles, this should have been the end of the grand manner of writing history; but the manner was revived and in certain respects very brilliantly revised, by Macaulay and Motley.

Macaulay is a master of the long sentence, but he tends to shorten its units and hasten its movement; and he deliberately employs the short sentence to achieve flexibility and variation. The prose remains heroic, but has ceased to be grandiloquent; the stereotyped phrase is rare; there is no difficulty in rendering the dagger left sticking in the body or the dungheaps beneath the windows of the country gentlemen. These few lines from the account of the execution of Monmouth represent a revolution in the practice of historical prose:

> The head sank down once more. The stroke was repeated again and again; but still the neck was not severed, and the body continued to move. Yells of rage and horror rose from the crowd. Ketch flung down the axe with a curse. "I cannot do it," he said; "my heart fails me." "Take up the axe, man," said the sheriff. "Fling him over the rails," roared the mob. Two more blows extinguished the last remains of life; but a knife was used to separate the head from the shoulders.

This is near the end of one of the greatest pieces of narrative in Macaulay's history, and indeed in English literature, the account of Monmouth's rebellion. The men, the country, the mud, the weather, as well as the blood and disaster, are rendered unforgettably, and this passage is followed immediately by the magnificent meditation on Monmouth's burial, a meditation worthy of Shakespeare. But no detail damages the prose. The prose is quick as well as intricate. It changes pace rapidly, and moves easily from subject to subject, but it never loses its identity. Whatever Macaulay's defects as an historical scholar —and he resembles most scholars in this, that his errors appear to have been many and serious—his contribution to the development of historical prose was one of the greatest. Motley's virtues are similar and perhaps not greatly inferior, although there is a stronger trace in Motley of the heroic stereotype.

Parkman has similar virtues at his best, but even to the end of his career the opportunity of describing a forest scene will demoralize him completely and reduce his style to a cold delirium of academic pseudo-poeticism. And the hardships of his private life, his engrossing and exhausting struggle with blindness, insanity, rheumatism, arthritis and perhaps other disorders, although one cannot but admire him for his strength of character in dealing with them, unquestionably limited both his scholarship and his understanding to the point where he is relatively a minor figure. He was forced to concentrate on the immediate data of his subject: he knew to perfection what the priests had done in the wilderness, but his understanding of the religious mind was that of Hume; he knew how the Iroquois and the Hurons appeared to the priest and how they behaved in war, but he knew nothing of anthropology and seems not to have considered even the lessons to be drawn from Prescott's treatment of the civilized tribes. The Indian and priest in juxtaposition, and in certain kinds of action, as seen from without by a man of heroic temperament and limited understanding, he could depict to perfection. He was at his best in dealing with the simple military man or adventurer, whose qualities he was easily able to comprehend.

But to the best of my knowledge, Parkman is the last distinguished historian of the heroic line.[40] Adams introduces a new style and an entirely new conception of historiography. The Adams who wrote the history was in the full possession of his intellectual powers, but he was the same Adams who was to deteriorate in the particular manner which we have seen. He was not heroic, and he did not see men as heroic, or at least he did not see those as heroic who were close to him in time and civilization. But he had a curiosity about psycho-

[40] I am simply taking it for granted that my reader feels, as I do, that the less said about Carlyle the better.

logical motives and action comparable to that of Henry James; his gift was for high comedy.

Gibbon chose for his subject the decline and fall of the Roman Empire; and the other historians whom I have mentioned did their best to rival this selection among the subjects remaining to them. The subjects were all essentially epic. Adams chose as his subject a period of sixteen years in the history of a nation which was, at the period which he examined, of about the same importance as Ecuador or Bolivia in the world of today; and which was, at the time of his writing, in spite of its astonishing growth, in a period of economic, political, and moral confusion which may well have made its future seem doubtful. But it was Adams' own country, and his forbears had helped to make it; so the subject was serious. Yet although it was a subject which called for serious investigation, it could scarcely hope for better than disinterested examination from Adams: if comedy was inherent in the subject, then comedy would certainly result in the literary product.

I have already spoken of Adams' admiration for James's treatment of character; I have quoted Adams on the "pleasure of seeing the lights of his burning glass turned on alternate sides of the same figure." He was fascinated with the manner in which the Jamesian character tends to shift and dissolve and assume new aspects under scrutiny, and he was conscious that he possessed the same kind of sensibility. And his central figure, Thomas Jefferson, probably lent itself better to representation by a man of Adams' talents than any other major American statesman would have done.

The history opens with six chapters of analysis of general conditions, and the last volume closes with a similar analysis. The narrative proper begins with the seventh chapter, which gives a picture of Jefferson's inauguration and an introductory portrait of each of the main figures in the administration, a portrait which is brief, mainly physical, and skillfully suggestive. His final summary of Jefferson's appearance and mannerisms is as follows: [41]

For eight years this tall, loosely built, somewhat stiff figure, in red waistcoat and yarn stockings, slippers down at the heel, and clothes that seemed too small for him, may be imagined as Senator Maclay described him, sitting on one hip, with one shoulder high above the other, talking almost without ceasing to his visitors at the White House. His skin was thin, peeling from his face on exposure to the sun, and giving it a tettered appearance. This sandy face, with hazel eyes and sunny aspect; this loose shackling person; this rambling and often brilliant conversation, belonged to the controlling influences of American history, more necessary to the story than three fourths of the official papers, which only hid the truth.

And later, when the narrative has progressed sufficiently for the statement to be comprehensible, he writes: [42]

The contradictions in Jefferson's character have always rendered it a fascinating study. Excepting his rival, Alexander Hamilton, no American has been the object of estimates so widely differing and so difficult to reconcile. Almost every other American statesman might be described in a parenthesis. A few broad strokes of the brush would paint the portraits of all the early Presidents with this exception, and a few more strokes would answer for any member of their cabinets; but Jefferson could be painted only touch by touch, with a fine pencil, and the perfection of the likeness depended upon the shifting and uncertain flicker of its semitransparent shadows.

To attempt a summary or description of his method of depicting this character would be useless, for he does it only in rendering fully and cautiously the manner in which Jefferson dealt with the many confusing situations encountered in his position; but one can illustrate it on a very small scale by

[41] Op. cit., Vol. I, p. 187.   [42] Ibid., p. 277.

quoting complete his account of a minor incident, the Callender scandal: [43]

James Thompson Callender, a Scotch adventurer compared with whom the Cobbetts, Duanes, Cheethams, and Woods who infested the press were men of moral and pure life, had been an ally of Jefferson during the stormy days of 1798, and had published at Richmond a volume called "The Prospect before Us," which was sufficiently libellous to draw upon him a State prosecution, and a fine and some months imprisonment at the rough hands of Judge Chase. A few years later the Republicans would have applauded the sentence, and regretted only its lightness. In 1800 they were bound to make common cause with the victim. When Jefferson became President, he pardoned Callender, and by a stretch of authority returned to him the amount of his fine. Naturally Callender expected reward. He hastened to Washington, and was referred to Madison. He said that he was in love, and hinted that to win the object of his affections nothing less than the post-office at Richmond was necessary for his social standing. Meeting with a positive refusal, he returned to Richmond in extreme anger, and became editor of a newspaper called "The Recorder," in which he began to wage against Jefferson a war of slander that Cobbett and Cheetham would have shrunk from. He collected every story he could gather, among overseers and scandalmongers, about Jefferson's past life,—charged him with having a family of negro children by a slave named Sally; with having been turned out of the house of a certain Major Walker for writing a secret love-letter to his wife; with having swindled his creditors by paying debts in worthless currency, and with having privately paid Callender himself to write "The Prospect before Us," besides furnishing materials for the book. Disproof of these charges was impossible. That which concerned Black Sally, as she was called, seems to have rested on a confusion of persons which could not be cleared up; that relating to Mrs. Walker had a foundation of truth, although the parties were afterwards reconciled; that regarding the payment of debt

[43] Ibid., pp. 322 to 327.

was true in one sense, and false only in the sense which Callender gave it; while that which referred to "The Prospect before Us" was true enough to be serious. All these charges were welcomed by the Federalist press, reprinted even in the New York "Evening Post," and scattered broadcast over New England. There men's minds were ready to welcome any tale of villainy that bore out their theory of Jefferson's character; and at the most critical moment, a mistake made by himself went far to confirm their prejudice.

Jefferson's nature was feminine; he was more refined than many women in the delicacy of his private relations, and even men as shameless as Callender himself winced under attacks of such a sort. He was sensitive, affectionate, and, in his own eyes, heroic. He yearned for love and praise as no other great American ever did. He hated the clergy chiefly because he knew that from them he could expect neither love nor praise, perhaps not even forbearance. He had befriended Callender against his own better judgment, as every party leader befriended party hacks, not because the leaders approved them, but because they were necessary for the press. So far as license was concerned, "The Prospect before Us" was a mild libel, compared with Cobbett's, Coleman's, and Dennie's cataracts of abuse; and at the time it was written, Callender's character was not known and his habits were still decent. In return for kindness and encouragement, Callender attempted an act of dastardly assassination, which the whole Federalist press cheered. That a large part of the community, and the part socially uppermost, should believe this drunken ruffian, and should laugh while he bespattered their president with his filth, was a mortification which cut deep into Jefferson's heart. Hurt and angry, he felt that at bottom it was the old theological hatred in Virginia and New England which sustained this mode of warfare; that as he had flung Paine at them, they were flinging Callender at him. "With the aid of a lying renegade from Republicanism, the Federalists have opened their sluices of calumny," he wrote; and he would have done wisely to say no more. Unluckily for him, he undertook to contradict Callender's assertions.

James Monroe was Governor of Virginia. Some weakness in

Monroe's character caused him more than once to mix in scandals which he might better have left untouched. July 7, 1802, he wrote to the President, asking for the facts in regard to Jefferson's relations with Callender. The President's reply confessed the smart of his wound:

"I am really mortified at the base ingratitude of Callender. It presents human nature in a hideous form. It gives me concern because I perceive that relief which was afforded him on mere motives of charity, may be viewed under the aspect of employing him as a writer."

He explained how he had pitied Callender, and repeatedly given him money.

"As to myself," he continued, "no man wished more to see his pen stopped; but I considered him still as a proper object of benevolence. The succeeding year he again wanted money to buy paper for another volume. I made his letter, as before, the occasion of giving him another fifty dollars. He considers these as proofs of my approbation of his writings, when they were mere charities, yielded under a strong conviction that he was injuring us by his writings."

Unfortunately, Jefferson could not find the press-copies of his letters to Callender, and let Monroe send out these apologies without stopping to compare them with his written words. No sooner had the Republican newspapers taken their tone from Monroe, and committed themselves to these assertions of fact, than Callender printed the two letters which Jefferson had written to him, which proved that not only had Jefferson given him at different times some two hundred dollars, but had also supplied information, of a harmless nature, for "The Prospect before Us," and under an injunction of secrecy had encouraged Callender to write. His words were not to be explained away: "I thank you for the proof-sheets you enclosed me; such papers cannot fail to produce the best effect."

No man who stood within the circle of the President's intimates could be perplexed to understand how this apparent self-contradiction might have occurred. Callender was neither the first nor the last to take advantage of what John Randolph called the "easy credulity" of Jefferson's temper. The nearest approach Jefferson could make toward checking an over-zealous friend was by shades of difference in the strength of his encouragement. To tell Callender that his book could not fail to produce the best effect was a way of hinting that it might do harm; and, however specious such an excuse might seem, this language was in his mind consistent with a secret wish that Callender should not write. More than one such instance of this kindly prevarication, this dislike of whatever might seem harsh or disobliging, could be found in Jefferson's correspondence.

A man's enemies rarely invent specious theories of human nature in order to excuse what they prefer to look upon as falsehood and treason. July 17, 1803, Callender was drowned in some drunken debauch; but the Federalists never forgot his calumnies, or ceased ringing the changes on the President's self-contradictions,—and throughout New England the trio of Jefferson, Paine and Callender were henceforth held in equal abhorrence. That this prejudice did not affect Jefferson's popular vote was true, but it seriously affected his social relations; and it annoyed and mortified him more than coarser men could understand, to feel in the midst of his utmost popularity that large numbers of his worthiest fellow-citizens, whose respect he knew himself to deserve, despised him as they did the vermin they trod upon.

One has in this account the portrait of a man who cannot quite gauge himself or his motives, and who appears extremely ambiguous, perhaps, to many of his observers; but we have a portrait of the man in action, a rich exhibition of his actions, feelings, and beliefs, no less rich than James could have exhibited in comparable space, in spite of the fact that every detail in Adams' account is firmly attached to an historical document. The exhibition of Jefferson's character is not only witty, but is honest and perceptive as well; it was only in Adams' later years that his interest in this aspect of human nature was to degenerate into a shallow mannerism, as we have seen it in the *Education*. The early incidents exhibiting Jefferson's nature in minor situations, suggest the man as we shall find him in the larger plan of the total work, dealing with the major problems of statesmanship.

Jefferson is obviously the character who most fascinates and amuses the historian; and Adams is fortunate that Jefferson's part was actually central. But he accepts his obligation as an historian with no qualms; he neither avoids adequate treatment of men of other types nor tries to remodel them. Burr, Jackson, Harrison, Tecumseh, Napoleon, Madison, Gallatin, and Barlow are only a few of the number portrayed at length: each one exists in his own right and is unforgettable. And each is portrayed as he should be portrayed by a careful historian: through his written words, or the written words of observers, and through his acts, one by one and in interrelation, each act taken carefully and curiously naked from the original document. Whether the subject is the maneuvering of Napoleon and the British ministry, whether it is the incidents leading to the death of Hamilton or those leading to the battle of Tippecanoe and the later death of that moderate and distinguished gentleman, Tecumseh, the story is clear and beautifully illuminated. All generalizations are made from the objective data actually presented, and the generalizations give the effect, at least, of caution and precision. We have human action of the most serious kind, the action of mature men affecting and governing the lives of nations. We have become so conditioned—I think that is the word—to the reading of novels, that we are likely to have the feeling that human nature cannot be depicted with depth or subtlety except as it appears in what we should call the personal adventures of the relatively young, in the private relationships arising in what is relatively the leisure time of the characters. To appreciate fully what Adams has done with his people, one must have, I suppose, a sufficient interest in history as bare fact not to be troubled by it; but the interest at least is adult and I can see no great harm in anyone's having it.

To the reader who habitually assumes that the great historians are necessarily in the heroic tradition, and that the only other historical type is that of the schoolroom text or the professional monograph, Adams' history may at first glance appear disappointing: it employs the method of the learned monograph, in a sense, but it raises the method to a form of art. This is what one should not overlook. The style is expert and flexible; it is never too exalted for its subject, as is sometimes the style of Gibbon; it never carries too much conviction to be convincing, as does sometimes the style of Macaulay or that of Motley. It is a style that can offer a sequence of dates or the summary of a document, without loss either of accuracy or of distinction. It is in the passages dealing with the play of character that the book is most brilliant, but if one reads and rereads it carefully, one discovers that the play of character is comprehensible as a result of the author's careful preparations, and that the style is adequate with respect to everything it touches.

The history is penetrated with precise intelligence in all its parts: it is in this quality, I think, that it surpasses any other historical masterpiece with which I am acquainted. There is greater magnificence in portions of Gibbon, Macaulay, and Motley, but there is seldom the skill of penetration, and there is not the uniformity of success in any of them. And the wit of Adams is invariably the result of understanding instead of the result of its absence.

What may have been the immediate cause of his turning away from the writing of history to the irresponsible activities of his later years, it might be hard to say. The death of his wife will not account for it, for a large part of the history was finished after that event; and the suggestion, which occurs in one of his letters, that the cause was the discouragement of his publishers, need be given but very little weight. Probably it was merely the accumulation of emotion, the result of an ancestral tendency, which finally reached a state where it influenced his action definitively. The letters indicate a regret for his past distinction, however. In 1899 he wrote to Elizabeth Cameron: [44]

So I read on and enjoyed my own history, which I am correcting in case of further editions. As a rule it bores me, and I have to drive myself up to the task, but yesterday I happened on the third volume, and was greatly amused by it. I was honestly surprised that no one ever mentioned it to me, or spoke of it in the press, so that I had never read it or heard of it before.

And to the same correspondent he wrote even more regretfully about two years later, referring to himself by a name of his own invention which he occasionally employs in his letters: [45]

The trouble is, and always has been, and always will be, with the greed and selfishness and jealousy and ambition of senators. On that subject you can read a now forgotten work written by one of your acquaintances long since dead, one Dordy d'Ullivier d' Angoulême, tedious enough but elaborately supported by historical evidence in nine volumes.

And in the same year he wrote to Henry Osborn Taylor, the eminent medievalist, who had formerly been his pupil: [46]

You have gone so far beyond me, both in horizon and in study, that I feel our situations reversed. You are the professor; I am the student. My role suits me better now, for I was always indolent and have always shirked responsibility. Between the admission that everything is right and everything wrong, I could never see my way to set up a sign-post.

[44] *Letters of Henry Adams,* op. cit., p. 215.　　[45] Ibid., p. 318.
[46] Ibid., p. 331.

In 1917, he wrote to Charles Milnes Gaskell, in one of his last letters: [47]

There are just three of my contemporaries living on this shore, but we have all lost our minds or our senses and no one thinks it worth while to tell us so. No books come out. I am not aware that there are any writers left, certainly none in my branch, which was extinct five and twenty years ago and more. No one even remembers the name of Lord Macaulay. I once wrote some books myself, but no one has even mentioned the fact to me for more than a generation. I have a vague recollection that once some young person *did* mention an anecdote to me that came from one of my books and that he attributed it to some one else.

[47] Ibid., p. 644.

WALLACE
STEVENS

OR THE HEDONIST'S PROGRESS [1]

THOUGH WALLACE STEVENS has published almost nothing in
the way of criticism, he has nevertheless been very clear in
stating his theories of life and of literature, and he may justifi-
ably be treated, I believe, in a series of essays on literary
theorists.

His fundamental ideas are stated in *Sunday Morning,* an
early poem, and in some ways his greatest. The poem consists
of eight stanzas in blank verse, each containing fifteen lines,
and it presents a clear and fairly coherent argument.

The first stanza sets the stage and identifies the protagonist.
We are given a woman, at home on a Sunday morning, medi-
tating on the meaning of death. The second stanza asks the

[1] All poems mentioned in this essay, unless otherwise identified, are to
be found in the second edition of *Harmonium,* by Wallace Stevens, published by Alfred A. Knopf, New York, 1931. The book is small, indexed,
and well known, and page references seem unnecessary.

question which provides the subject of the poem; it asks what divinity this woman may be thought to possess as a recompense for her ultimate surrender to death; and having asked the question, it replies that her divinity, which must live within herself, consists wholly in her emotions—not in her understanding of the emotions, but in the emotions as a good in themselves. This answer is not quite the orthodox romantic answer, which would offer us in the emotions either a true guide to virtue or a more or less mystical experience leading to some kind of union with some kind of deity. Any philosophy which offers the cultivation of the emotions as an end in itself, I suppose, is a kind of hedonism. In any event, that is the kind of philosophy which we find here.

The third stanza, by means of the allegory of Jove and his human loves, through his union with whom he crossed the heavenly strain upon the human, implies that man has a capacity which may at least figuratively be termed divine; the stanza is a subordinate commentary on the one preceding, and does not really advance the argument.

In the fourth stanza, however, the argument moves forward. The protagonist objects to the concept which has been offered her; she states that the beauties of this life are transient and that she longs to believe in a Paradise beyond them. The remainder of the stanza, and the greater part of it, is the poet's reply: in a passage of great rhetorical power, he denies the possibility of Paradise, at the same time that he communicates through the feeling of his language a deep nostalgic longing to accept the ideas which he is rejecting. In the first two lines of the fifth stanza, the woman repeats her objection, and the poet then replies with an explanation of the function of death: it is our awareness of the imminence of death which heightens our emotions and sharpens our perceptions; our knowledge of life's transience stimulates our perception of life's beauty.

In the sixth stanza the poet considers an hypothetical paradise, and, since he can imagine it only in terms of a projection of the good life as the hedonist understands the good life, he deduces that paradise would become tedious and insipid: we have in this stanza the first sharp vision of the ennui which is to obsess the later work of the poet and which is ultimately to wreck his talent, an ennui arising from the fact that emotion is not a good in itself, but that if cultivated for itself alone is merely a pleasant diversion so long as the novelty of a given experience endures, at most as long as new experiences can give us the illusion of novel excitement, and then becomes a disease of the spirit, a state of indifferency in which there is neither novelty nor significance.

The seventh stanza presents a vision of a future race of men engaged in a religious ritual, the generating principle of which is their joy in the world as it is given them and their sense of brotherhood as "men that perish." The stanza contains suggestions of a pantheism which goes beyond the bounds of a strict hedonism, but they are merely suggestions and they appear nowhere else. The eighth and last stanza begins by denying the immortality of Jesus, and, by implication, of man; and it places the protagonist finally and irretrievably on a small but beautiful planet, floating like a tropical island in boundless space, "in an old chaos of the sun."

This summary, even as summaries go, is extremely skeletalized. It has been my intention, here, merely to isolate the hedonistic theme for future consideration; the theme is not thus isolated in the poem, but is complicated by its interconnections with other human problems from which not even a hedonist can escape. Whatever the defects of the hedonistic theme, and with the possible but by no means certain exception of a few short poems by Stevens and of two or three poems by E. A. Robinson, *Sunday Morning* is probably the greatest American poem of the twentieth century and is certainly one of the greatest contemplative poems in English: in a blank

verse which differs, in its firmness of structure and incalcu-
lable sensitivity of detail, from all other blank verse of our time
save that of a few poems by Hart Crane which were in some
measure modeled upon it, it renders the acute uncertainty of
what we are inclined to consider the modern mind, but it does
so with no uncertainty of method or of statement; it renders
an acute consciousness of the imminence of death, of the sensory and emotional richness of life on this bewildering planet,
and of the heroic magnificence of the religious myths which
are lost to the poet and to many of the rest of us, except as
memories of things long past. If Stevens' career had stopped
with this poem, or a few years thereafter, it might seem an
unnecessary unkindness to insist upon the limitations of understanding which the poem discloses; but those limitations
appear very obviously in a few later poems, and they seem to
me to be very clearly related to the rapid and tragic decay of
the poet's style. As a poet in early maturity, Stevens brought
to this subject a style which was the result of a fine native gift
enriched by the study of English blank verse; the subject, once
formulated, and accepted as a guide to life and to expression,
destroyed the style in less than two decades. In *Sunday Morning* itself, we detect the limitations of the subject only by
rational analysis; in the later work we see the effect of those
limitations.

We may consider briefly, and perhaps as a kind of footnote
to *Sunday Morning,* one of the more obscure poems, called
The Stars at Tallapoosa. As far as I can penetrate this poem, I
judge that it postulates the absolute severance of the intellectual and the emotional: the lines between the stars are the
lines of pure intellect; the earth-lines and the sea-lines represent the non-intellectual experience (loosely speaking) of daily
human life. Both modes of experience have beauty and should
be pursued, but they are disparate and unrelated to each other;
and it follows, although this is not stated in the poem, that the

intellectual experience, since it bears no relationship to the rest of our life and hence is in no way useful, is valuable simply for the independent emotional excitement which one may derive from it.

If we turn to *A High-Toned Old Christian Woman*, a brief didactic and satirical poem, which is quite clear and unmistakable as regards its theoretic import, we get an additional step in the argument: we learn that the "moral law" is not necessary as a framework for art, but that "the opposing law" will do as well, and that in either event, the artists,

> Your disaffected flagellants, well-stuffed,
> Smacking their muzzy bellies in parade,
> Proud of such novelties of the sublime,
> Such tink and tank and tunk-a-tunk-tunk,
> May, merely may, madame, whip from themselves
> A jovial hullabaloo among the spheres.

Stevens, in becoming thus explicit, states his final doctrine, as do certain other contemporary theorists, in language surprisingly reminiscent of Poe:

> "It may be, indeed, that here this sublime end is, now and then, attained in fact. We are often made to feel with a shivering delight, that from an earthly harp are stricken notes which *cannot* have been unfamiliar to the angels." [2]

Poe's statement is made, of course, in the tone of saccharine sentimentality which is Poe's nearest approach to sincerity; Stevens' statement is made ironically, but one should not be misled by this fact. For though Stevens is ridiculing himself

---

[2] From *The Poetic Principle,* page 12 of Vol. I of the three volumes of criticism in Poe's works, the edition of Stedman and Woodberry. Quoted and elucidated in my essay on Poe, American Literature, Vol. 8, No. 4, page 392, and in my book of essays, *Maule's Curse* (New Directions, 1938), page 109.

and his artists, he is ridiculing his old Christian woman, the representative of the moralistic point of view, even more severely: he is offering his opinion as more nearly tenable than hers, notwithstanding the fact that he cannot offer his opinion with real seriousness. Stevens' self-ridicule is as irrational in its way as Poe's sentimentalism, and like that sentimentalism springs from a doctrine which eliminates the possibility of the rational understanding of experience and of a moral judgment deriving therefrom: since no idea is really tenable and since we cannot judge of the justice of a feeling but can only seek to heighten its intensity, all ideas and all feelings may fairly be, and sooner or later, in the history of a sensitive and witty man, are certain to be, subjected to merciless ridicule; but of this we shall see more interesting evidence later.

It is perhaps not important, but it is at least mildly interesting, to call attention at this point to a poem which has been at least twice misinterpreted by commentators who have not taken the trouble to understand Stevens as a whole. The poem is *Anecdote of the Jar:*

> I placed a jar in Tennessee,
> And round it was, upon a hill.
> It made the slovenly wilderness
> Surround that hill.
>
> The wilderness rose up to it,
> And sprawled around, no longer wild.
> The jar was round upon the ground
> And tall and of a port in air.
>
> It took dominion everywhere.
> The jar was gray and bare.
> It did not give of bird or bush,
> Like nothing else in Tennessee.

Stanley P. Chase has written of this poem:

"Very likely the little poem is meant to suggest nothing more than the superiority, to an intensely civilized person, of the simplest bit of handicraft over any extent of unregulated 'nature' . . ."[3]

And Howard Baker writes with the same obtuseness, but with greater elaborateness:

"Similarly a wild and disorderly landscape is transformed into order by the presence of a symmetrical vase. . . . The jar acts in the imagination like one of the poles of the earth, the imaginary order of the lines of latitude and longitude projecting around the pole. The jar itself—simple and symmetrical, a product of the human consciousness and not of nature—is a very fitting symbol for man's dominion over nature . . ."[4]

If the poem ended with the fourth line, there might be an imperfect justification of the interpretation offered by these writers, for in the first four lines the wilderness is not only dominated by the jar—as, in fact, it is dominated throughout the poem,—but it is called slovenly. If we examine the next two lines, however, we see that the phrase, "the slovenly wilderness," is in fact a slovenly ellipsis. The wilderness is slovenly after it has been dominated and not before: it "sprawled around, no longer wild." The jar is the product of the human mind, as the critics remark, and it dominates the wilderness; but it does not give order to the wilderness—it is vulgar and sterile, and it transforms the wilderness into the semblance of a deserted picnic ground. Its sterility is indicated in the last three lines, and if the jar is to be accepted as symbolic of the human intellect, then the poem is in part another example of

3 *Dionysus in Dismay*, by Stanley P. Chase, in *Humanism and America*, edited by Norman Foerster, Farrar and Rinehart, New York, 1930, page 211.
4 *Wallace Stevens and Other Poets*, by Howard Baker, The Southern Review, Vol. I, Number 2, Autumn 1935, page 376.

the same theme which we found in *The Stars at Tallapoosa*, but expressed this time with disillusionment and a measure of disgust. The poem would appear to be primarily an expression of the corrupting effect of the intellect upon natural beauty, and hence a purely romantic performance. To read any measure of neo-humanism into Stevens is as foolish as to endeavor, in the manner of certain young critics of a few years ago, to read into him a kind of incipient and trembling consciousness of the beauty of Marxism.

I have already pointed out that in the sixth stanza of *Sunday Morning*, the stanza in which Stevens projects into the eternity of paradise the highest good which he can imagine, there appears a weary dissatisfaction with the experience, a hint of the dissatisfaction which might imaginably appear in our present life if the experience were too long protracted. This dissatisfaction is familiar to students of romantic literature under the name of ennui; it is the boredom which eventually overtakes the man who seeks for excitement instead of understanding. In the poem entitled *The Man Whose Pharynx Was Bad* we find a statement of this boredom which is both extreme and explicit. The poem as it appears in *Harmonium* lacks four lines of the original version, lines ten to thirteen inclusive, which appeared in The New Republic for September 14, 1921. Those lines are essential to the poem and to the understanding of Stevens, and I shall quote the entire poem in its original version:

> The time of year has grown indifferent.
> Mildew of summer and the deepening snow
> Are both alike in the routine I know;
> I am too dumbly in my being pent.
>
> The wind attendant on the solstices
> Blows on the shutters of the metropoles,

Stirring no poet in his sleep, and tolls
The grand ideas of the villages.

The malady of the quotidian . . .
Perhaps if summer ever came to rest
And lengthened, deepened, comforted, caressed
Through days like oceans in obsidian

Horizons, full of night's midsummer blaze;
Perhaps, if winter once could penetrate
Through all its purples to the final slate,
Persisting bleakly in an icy haze;

One might in turn become less diffident,
Out of such mildew plucking neater mould
And spouting new orations of the cold.
One might. One might. But time will not relent.

The poet has progressed in this poem to the point at which the
intensity of emotion possible in actual human life has become
insipid, and he conceives the possibility of ultimate satisfaction only in some impossible emotional finality of no matter
what kind. In fact, the figurative opposites of summer and
winter here offered suggest the opposites of the moral and the
anti-moral which appear in *A High-Toned Old Christian
Woman.*

The situation in which Stevens may here be observed is
similar to a difficulty in which Poe found himself. Poe, like
Stevens, sought only emotional stimulation in the arts, and
hence he considered novelty, and novelty of a fairly crude
kind, to be an essential of good art. He wrote:

"Nothing is more clear than this proposition, although denied
by the chlorine critics (the grass-green). The desire of the new is an
element of the soul. The most exquisite pleasures grow dull in

repetition. A strain of music enchants. Heard a second time, it pleases. Heard a tenth it does not displease. We hear it a twentieth, and ask ourselves why we admired. At the fiftieth, it produces ennui, at the hundredth disgust." [5]

Both men are in search of intense feeling; neither is in search of just feeling, of feeling properly motivated. The poem as an exercise in just feeling is an act of moral judgment, as I have repeatedly indicated; and though all such judgments must of necessity be governed by general principles, yet each particular judgment, since it arises from an individual relationship between unique persons and events, will be, if truly just, unique, as individual men are unique, and will have its own inexhaustible fascination as a living entity. But if one does not recognize this principle of justice, then the poem can have no true uniquenesss: the poet and the reader alike are bent, as are Poe and Stevens, on a quest for the new, which, in the realm of emotion divorced from understanding or any principle of propriety, can be found only in new degrees of intensity and of strangeness; and as each new degree achieved becomes familiar it is submerged in the monotone of that which is no longer new, so that the search is equally devoid of hope and of significance. Poe never had the wit to perceive the futility of this search; Stevens has the wit not only to see the futility but to be both depressed and ironic in consequence, yet he is unable to think himself out of the situation into which he has wandered.

Unless one change one's entire philosophy, having arrived at this impasse, there can remain open to one only two modes of action: one may renounce one's art and subside into a kind of stoical silence; or one may pursue, not greater intensity of experience, for human language and the human organism alike set a certain limit to progress in that direction, but ex-

[5] Op. Cit. Vol. III, p. 107.

perience increasingly elusive and incomprehensible. Stevens has considered both of these possibilities, but since he has chosen the latter, we may fairly examine first the mode of action which he has considered and discarded. It so happens, incidentally, that his meditation upon the possibility of renunciation has resulted in his longest single work.

The Comedian as the Letter C (the significance of the title, I regret to say, escapes both my learning and my ingenuity) is a narrative poem in six parts, dealing with a poet who begins with romantic views of the function of his art and who, in reforming them, comes to abandon his art as superfluous. The first part of the poem deals with Crispin's encounter with the sea, that is, with his realization of a universe vast, chaotic, and impersonal beyond his power of formulation or imagination, and rendering him contemptible by contrast. In the second part, Crispin arrives in Yucatan, disillusioned as to his old convictions, but finding a heightened experience and new food for his art in the barbaric violence of the tropical landscape; finding these, that is, until he is overwhelmed by a thunderstorm, of which the symbolic function is similar to that of the sea in the first part, and is driven with the terrified crowd about him into the cathedral. In the third part he returns to North America, intent now, not on the extreme and unnatural excitements of the southern landscape which he has left, but on the discovery of reality:

> He gripped more closely the essential prose
> As being, in a world so falsified,
> The one integrity for him, the one
> Discovery still possible to make,
> To which all poems were incident, unless
> That prose should wear a poem's guise at last.

But he is bent on discovering not the reality of his own nature, but rather the reality of his native country. Man is no longer,

as in the first line of the first part, the intelligence of his soil;
but the soil, as we note in the first line of the next and fourth
section, is man's intelligence. These statements do not have
the philosophical lucidity which would delight the present
simple paraphraser, but they seem to mean, in their relationship to this poem, that Crispin has been turned away first
from the attempt to study himself directly, and second from
the attempt to indulge in exotic experiences, and that he has
been turned instead to the attempt to master his native environment—to master it, that is, for the purposes of poetry. The
nature of this last procedure I do not pretend to understand,
and since the words which I have just used are my own and are
not quoted from Stevens, it is possible that my confusion is of
my own contriving. But in general, I should say that Stevens
appears to have slipped here into the Whitmanian form of a
romantic error common enough in our literature, but current
especially in Stevens' generation and espoused in particular
by Stevens' friend W. C. Williams: the fallacy that the poet
achieves salvation by being, in some way, intensely of and
expressive of his country. A common variant of this notion is
the idea that the poet should bear the same relationship to his
time, and in fact the two versions are perhaps most commonly
combined, as they are in Williams. Felt with sufficient intensity, they become indistinguishable, as in Crane or even in
Whitman, from pantheism, and go quite beyond the bounds
of hedonism; but the notions in question represent merely a
casual subject for meditation in Stevens, a subject which he
considers because he is confused but which involves a spiritual
quality, a capacity for naively whole-hearted enthusiasm, which
is quite foreign to his nature. The ideas are the attempt to
justify a kind of extroversion: the poet, cut off from human
nature, which is his proper subject-matter, seeks to find a subject in the description, or, as the saying goes, in the expression,
of what is round about him. In practice, this results mainly,

as in Williams, in a heavy use of the native landscape, sometimes as legitimate symbolism or background, sometimes as
the subject of mere description, sometimes as false symbolism [6]:
in the first of these three instances, the poet is actually intent
on doing something not adequately explained by his theory;
in the second he is doing something relatively easy and unimportant; and in the third he is writing badly. Crispin seeks,
then, an understanding not of himself but of his native landscape, and his native landscape is a temperate one, which does
not offer the flamboyant and succulent excitements of Yucatan:

> The spring came there in clinking pannicles
> Of half-dissolving frost, the summer came,
> If ever, whisked and wet, not ripening,
> Before the winter's vacancy returned.

This landscape is the one which appears in *The Man Whose
Pharynx Was Bad,* and which Stevens there uses to symbolize
his own frustration. But Crispin, having returned from
Yucatan, hopes now to achieve the beatific pleasure reserved
for the successful hedonist, not by extravagance of experience,
but by honesty and accuracy of experience: by honesty and
accuracy, however, so far as we can judge from the poem,
merely in describing the scenery which surrounds him, as if,
perhaps, there were some ulterior virtue in this process which
cannot quite be defined in words. The fourth section of the
poem is really an elaboration upon the central ideas of the
third, and it scarcely calls for comment at present. In the fifth
and sixth parts, Crispin's concentration upon the normal
world about him results in his marrying and begetting
daughters; and finding that the facts which he had set out to
describe with such exemplary honesty are more engrossing

[6] This whole topic is discussed at length in the second essay (the section
on Pseudo-reference) of my book called *Primitivism and Decadence,* The
Arrow Editions, New York, 1937.

than the description of them, he abandons his art, in order, as very young people are sometimes heard to say, to live. This is not surprising, for the honest description which Crispin set out to achieve is in itself a moral experience, though of a very limited kind: honest description renders the feeling appropriate to purely sensory experience, and is hence a kind of judgment of that experience. But if Crispin had realized this, he would have realized the whole moral basis of art, and would have proceeded to more complex subjects; not realizing this, he lost interest in his simplified art, and found the art even in this simplified form to be the last element of confusion remaining in his experience: to achieve intelligent objectivity, Crispin is forced to abandon his description and merely enjoy the subject-matter of his description in the most naked possible of conditions:

> He first, as realist, admitted that
> Whoever hunts a matinal continent
> May, after all, stop short before a plum
> And be content and still be realist.
> The words of things entangle and confuse.
> The plum survives its poems . . . . .
> . . . . it survives in its own form,
> Beyond these changes, good fat guzzly fruit.

We have now the complete argument, I believe, which leads to Crispin's renunciation. The passage in which the renunciation takes place, however, is interesting for another reason; for the quality of the rhetoric employed at this particular juncture helps us profoundly to understand Stevens himself. The passage follows closely upon the lines just quoted and will be found about half-way through the fifth section:

> Was he to bray this in profoundest brass
> Arointing his dreams with fugal requiems?

Was he to company vastest things defunct
With a blubber of tom-toms harrowing the sky?
Scrawl a tragedian's testament? Prolong
His active force in an inactive dirge,
Which, let the tall musicians call and call,
Should merely call him dead? Pronounce amen
Through choirs infolded to the outmost clouds?
Because he built a cabin who once planned
Loquacious columns by the ructive sea?
Because he turned to salad beds again?

What I wish the reader to note is this: that the passage describes Crispin's taking leave of his art, and describes also his refusal to use his art in the process of leave-taking, because the art is, after all, futile and contemptible. Yet for Stevens himself the entire poem is a kind of tentative leave-taking; he has not the courage to act as his hero acts and be done with it, so he practices the art which he cannot justify and describes it in terms of contempt. Furthermore, the chief instrument of irony in this passage, and throughout the poem, and indeed throughout much of the rest of Stevens, is a curious variant on the self-ridicule, the romantic irony, with which we are familiar from Byron through Laforgue and his modern disciples; [7] the instrument is self-parody, a parody occasionally subtle, often clumsy, of the refined and immutable style of Stevens at his best. To estimate at least a part of the tragedy represented by Stevens' career, the reader can scarcely do better than compare the lines quoted above with the last section of the much earlier Sunday Morning:

She hears upon that water without sound,
A voice that cries, "The tomb in Palestine
Is not the porch of spirits lingering.

[7] This entire subject is discussed in the latter part of my second essay in Primitivism and Decadence, already mentioned.

It is the grave of Jesus where he lay."
We live in an old chaos of the sun,
Or old dependency of day and night,
Or island solitude, unsponsored, free,
Of that wide water, inescapable.
Deer walk upon our mountains, and the quail
Whistle about us their spontaneous cries;
Sweet berries ripen in the wilderness;
And, in the isolation of the sky,
At evening, casual flocks of pigeons make
Ambiguous undulations as they sink,
Downward to darkness, on extended wings.

Since the poet, having arrived at the predicament to which we have traced him, however, is not to abandon his art, there remains only the possibility that he seek variety of experience in the increasingly perverse and strange; that he seek it, moreover, with no feeling of respect toward the art which serves as his only instrument and medium. In the poem entitled *The Revolutionists Stop for Orangeade,* we are given the theory of this type of poetry:

Hang a feather by your eye,
Nod and look a little sly.
This must be the vent of pity,
Deeper than a truer ditty
Of the real that wrenches,
Of the quick that's wry.

And from this point onward there remains little but the sly look and a perverse ingenuity in confusing the statement of essentially simple themes. *The Man with the Blue Guitar,*[8] for example, which is one of his most recent performances, is merely a jingling restatement of the old theme of the severance

8 *The Man with the Blue Guitar,* by Wallace Stevens, Alfred A. Knopf, N. Y., 1937.

between the rational understanding and the poetic imagination. But the statement is never quite clear; and since the theme, though unsound, is far from difficult to understand, one is inclined to suspect that the lack of clarity is the result of a deliberate choice, a choice motivated, perhaps, by the hope that some note more moving than the poet has a right to expect may be struck from the obscurity. And if one does not always encounter such wilful semiobscurity in the later poems, one much too commonly encounters the kind of laborious foolishness to be found in the following poem, entitled *The Mechanical Optimist,* published in *New Directions* for 1936:

> A lady dying of diabetes
> Listened to the radio,
> Catching the lesser dithyrambs.
> So heaven collects its bleating lambs.
>
> Her useless bracelets fondly fluttered,
> Paddling the melodic swirls,
> The idea of God no longer sputtered
> At the roots of her indifferent curls.
>
> The idea of the Alps grew large,
> Not yet, however, a thing to die in.
> It seemed serener just to die,
> To float off on the floweriest barge,
>
> Accompanied by the exegesis
> Of familiar things in a cheerful voice,
> Like the night before Christmas and all the carols.
> Dying lady, rejoice, rejoice!

The generating mood is one of ennui; the style represents an effort, half-bored and half desperate, to achieve originality; the victim of the irony is very small game, and scarcely worthy of the artillery of the author of *Sunday Morning;* the point of view is adolescent. The author of *Sunday Morning* and of *Le Monocle de Mon Oncle,* the heir of Milton and of Jonson, is endeavoring, in his old age, to épater les bourgeois. The poem is the work of a man who twenty or twenty-five years earlier was one of the great poets of the English language.

This is the outline, I believe, of the sequence of ideas and states of mind which have debased the greatest American poetic talent of the twentieth century. The sequence is offered merely as a species of logical sequence; it is only imperfectly chronological. Stevens was a hedonist from the beginning, and the entire complex of ideas and feelings which I have recounted are to be found in his work from the beginning. But although it is possible to find some of his most willful nonsense —*Earthy Anecdote*, let us say, or *Metaphors of a Magnifico*— among his earlier poems, it is likewise true that all of his great poetry is early. *Sunday Morning* is one of the earliest compositions; *The Snow Man, Le Monocle de Mon Oncle, Of the Manner of Addressing Clouds, Of Heaven Considered as a Tomb, The Death of the Soldier* are all of the next few years. All of these poems were written and first published before 1923, the date of the first edition of *Harmonium;* and if there is a later poem as good I do not know it or cannot appreciate it. There are other poems, more or less early, less perfect or of smaller scope but still of considerable beauty, such as *Peter Quince at the Clavier* or *Cortège for Rosenbloom,* and such poems as these one may find equalled occasionally, though very rarely, at a later date; but these two surpass anything by the author which I have read in the past decade.

Some of the virtues of *Sunday Morning* I have indicated in very general terms, but one cannot turn from the poem that may be the greatest American work of our century without

considering briefly some of its more haunting beauties, if it
be only as an act of piety.

I have already quoted the final stanza of the poem, and its
beauty should be obvious; yet as removed from its context, the
stanza loses much of its complexity. The "water without
sound," the "wide water inescapable," is not only an image
representing infinite space; it is an image, established in the
first stanza, representing a state of mind, a kind of bright and
empty beatitude, over which the thought of death may darken
suddenly and without warning:

> She dreams a little, and she feels the dark
> Encroachment of that old catastrophe,
> As a calm darkens among water-lights.

The language has the greatest possible dignity and subtlety,
combined with perfect precision. The imminence of absolute
tragedy is felt and recorded, but the integrity of the feeling
mind is maintained. The mind perceives, as by a kind of
metaphysical sense, the approach of invading impersonality;
yet knowing the invasion to be inevitable and its own identity,
while that identity lasts, the only source of any good whatever,
maintains that identity in its full calm and clarity, that nothing
may be sacrificed without need. This combination of calm
and terror, in dealing with this particular theme, will be
found in only one other poet in English, in Shakespeare as
one finds him in a few of the more metaphysical sonnets.[9] The
calm clarity of tone enables the poet to deal with a variety of
kinds of feeling which would be impossible were the terror
emphasized for a moment at any point, were the complete and
controlled unity of the experiencing mind for a moment dis-

[9] I have discussed this attitude of Shakespeare and some of its historical
background in Poetry: A Magazine of Verse for February, March, and
April, 1939; and have analyzed the 77th sonnet with this attitude in
mind on page 49 of the issue for April.

ordered by its own perceptions. The same poem, for example, is able to contain the following lines, of a sweetness and of an illusory simplicity which again are scarcely less than Shakespearean:

> She says, "I am content when wakened birds,
> Before they fly, test the reality
> Of misty fields, by their sweet questionings;
> But when the birds are gone, and their warm fields
> Return no more, where, then, is paradise?"

And out of this passage proceeds the great lament for the lost myths, which I have already mentioned. This passage and others similar, though beautiful in themselves, are a preparation for the descriptive lines in the last stanza, and when we finally come to those lines, they are weighted with meaning and feeling accumulated from all that has gone before. It is difficult for this reason to quote from the poem for the purpose of illustrating its beauty.

One aspect of the poem may perhaps be mentioned, however, with some small profit, and it may best be indicated, I believe, through a brief comparison with Bryant's *Thanatopsis*. Bryant's poem is a great poem and is worthy of the comparison, and its resemblance to Stevens' poem in certain ways is both surprising and illuminating. Both poems are semididactic meditations on death, written in a firm but simplified Miltonic blank verse, the verse of Stevens, possibly, being somewhat smoothed and softened by the intervention of Tennyson. Both poems are pagan in their view: but that of Bryant, the New Englander of the early 19th century, is essentially stoical, whereas that of Stevens, the Pennsylvanian of the 20th century, is Epicurean. Both poems find man, a spiritual being, isolated in a physical universe: but for Bryant that universe is the Earth, hairy, vast, and almost against the eye; for Stevens it is the tropical Pacific of infinity, in which the earth appears as an infinitesimal floating island.

The poems resemble each other more curiously, however, in that each bears a particular relationship to an antecedent body of more or less decadent poetry.

The deistic philosophy of the 18th century had early generated in its numerous followers a combination of ideas and attitudes which was to mark literary style, and especially poetic style, more strongly, perhaps, than any other philosophy has ever done. Deism was an amateur philosophy, a fact which may account in part for its rapid rise to popularity among men of letters and gentlemen at large: it received its definitive philosophical outline from the third Earl of Shaftesbury and its definitive literary expression from Alexander Pope, in *The Essay on Man*. Roughly speaking, one may say that these writers taught: [10] that the world is ruled by a beneficent mind, that everything is as it must be, that what appears to be evil is actually good as relative to the whole, that because the ruling mind is beneficent man will find happiness in all his benevolent affections and beneficent actions and misery in their opposites. They taught likewise [11] that virtue is natural to man and that the instincts and emotions are more reliable guides to conduct than the reason, though training and cultivation may refine these guides; that, in the words of Robertson,[12] "to be good humored and truly cultivated is to be right in religion and conduct, and consequently happy." The contradictions in this philosophy have been so often recounted that I need scarcely remark upon them here. What I wish to

[10] *Shaftesbury's "Characteristics,"* edited by J. M. Robertson, London, Grant Richards, 1900; editor's introduction pp. xxix and xxx.

[11] Pope, *Essay on Man*, especially Epistle III, more especially section II thereof; e.g., lines 97-8: And Reason raise o'er Instinct as you can,/ In this 'tis God directs, in that 'tis Man.

[12] J. M. Robertson, op. cit., p. xxxi.

point out is this: that in spite of all contradictions the philosophy represents an attack on the rational faculty and a fairly complete outline of later romanticism; that the attack is made by means of what purport to be the methods of the rational faculty—that is, the attack is composed of a small set of concepts which are supposed to explain all experience, and which are moved about in various pseudo-rational relationships in order that certain philosophical conclusions may be reached. The deists appear to have achieved the delusion that they were reasoning with a final and immutable clarity, at the same time that they were attacking with all their small but apparently sufficient intellectual powers the very foundations of reason itself.

Their ideas generated an attitude of smug imperception in at least two ways: they were sure, in the first place, that they had solved all the essential problems of philosophy, history,[13] and morals, with the result that moral ideas and feelings were with increasing regularity expressed in a fixed set of stereotyped expressions or literary counters, which of necessity had for the most part a somewhat sentimental quality; and the general tendency of their philosophy worked to destroy the belief in the value of rational criticism, so that in spite of the composition of a good deal of literary criticism in the period, most of it somewhat superficial, the virtue of these counters long passed unchallenged, and when the challenge came, it came, strangely enough, not in the name of the intellect but in the name of the sensibility. Christian doctrine, and to some extent the best classical philosophy preceding it, had taught man to examine himself according to sound and intricate rules, in order that he might improve himself, and, if a Christian,

[13] See *The Art of History,* by J. B. Black, Methuen and Co., Ltd., London, 1926. This book, which I fear is out of print, is one of the most brilliant pieces of criticism of our century, and ought to be more widely available.

achieve salvation. Deistic doctrine taught him that he was
fairly certain of achieving any salvation that there might be
available if he would only refrain from examining himself:
"There needs but thinking right [i.e., deistically], and meaning well." [14] The result was the 18th century cliché, the most
obvious symptom of the neat and innocent reasoning and per-
ceiving of so many 18th century writers.

The Age of Reason has won that name from its heirs: from
those who have agreed with it so completely as to abandon
its literary methods, which were merely the methods of the
preceding age, and too often unduly simplified.[15] The reasoning of the Age of Reason was very largely directed toward
the destruction of the authority of Reason. Later romantic
writers accepted the notion of the essential baseness of Reason
with no real argument, and, when they began to see the mo-
notony of 18th century language at its worst, they had recourse to the standard romantic explanation of dullness, that
it was caused by excessive intellectualism; and we have as a
result the nineteenth century judgment, which still prevails,
of eighteenth century poetry, that it is bad because too intellectual, whereas in reality eighteenth century poetry is commonly good and is often great but displays defects which are
primarily due to intellectual deficiency. The eighteenth century poetic language had become so well established by the
middle of the century that it could dominate men with no
respect for the ideas which seem to have generated it: Samuel
Johnson had nothing but contempt for deism, yet his style

14 Pope, *The Essay on Man,* Epistle IV, l. 32.
15 The conclusion of *The Dunciad,* though not unduly simplified, is an
example of the continuance: it is the natural development of the procedure established by Gascoigne, Ben Jonson, Greville, Donne, and
others, and is one of the greatest passages in English poetry. *The Essay
on Man* discloses a related procedure weakened by nonsense and sentimentalism.

shows the influence of deism; the influence upon his prose was small, for that was the medium which he cultivated most assiduously, but the influence upon his verse was great. The prologues to *Comus* and to *A Word to the Wise,* which are probably his greatest poems, are stereotyped in almost every detail of language, but are poems of extraordinary power because of the conviction and intelligence of the author, which are expressed mainly in the plot and rational outline, and in a certain tragic irony with which the stereotypes are occasionally used: these poems are the work of a great genius employing a decadent language. The Reason, at this time, was tending toward immobility; and in those who accepted the doctrine, the emotions were freed: the natural outcome was to be found in Gray and Collins, men who in a discreet and sophisticated manner cultivated the feelings for their own sake, who generalized about the feelings with facile elegance but with small understanding, and who in varying degrees were the victims of uncomprehended melancholy.

These men and others of less talent but closely related, such as Blair and Macpherson, formed much of the immediate background of Bryant. The influence of Blair is to be seen in the form and matter of *Thanatopsis*; the influence of Ossian has been seen in Bryant's taste for panoramic landscape, though as a matter of fact Gray, Collins, and others of the period might be cited in this connection with equal justice. One of the most obvious relationships to these poets is to be seen in Bryant's early taste for the semi-epigrammatic epithet, which marks Gray's *Elegy* so strongly, a type of phrase which seems to show the breaking down of the Popian epigram in the direction of the standard cliché of the period: Gray's "mute inglorious Miltons" meet their milder descendants in Bryant's "solemn brood of care." The most interesting resemblance of Bryant to these romantic predecessors, however, is to be found in moments of a kind of melancholy, which though in a measure

formal and even arbitrarily imposed upon the matter, is deeply
felt by the poet.

> . . . . the vales
> Stretching in pensive quietness between . . .
> Where thy pale form was laid with many tears. . . .

These lines are very beautiful in their way, but they are far
from specific: a sadness deriving in part from the general
theme of the poem, and in part from a traditionally fixed
rhetoric and emotional approach, is spread like a fine haze
across the whole body of detail. This rhetoric, with its cognate
melancholy, which, though formulary, is none the less profoundly a state of mind, is the most obvious characteristic of
early romanticism: it is obvious in Gray and Collins and
faintly discernible in the early Bryant.

Blake and Wordsworth broke the somewhat narrow frame
of this early romanticism by freeing new emotions, mainly
the obscurely prophetic; Wordsworth freed himself from the
rhetorical forms of the preceding century by scrutinizing with
literal exactness not his own human nature but the external
nature of landscape, and Blake and Coleridge achieved a comparable freedom by a similar literalness in treating the phan-
tasmagoria of the supernatural. The scope of romantic poetry
was thus widened, but it remained essentially romantic poetry:
poetry, that is, which sought to free the emotions rather than
to understand them. Romantic poetry developed in the nineteenth century in England more or less along the lines indicated by these poets, and with no radical innovations of method
after their time: the English romantics sought to free the emotions by writing about them in a more or less emotional manner; Wordsworth, of course, became less consistently Romantic
as he matured.

The next step in the development of romantic practice,
though it was suggested by Coleridge in the doctrine of or-

ganic form, was first indicated more or less fully by Poe, and in the matter of actual poetic practice was perhaps first taken by Poe, though very haltingly. One sees its nature precisely in the great French Symbolists. If it is the business of the poem to "express" emotion, then the form itself of expression should be expressive and if we are rigorously reasonable, as a few of the romantics are, in the pursuit of their unreasonable ends, we shall see that language can best be purely expressive of emotion if it is so used that all except emotional content is as nearly as possible eliminated. Mallarmé was quite clear as to the necessity of eliminating rational content from language [16] and was more brilliant and more elaborate than any other poet has ever been, in his technique of elimination. The later poems especially display extremely obscure symbolism and reference, stated in a syntax so perverse as to be barely and very uncertainly explicable, at the same time that the individual phrases communicate feelings and perceptions more sharp and interesting, when viewed in isolation, than they frequently have a right to communicate when viewed as a part of any deducible whole. The suggestiveness of the details is forced into startling isolation by the difficulty of comprehending the poems as wholes; and this effect appears, at least, to be deliberately sought. The reader who is curious may profitably study the three sonnets beginning respectively *Tout Orgueil fume-t-il du soir, Surgi de la croupe et du bond*, and *Une dentelle s'abolit* in the Fry-Mauron edition.[17] In the last of these, the technique of negation, by which gross matter is eliminated, and feeling, it is hoped, is preserved, approaches the quality of unintentional parody: "A lace curtain is effaced

[16] See his *Avant-dire* to René Ghil's *Traité du Verbe*. An extensive quotation from this, with a brief commentary upon it, will be found on page 2 of my work *Primitivism and Decadence*.

[17] Poems by Mallarmé. Translated by Roger Fry, with commentaries by Charles Mauron. 1936, Chatto & Windus, London.

in doubt of the supreme Game [the nature of the supreme Game, one should observe, is more than uncertain] to display like a blasphemy nothing but the eternal absence of any bed." The same doctrine is stated, perhaps less clearly, but in terms approaching those of Stevens in *The Revolutionists Stop for Orangeade*, by Paul Verlaine, in *Art Poétique*:

> *Il faut aussi que tu n'ailles point*
> *Choisir tes mots sans quelque méprise:*
> *Rien de plus cher que la chanson grise*
> *Où l'Indécis au précis se joint. . . .*
>
> *Car nous voulons la Nuance encor,*
> *Pas la couleur, rien que la Nuance!* [18]

And Rimbaud, in the version of *Bonheur* which appears in *Les Illuminations*, informs us that the beatitude of which he has made a magic study has made his speech incomprehensible, has caused it to take wing and escape; and earlier in the same poem he states that he has eliminated rational control from his life as well, for the same beatitude has taken possession of his life, both body and soul, and dispersed all effort. Just as

[18] In spite of this statement Verlaine is more innocent than Mallarmé, and less capable of intellectual perversity, as he is less capable than Rimbaud of consistent anti-moral energy and passion. On page 89 of my work *Primitivism and Decadence* I refer to Verlaine as primitive—that is, limited, or minor, but relatively sound in method—rather than decadent. Such a view is supported by some of his best poems—*Malines* or *Le piano que baise une main frêle*, for example—but not by all. The poem beginning *Dans l'interminable* differs not at all in method from Rimbaud's *Larme*; both employ a description of strange landscape to communicate a feeling; but what is more or less conventionally obscure melancholy in Verlaine—obscure in the sense that the motive of the melancholy is nowhere suggested—is pushed to pure hallucination in Rimbaud. And many other poems by Verlaine use the same method: *C'est l'extase langoureuse*, for example, or *Green*. And it is worth remembering that the title of his best collection is *Romances Sans Paroles*.

the first great English romantics released the new subject matter, these poets, who were in rebellion against the stylistic looseness of their immediate predecessors in France, released the method which was, essentially, the proper method of romantic poetry. They released it, that is, within the bounds imposed by more or less traditional forms and by their own considerable talents and training: in their less fortunate successors we can observe the rapid progression toward le surréalisme. Mallarmé, like Gray, is a scholarly and sophisticated enemy of Reason; the body of his work, like that of Gray, is small; and similarly its generative power is very great. Mallarmé and his coadjutors seem to have played a part in the career of the young Stevens similar to that of Gray and Collins in the work of the young Bryant.

Mallarmé and Verlaine resemble Gray and Collins in their precise artistry and in their sophisticated melancholy, a melancholy which arises in both generations for much the same reasons, and which is kept within fairly close stylistic bounds in both pairs of poets by comparable sophistication of style. But the Frenchmen surpass the two Englishmen of a century earlier in the elusive fluctuation of their perception; they have come closer to writing not merely about their emotions but with their emotions, and in addition to being in certain ways more sensitive, they are harder to understand. In fact, they seem to exist very close to that precarious boundary beyond which meaning will become so diminished that sensitivity must rapidly diminish with it, since the feeling contained in language is indissolubly connected with the abstract sense of language and must vanish if that abstract sense is wholly destroyed.

It is in relationship to this resemblance and to this difference that it is most interesting to compare *Thanatopsis* to *Sunday Morning*. Both Stevens and Bryant in these poems were influenced perceptibly by the preceding decadent masters; both

seem to have recovered from the influence to such an extent
that the influence appears as a faint memory, as the super-
sensitivity of a kind of convalescence, in poets who are even
more heavily influenced by antecedent and stronger tradition.
But in Bryant this recovery was aided by more than mere
literary tradition: he found his support in the skeletalized
morality and etherealized theology of Unitarianism. From
these he derived concepts over-simplified much as were those
of deism, but over-simplified, at least, from something that
was originally sound. The best of his later poems, *To a Waterfowl, The Past, The Battlefield,* and *The Tides,* are written
on themes which are clear and reasonably sound but which he
was able to apprehend only in terms so general as to approach
without quite impinging upon vagueness. There is in these
poems a good deal of the moral conviction that we find in the
best poets of the English Renaissance, along with a remarkable
gift for style, but there is very little left of the old moral
intelligence, the diversity, the subtlety, and the precision.
Bryant had not the intellect requisite to surpass the dominant
ideas of his generation in New England and recapture anything of the earlier intelligence, but the ideas at least supported him, and he had enough either of simplicity or of
stubbornness not to exchange them for anything worse. But
Stevens appears to have been supported at this point in his
career by little except literary tradition; like Bryant he accepted one of the current philosophies of his time, but one
more beguiling and at the same time more dangerous than
that of Bryant, and like Bryant he seems to have accepted it
with no trace of scepticism, and with the result that we have
seen. His history epitomizes that of four generations of French
poets.

But we have done with the outline of Stevens' general history; it is with the moments of dangerous but successful balance in his earlier years that we are now concerned. I have

spoken of the elusive fluctuation of perception in Mallarmé
and Verlaine, and I have referred to the extraordinary subtlety
with which Stevens perceives the impingement of death, as
well as other matters, in *Sunday Morning*; and I have compared this quality in Stevens to a similar quality in some of
Shakespeare's sonnets. This particular kind of sensitivity is
fairly common in modern poetry, but nowhere at so high a
level of excellence, I think, except in Valéry, certainly nowhere in English: at a lower level, or in another language and
rhetorical tradition, it would probably display nothing that
we should think of as Shakespearean.

Le Monocle de Mon Oncle, a work produced a few years
later than *Sunday Morning*, endeavors to treat the subject of
love in hedonistic terms and confesses ironically to encountering more than one difficulty. The poem is often obscure, and,
perhaps because one cannot easily follow it, appears far less
a unit than *Sunday Morning*; it contains extraordinary writing, however. The second stanza may fairly illustrate what I
have said:

> A red bird flies across the golden floor.
> It is a red bird that seeks out his choir
> Among the choirs of wind and wet and wing.
> A torrent will fall from him when he finds.
> Shall I uncrumple this much-crumpled thing?
> I am a man of fortune greeting heirs;
> For it has come that thus I greet the spring.
> These choirs of welcome choir for me farewell.
> No spring can follow past meridian.
> Yet you persist with anecdotal bliss
> To make believe a starry connaissance.

The first four lines are incomprehensible, except as description, and the claim of the fifth line is unjustified; the remainder
of the stanza, however, displays a combination of bitterness,

irony, and imperturbable elegance not unworthy of Ben Jonson.

Of the Manner of Addressing Clouds deals essentially with the same subject as the passage in which Crispin contemplates the plum, but deals with it in a different mood; that is, the poet sees much the same relationship between his art and his subject as does Crispin, but since he sees himself alone in the "old chaos of the sun," "that drifting waste," amid the "mute bare splendors of the sun and moon," he is glad to retain his art as a mitigation of his solitude: what kind of mitigation he does not venture to say, but the mere fact of mitigation suffices him. The opening lines of this poem display a faint suggestion of Stevens' self-parody in one of its most frequent forms, an excess of alliteration which renders the style perversely finical. If one will compare these lines to the opening of *The Comedian as the Letter C*, he may readily see how rapidly the method can degenerate into very crude comedy. *Of Heaven Considered as a Tomb* is a vision of death as extinction. These two poems deal with the evaluation of the central theme of *Sunday Morning*, with the irremediable tragedy, and they are free from all in that poem which invites question as well as much that provides richness and variety. The style of both has a cold concentration, related to this purity of motive, which almost surpasses, for me, the beauty of the longer poem. *The Snow Man* and *The Death of the Soldier* deal respectively with life and with death in a universe which is impersonal and devoid of any comfort except that which one may derive from the contemplation of the mute bare splendors. They have great power, but probably less than the other short poems which I have just mentioned, perhaps because of the metrical form.[19]

19 The scansion of free verse and the influence of the meter on the total poetic result may be found discussed at great length in the last essay of my book, *Primitivism and Decadence*. The scansion of *The Snow Man*

There appears to be in the best of the early poems, as I have said, a traditional seriousness of attitude and a traditional rhetoric cognate with that attitude and precisely expressive of it. This traditional element in the early work enables Stevens' talent to function at its highest power; but it is not only unjustified and unsupported by Stevens' explicit philosophy, it is at odds with that philosophy. And the conflict between the traditional element and the element encouraged by the philosophy results little by little in the destruction of the traditional element and the degradation of the poet's style. It is extremely important that we understand Stevens for more reasons than one; he has written great poems, and we should know them and know why they are great; and we should know what is bad, and why it is bad, so that we may separate the bad from the good and the more surely preserve the good. But beyond this, he gives us, I believe, the most perfect laboratory of hedonism to be found in literature. He is not like those occasional poets of the Renaissance who appear in some measure to be influenced by a pagan philosophy, but who in reality take it up as a literary diversion at the same time that they are beneath the surface immovably Christian. Stevens is released from all the restraints of Christianity, and is encouraged by all the modern orthodoxy of Romanticism: his hedonism is so fused with Romanticism as to be merely an elegant variation on that somewhat inelegant System of Thoughtlessness. His ideas have remained essentially unchanged for more than a quarter of a century, and on the whole they have been very clearly expressed, so that there is no real occasion to be in doubt as to their nature; and he began as a great poet, so that when we examine the effect of those ideas upon his work, we are examining something of very great importance.

---

is there marked. That of *The Death of the Soldier* is similar in principle, but simpler in form.

T. S.
ELIOT

OR THE ILLUSION OF REACTION

T. S. ELIOT is probably the most widely respected literary figure of our time; he is known primarily as the leader of the intellectual reaction against the romanticism of which he began his career as a disciple. It is my purpose to show that his intellectualism and his reactionary position are alike an illusion. It is perhaps needless to say that I use the word *reactionary* in no emotional or pejorative sense, but in a simple and literal one; I regard myself as a reactionary.

Eliot is a theorist who has repeatedly contradicted himself on every important issue that he has touched, and he has dealt in some fashion with most of the important literary issues of our time. Between some of his contradictory statements there is a greater or less lapse of time, and one might account for them by a change of view if he showed any consciousness of contradiction; but many of them occur within the same book or even within the same essay. In this connection, however, the year 1928 should be held in mind as a crucial one if any important change is to be demonstrated, for it was in this year, in his book of essays *For Lancelot Andrewes*, that he announced his conversion to Catholicism and to classicism.

The first aim of this essay will be to demonstrate the existence of these contradictions; the second will be to determine as far as possible the main tendency in his theories; and the last will be to show the effect of this tendency upon his poetry and to indicate the effect upon his disciples.

Eliot's critical discussion deals with a fairly definite number of topics, and in the interests of clarity I shall do my best to treat each topic separately, though a certain amount of overlapping will be inevitable.

I. *Autotelic Art*

In *The Function of Criticism* [1] Eliot writes:

"No exponent of criticism . . . has, I presume, ever made the preposterous assumption that criticism is an autotelic activity. I do not deny that art may be affirmed to serve ends beyond itself; but art is not required to be aware of these ends, and indeed performs its functions, whatever they may be, according to various theories of value, much better by indifference to them. Criticism, on the other hand, must always profess an end in view, which, roughly speaking, appears to be the elucidation of works of art and the correction of taste."

One is confronted here with several problems. How, for example, can an artist perform a function better for not knowing what it is? Is Eliot assuming an automatic, or unconscious art, an art which is an extreme form of romantic mysticism? Where also is the line between prose which is art and prose which is not art? Are we to assume that there is no art in

[1] Selected Essays, by T. S. Eliot. Harcourt, Brace & Co. P. 13. (1932).

expository prose, let us say in Johnson's Introduction to his dictionary? Or merely that there is no art in that branch of expository prose which we call literary criticism? And if there is no art in expository prose, then what shall we say about expository verse? What shall we do, let us wonder in passing, with the first of Donne's *Holy Sonnets*, with the *Epistle to Dr. Arbuthnot*, or with much of *The Divine Comedy*? In the same essay he adds: [2]

"I have assumed as axiomatic that a creation, a work of art, is autotelic; and that criticism is about something other than itself."

Art, then, is about itself, but this information does not help me to answer my questions, for I do not understand it. What, for example, would Pope or Dante have understood if this statement had been made to them regarding the poems which I have just mentioned? Or what can we understand with regard to these poems? About all we can deduce from such a passage is that the artist does not really know what he is doing; a doctrine which we shall find suggested and elucidated elsewhere, and which leads directly to the plainest kind of determinism.

Yet every poem appears to the unpracticed eye to say something about some aspect of human experience. What are we to make of this? In one of his earliest and most famous essays, Eliot deals with this problem by way of a figure of speech: [3]

"The analogy was that of the catalyst. When the two gases previously mentioned are mixed in the presence of a filament of platinum, they form sulphurous acid. This combination takes place only if the platinum is present; nevertheless the newly formed acid contains no trace of platinum, and the platinum itself is apparently unaffected: has remained inert, neutral, and unchanged. The mind of the poet is the shred of platinum. It may

[2] Ibid., p. 19.
[3] *Tradition and the Individual Talent,* Ibid., p. 7 and thereafter.

partly or exclusively operate upon the experience of the man himself; but the more perfect the artist, the more completely separate
in him will be the man who suffers and the mind which creates;
the more perfectly will the mind digest and transmute the passions
which are its material.

"The experience, you will notice, the elements which enter the
presence of the transforming catalyst, are of two kinds: emotions
and feelings. The effect of a work of art upon the person who
enjoys it is an experience different in kind from any experience
not of art. It may be formed out of one emotion, or may be a combination of several; and various feelings, inhering for the writer in
particular words or phrases or images, may be added to compose
the final result. Or great poetry may be made without the direct
use of any emotion whatever: composed out of feelings solely.
Canto XV of the *Inferno* (Brunetto Latini) is a working up of the
emotion evident in the situation; but the effect, though single as
that of any work of art, is obtained by a considerable complexity
of detail. The last quatrain gives an image, a feeling attaching to
an image, which 'came,' which did not develop simply out of what
precedes, but which was probably in suspension in the poet's mind
until the proper combination arrived for it to add itself to. The
poet's mind is in fact a receptacle for seizing and storing up num-
berless feelings, phrases, images, which remain there until all the
particles which can unite to form a new compound are present
together.

"If you compare several representative passages of the greatest
poetry you see how great is the variety of the types of combination,
and also how completely any semi-ethical criterion of sublimity
misses the mark. For it is not the 'greatness,' the intensity, of the
emotions, the components, but the intensity of the artistic process,
the pressure, so to speak, under which the fusion takes place, that
counts. The episode of Paolo and Francesca employs a definite
emotion, but the intensity of the poetry is something quite different from whatever intensity in the supposed experience it may
give the impression of . . . the murder of Agamemnon, or the
agony of Othello, gives an artistic effect apparently closer to a

possible original than the scenes from Dante. In the *Agamemnon*, the artistic emotion approximates to the emotion of an actual spectator; in *Othello* to the emotion of the protagonist himself. But the difference between art and the event is always absolute."

This passage requires a good deal of comment. In the first place, one should note the words *emotion* and *feeling*: the first refers to an emotion, as we commonly use the term, which arises from an experience outside of literature; the second to an emotion stirred by a work or a fragment of literature. Emotion and feeling are the ingredients of literary art; there is no reference to rational understanding. Emotion, moreover, in Eliot's sense of the word, is transformed by the artistic process into something which differs absolutely from that which it was originally, so that semi-ethical criteria are irrelevant to our judgment of the work of art. Art appears to be in this passage, as in Poe, a matter of the novel combination of materials; and there is no question of the artist's understanding what he is saying: the criterion, as in Poe, is one of *effect*. This is interesting, for in reading Eliot, one cannot avoid the conclusion that he has absorbed much from Poe, but through early or fragmentary or otherwise uncritical reading: many of Eliot's theories resemble those of Poe without Eliot apparently knowing it, and his references to Poe are almost invariably inaccurate.[4]

There is further evidence in this passage that Eliot regards the poet as passive: he refers to him as "inert, neutral, un-

[4] In the essay on Marvell (Selected Essays, New York, p. 259), for example, Eliot writes: "There is here the element of *surprise*, as when Villon says: Necessité faict gens mesprendre Et faim saillir le loup des bois, the surprise which Poe considered of the highest importance." But it was *originality* not *surprise*, about which Poe theorized, and he conceived it as a more or less arbitrary effect of scenery or meter, not as simple precision of comparison. See my essay on Poe in *Maule's Curse*, New Directions, 1938, or in American Literature VIII-4, p. 379.

changed," during and after the act of creation. Yet the figure
is not developed consistently, for later Eliot asserts that it is
"the intensity of the artistic process, the pressure, so to speak,
under which the fusion takes place that counts." He does not
say whether this intensity is a function of the inert mind of
the poet or an accident affecting the mind from without. Nor,
if we try to interpret the figure, to translate it into plain language, can we determine what is meant either by inertness or
by intensity; nor can we guess what occurs when the poet
writes: the entire process is a mystery, and if the critic can say
no more about it than he has said, he would have done well
to employ less and simpler language.

If I may be pardoned for insisting, for a moment, on my
own view of these matters, I should like to suggest that it
describes more accurately the facts which Eliot appears to have
in mind than does the theory of Eliot himself. According to
my view, the artistic process is one of moral evaluation of
human experience, by means of a technique which renders
possible an evaluation more precise than any other. The poet
tries to understand his experience in rational terms, to state
his understanding, and simultaneously to state, by means of
the feelings which we attach to words, the kind and degree of
emotion that should properly be motivated by this understanding. The artistic result differs from the crude experience
mainly in its refinement of judgment: the difference in really
good art is enormous, but the difference is of degree rather
than of kind. The "intensity" of the work of art, which is
different from the intensity of the crude experience, lies in
this: that what we call intensity in a work of art is a combination of the importance of the original subject and the precision
of the judgment; whereas that which we call intensity in life
is most often the confused and therefore frightening emotion
resulting from a situation which we have not yet had time to
meet and understand, and our feeling toward which, as it ap-

proaches clarity and control, approaches, though from a considerable distance, the condition of art.

I must ask the reader to bear carefully in mind not only the passage just quoted from Eliot but my statement of my own point of view, while he is considering the following passage from the essay called *The Metaphysical Poets*: [5]

"In the seventeenth century a dissociation of sensibility set in, from which we have never recovered; and this dissociation, as is natural, was aggravated by the two most powerful poets of the century, Milton and Dryden. Each of these men performed certain poetic functions so magnificently well that the magnitude of the effect concealed the absence of others. The language went on and in some respects improved; the best verse of Collins, Gray, Johnson, and even Goldsmith satisfies some of our fastidious demands better than that of Donne or Marvell or King. But while the language became more refined, the feeling became more crude. The feeling, the sensibility, expressed in the *Country Churchyard* (to say nothing of Tennyson and Browning) is cruder than in the *Coy Mistress*."

The significance of this passage is not quite clear, but Eliot returns to the subject and elucidates it in his essay on Marvell: [6]

"When we come to Gray and Collins, the sophistication remains only in the language, and has disappeared from the feeling. Gray and Collins were masters, but they had lost that hold on human values, that firm grasp of human experience, which is a formidable achievement of the Elizabethan and Jacobean poets."

But how does this firm grasp of human values get into an autotelic art, to which ethical criteria are irrelevant? Has Eliot changed his mind radically over a period of years? *The Function of Criticism*, from which the first quotation in this essay is drawn is dated [7] 1923. *Tradition and the Individual Talent*,

[5] Op. Cit., p. 247.   [6] Ibid., p. 256.
[7] Ibid. see list of dates in table of contents.

which provides the second quotation is dated 1917, and first appeared in book-form in *The Sacred Wood*, in 1921. The two other essays, however, are both dated 1921, and the essay on Swinburne, which appears in *The Sacred Wood*, finds Swinburne a poet of very limited value because his poetry was not nourished on human experience, and it ends with the statement: [8]

". . . the language which is more important to us is that which is struggling to digest and express new objects, new feelings, new aspects, as, for instance, the prose of Mr. James Joyce or the earlier Conrad."

How does the language "digest" these subjects, without being "about" them? This passage and the passage from the essay on Marvell, though carelessly put, are comprehensible in my terms but not in the terms of the other essays cited. Eliot has not changed his mind over a given period, for the dates of the essays forbid such a view. The fact of the matter is that at any given time he can speak with equal firmness and dignity on both sides of almost any question, and with no realization of the difficulties in which he is involved.

II. *The Theory of the Objective Correlative*

My own view of poetry, which I have already indicated, is a simple one: I believe that the feeling expressed by the work is, or should be, motivated by the artist's comprehension of his subject, which is drawn from human experience; and that the value of the work depends upon the justness of the motivation, in whole and in detail. Eliot sometimes adopts this view, but in the main he prefers to assume the emotion as initial:

[8] Ibid., p. 285.

the result is his famous and widely influential theory of the objective correlative. In his essay on Hamlet [9] he writes:

"The only way of expressing emotion in the form of art is by finding an 'objective correlative'; in other words, a set of objects, a situation, a chain of events which shall be the formula for that *particular* emotion; such that when the external facts, which must terminate in sensory experience, are given, the emotion is immediately evoked."

This seems to me, I confess, a reversal of the normal processes of understanding human experience, and a dangerous reversal. Mario Praz traces this concept to Pound: [10]

"Pound's idea of poetry as 'a sort of inspired mathematics which gives us equations, not for abstract figures, triangles, spheres, and the like, but for the human emotions,' may be said to be the starting point for Eliot's theory of the 'Objective correlative.' "

Praz continues:

"That influence is closely connected with Eliot's interpretation of Dante's allegory along the lines suggested by Ezra Pound—as we have seen above. Clear visual images, a concise and luminous language: these are the two qualities of Dante Eliot has in mind. The former is the 'objective correlative' of the emotions they intend to suggest, the latter appeals to the auditory imagination: there is an element of extreme precision and extreme vagueness in both ... The pattern of images in *Ash Wednesday* seems thus suggested by Dante, but in a peculiar way. It is as if Eliot had been reading Dante without giving much heed to the meaning, but letting himself be impressed by a few clear visual images."

Praz is unquestionably correct in his claims for the extensive influence of Pound upon Eliot's critical theories. Nevertheless,

[9] Ibid., p. 124.
[10] Southern Review, Vol. II, No. 3, pp. 525-548. The passage from Pound occurs on p. 5, *The Spirit of Romance.*

this particular theory is at least as old as Poe and is more than likely older, and Poe states it much more nearly in Eliot's terms. Poe writes in his essay on Hawthorne: [11]

" . . . having conceived, with deliberate care, a certain unique or single *effect* to be wrought out, he [the skillful literary artist] then invents such incidents—he then combines such events as may best aid him in establishing this preconceived effect."

One will find the same procedure elaborated in *The Philosophy of Composition.*

Eliot, however, is unable to adhere to his position. In the same essay—indeed on the same page—he writes:

"Hamlet is up against the difficulty that his disgust is occasioned by his mother, but that his mother is not an adequate equivalent for it; his disgust envelops and exceeds her. It is thus a feeling which he cannot understand . . ."

And the play as a whole is found at fault in the end for the same reason with relation to Shakespeare: the events of the play are not an adequate equivalent for the disgust which Shakespeare, in Eliot's opinion, was trying to express. Now finding an "objective correlative" for an emotion is not the same thing as understanding it: to understand it we must know and correctly judge its motive. There seems to be a suggestion here that Eliot's theory is inadequate to his feeling about the play. There is a similar suggestion in this passage from the essay on Cyril Tourneur: [12]

"The cynicism, the loathing and disgust of humanity, expressed consummately in *The Revenger's Tragedy,* are immature in the respect that they exceed the object."

[11] Stedman and Woodberry edition, p. 31 of the second of the three volumes of Poe's criticism. For further comment see my essay on Poe, already mentioned.

[12] Op. cit., p. 166.

And a few years earlier he is even more explicit. In the essay on Lancelot Andrewes, he writes: [13]

"Andrewes' emotion is purely contemplative; it is not personal, it is wholly evoked by the object of contemplation, to which it is adequate; his emotion is wholly contained in and explained by its object. But with Donne there is always something else, the 'baffling' of which Mr. Pearsall Smith speaks in his introduction. Donne is a 'personality' in a sense in which Andrewes is not: his sermons, one feels, are a 'means of self-expression.' He is constantly finding an object which shall be adequate to his feelings: Andrewes is wholly absorbed in the object and therefore responds with the adequate emotion. Andrewes has the *goût pour la vie spirituelle,* which is not native to Donne."

Now it is immaterial with respect to my present purposes whether this comparison of the two men is a just one; the point which interests me is this: that Andrewes is praised because he adheres to my principles, whereas Donne is blamed because he adheres to those of Eliot. Eliot does not explain his self-contradiction, nor does he give any evidence that he is aware of it.

III. *Thought and Emotion in Poetry*

The theory of the "objective correlative" rests, as Eliot says in discussing Andrewes, on the assumption that the poet is trying to express an emotion, not on the theory that he is trying to understand it. It is as good a fundamental principle as one is likely to find to serve as a justification for the sort of confused motivation which I have discussed under the name of pseudo-reference in an earlier collection of essays called *Primitivism and Decadence.* I should like to reiterate what I

[13] Ibid., p. 298. The last three essays mentioned are dated 1919, 1931, and 1926 respectively.

shall be able to show in great detail later, that this primacy which Eliot gives to the emotions leads directly to a thorough determinism of the most dangerous sort: if we are bound to express our emotions without understanding them, we obviously have no way of judging or controlling them, but must take them as they come. Eliot deals with the general subject of the relation of thought to emotion in a great many passages, of which I must confine myself to a relatively small number for comment.

In the essay on *Shakespeare and the Stoicism of Seneca*[14] he says:

"The poet who 'thinks' is merely the poet who can express the emotional equivalent of thought. But he is not necessarily interested in the thought itself. We talk as if thought was precise and emotion was vague. In reality there is precise emotion and there is vague emotion. To express precise emotion requires as great intellectual power as to express precise thought."

This passage is a startling one. What, for example, is the emotional equivalent of thought, unless it is the emotion motivated by thought? We are not concerned, here, with the objective correlative of an emotion, but with the emotional correlative of a thought, which must then be expressed by means, I presume, of an objective correlative. What is the nature of the extraordinary sequence of relationships here implied? And if the emotion is to be considered as motivated by the thought, what are we to think of the poet who can express such emotion when he is not "interested in the thought itself"? Furthermore, how can such emotion be expressed except in terms of the motivating thought unless we are to falsify it utterly? And how can it be precise unless the motivating thought is precise?

In the same essay and on the next page Eliot writes:

14 Ibid., p. 115.

"The difference between Shakespeare and Dante is that Dante had one coherent system of thought behind him; but that was just his luck, and from the point of view of poetry is an irrelevant accident. It happened that at Dante's time thought was orderly and strong and beautiful, and that it was concentrated in one man of the greatest genius; Dante's poetry receives a boost which in a sense it does not merit, from the fact that the thought behind it is the thought of a man as great and lovely as Dante himself: St. Thomas . . . In truth, neither Shakespeare nor Dante did any real thinking—that was not their job; and the relative value of the thought current at their time, the material enforced upon each to use as the vehicle of his feeling, is of no importance."

Now Eliot, as we shall see elsewhere, is usually of the opinion that Shakespeare was the inhabitant of a very inferior intellectual milieu, so that this passage is in effect a comparison of two very great poets one of whom is supposed to have inherited (without much effort) the clearest and most intricate philosophy of all time and the other a ragbag of disparate philosophical fragments. But what, then, is the meaning of the passage? In what sense does Dante's poetry "receive a boost," irrespective of the question of merit? Is Dante's poetry better for the clarity of its thought, or is it not? If it is better, in what sense is the clarity of its thought an irrelevant accident? It is not Dante's personal merit with which we are concerned, but the quality of his poetry. The last sentence, however, is emphatic, and it is emphatically anti-intellectual and deterministic at the same time: "the relative value of the thought current at their time, the material enforced upon each to use as the vehicle of his feeling, is of no importance." We may observe from this that the quality of a writer's thought is at once enforced upon him and is irrelevant to the quality of his work.

Much the same view is expressed more fully a little later: [16]

[16] Ibid., p. 117.

"What every poet starts from is his own emotions. . . . The great poet, in writing himself, writes his time. Thus Dante, hardly knowing it, became the voice of the thirteenth century; Shakespeare, hardly knowing it, became the representative of the end of the sixteenth century, of a turning point in history. But you can hardly say that Dante believed, or did not believe, the Thomist philosophy: you can hardly say that Shakespeare believed, or did not believe, the mixed and muddled scepticism of the Renaissance. If Shakespeare had written according to a better philosophy, he would have written worse poetry; it was his business to express the greatest emotional intensity of his time, based on whatever his time happened to think. Poetry is not a substitute for philosophy or theology or religion, as Mr. Lewis and Mr. Murry sometimes seem to think; it has its own function. But as this function is not intellectual but emotional, it cannot be defined adequately in intellectual terms. We can say that it provides 'consolation': strange consolation, which is provided equally by writers so different as Dante and Shakespeare. . . .

"I doubt whether belief proper enters into the activity of a great poet, qua poet. That is, Dante, qua poet, did not believe or disbelieve the Thomist cosmology or theory of the soul: he merely made use of it, or a fusion took place between his initial emotional impulses and a theory, for the purpose of making poetry. The poet makes poetry, the metaphysician makes metaphysics, the bee makes honey, the spider secretes a filament; you can hardly say that any of these agents believes: he merely does."

This passage also is curious in a great many ways. In the first place we have no authority for Shakespeare's intellectual equipment save Eliot's unsupported impression; and Eliot's impression even of so monumental a subject as this, as we shall ultimately have occasion to see, is not incapable of sudden and unpremeditated reversal; but let us suppose Shakespeare to be what Eliot here says he is. Eliot displays a knowledge of the personal beliefs and motives of two poets of distant ages that can be matched for its clairvoyance, I imagine, only by the perceptions of certain characters of Henry James; and he refines upon this clairvoyance in the case of Dante by distinguishing between Dante *qua* Dante and Dante *qua* poet. Anyone who can take this sort of thing seriously is welcome to do so. These points are all trivial, however, as compared to another; namely a kind of mystical determinism which has seldom been stated with such naive emphasis except by Emerson himself. Eliot writes: "Thus Dante, hardly knowing it, became the voice of the thirteenth century . . ." And Emerson: "Great men have always confided themselves childlike to the genius of their age . . ." And again:

> "The hand that rounded Peter's dome,
> And groined the aisles of Christian Rome,
> Wrought in a sad sincerity;
> Himself from God he could not free."

A passage in which God, the universe, and the period are conceived to be one. And it is worth noting in passing that Eliot's belief that only intellectual matter may be treated by the intellect introduces a new complication, with really extraordinary irradiations, into the practice of philosophy and of criticism.

Eliot is not without his hesitations, however. In writing elsewhere of Dante,[17] he says:

"And clear visual images are given much more intensity by having a meaning—we do not need to know what the meaning is, but in our awareness of the image we must be aware that the meaning is there too. Allegory is only one poetic method, but it is a method which has very great advantages.

"Dante's is a *visual* imagination. It is a visual imagination in a different sense from that of a modern painter of still life: it is visual in the sense that he lived in an age in which men still saw visions. It was a psychological habit, the trick of which we have forgotten,

17 Ibid., p. 204.

but as good as any of our own. We have nothing but dreams, and we have forgotten that seeing visions—a practice now relegated to the aberrant and uneducated—was once a more significant, interesting, and disciplined kind of dreaming. We take it for granted that our dreams spring from below: possibly the quality of our dreams suffers in consequence."

It is possible, of course, as Eliot somewhere else remarks, to admire a poem deeply without wholly understanding it; but such admiration must rest on an understanding at least imperfect, and the idea that this admiration is adequate as compared with that which comes with full understanding is mere nonsense. Dante's visions, with their meaning obscured, are dreams, as Praz points out; though in Dante, at least, and in part by virtue of the meaning which helped Dante to see them, they may be dreams of unusual clarity. If the meaning is important in the creation of the poem, at any rate, it is foolish to suppose that one can dispense with it in reading the poem or that the poet did not take his meaning seriously. Only the frailest barrier exists between the idea of this passage and Poe's theory that the poet should lay claim to a meaning when he is aware of none.

Eliot goes still farther, in his essay on Marvell, in the direction of admitting the importance of thought in the poem, but the passage is merely an undeveloped hint, and one does not really know what he meant by it: [18]

"These verses have the suggestiveness of true poetry; and the verses of Morris, which are nothing if not an attempt to suggest, really suggest nothing; and we are inclined to infer that the suggestiveness is the aura around a bright clear center, that you cannot have the aura alone."

And in writing of Dryden, he says likewise: [19]

[18] Ibid., p. 259.   [19] Ibid., p. 273.

"Swinburne was also a master of words, but Swinburne's words are all suggestions and no denotation; if they suggest nothing, it is because they suggest too much."

This is a good statement, but there is small reason to believe that Eliot knows what it means. He concludes his essay on the Metaphysical poets, for example,—an essay, which, incidentally, comments with a certain penetration on some of the qualities of metaphysical poetry—with this remarkable judgment: [20]

"It is not a permanent necessity that poets should be interested in philosophy, or in any other subject. We can only say that it appears likely that poets in our civilization, as it exists at present, must be *difficult* . . . The poet must become more and more comprehensive, more allusive, more indirect, in order to force, to dislocate if necessary, language into his meaning . . . Hence we get something which looks very much like the conceit—we get, in fact, a method curiously similar to that of the metaphysical poets . . ."

The idea is illustrated by a passage of fragmentary and weakly allusive French symbolism. This statement by Eliot has been often quoted, and is probably one of the main reasons why so many of the young and decadent romantics of our own period are convinced that they are in the tradition of Donne. If one cannot be profound, it is always fairly easy to be difficult.

Only one deduction is possible from Eliot's many comments upon this subject: namely that he believes that a poet who merely pretends to be saying something may be as successful as one who succeeds in saying something, that, as he said clearly in the passages quoted earlier in this section, the intellectual content of a poem is irrelevant to its value. That the intellectual content of a poem, whether good, bad, or fraudulent is an inseparable part of the poem and is inextricably involved

[20] Ibid., p. 248.

in the emotion, simply by virtue of the fact that the poem is composed of words, he does not seem to consider.

IV. *Poetry and Belief*

The subject of poetry and belief is little more than a subsidiary topic under the preceding head; for this reason, I shall consider only one passage from Eliot, a characteristic one, and shall try to make a few elementary distinctions of my own. This may seem presumptuous, but the problem of poetry and belief does not seem to me nearly so difficult as more learned authorities than myself have apparently thought it. In writing of Dante, Eliot comments as follows on certain ideas of I. A. Richards: [21]

"We may raise the question whether 'literature' exists; but for certain purposes, such as the purpose of this essay on Dante, we must assume that there is literature and literary appreciation; we must assume that the reader can obtain the full 'literary' or (if you will) 'aesthetic' enjoyment without sharing the beliefs of the author. . .

"I deny, in short, that the reader must share the beliefs of the poet in order to enjoy the poetry fully. I have also asserted that we can distinguish between Dante's beliefs as a man and his beliefs as a poet. But we are forced to believe that there is a particular relation between the two, and that the poet 'means what he says'. If we learned, for instance, that *De Rerum Natura* was a Latin exercise which Dante had composed for relaxation after completing *The Divine Comedy*, and published under the name of one Lucretius, I am sure that our capacity for enjoying either poem would be mutilated . . .

"And I confess to considerable difficulty in analyzing my own feelings, a difficulty which makes me hesitate to accept Mr. Rich-

[21] Ibid., p. 229.

ards' theories of 'pseudo-statements'. On reading the line which
he uses,

> Beauty is truth, truth beauty . . .

"I am at least inclined to agree with him, because this statement
of equivalence means nothing to me. But on rereading the whole
ode, this line strikes me as a serious blemish on a beautiful poem;
and the reason must be either that I fail to understand it, or that
it is a statement which is untrue . . ."

Like Eliot, I find the statement of Keats a blemish, and for
the reason given, a reason which, however, Eliot has no right
to give, for the general theories which we have been examining
will not support it. What "particular relation" can there be
between the beliefs of the two Dantes, or how can the poet
"mean what he says" if he is "not necessarily interested in the
thought itself"? Eliot is not making fine distinctions when he
writes thus; he is indulging in unpardonable confusion.

The difficulty in the statement by Keats, however, is not
the same difficulty that Dante might be supposed to encounter
in Lucretius or Lucretius in Dante; the difficulty is one of
simple incomprehensibility. Beauty and Truth are abstract
terms with distinct meanings; to say that they are interchangeable without explaining oneself leads to confusion. The non-
Christian, however, might easily share a wide community of
belief with Dante. The portraits of the damned are portraits
of human beings, represented in Hell as they might be seen
in life, suffering for sins most of which are acknowledged to
be sins by intelligent men, whether Christian or not. As we
proceed, however, toward the final vision of beatitude, we
find ourselves dealing with concepts which are more and more
purely Christian, and it is more than likely that only the convinced Christian can feel the poetry at something like its full
value: for the rest of us, the poetry offers a theoretic projection
of the imagination, a representation more or less dramatic.
Not purely, however: for such poetry will of necessity be col-

ored by feelings, desires, and ideas common to all men, and this alloy renders easier our entrance into the Christian state of feeling.

Let us consider another case. One of the few great poems of the twentieth century in America, I imagine, is *Sunday Morning*, by Wallace Stevens. The poem is a meditative composition, discreetly didactic in form; and its doctrine is one of more or less Paterian hedonism. Now I am not, myself, a hedonist of any variety; my dislike for the philosophy is profound, and I believe that it has, in the long run, done serious damage to the style of Wallace Stevens. But I know that hedonists exist, and the state of mind portrayed in the poem seems proper to them, and moreover it seems beautifully portrayed. It is no more necessary that one be a hedonist in order to enjoy this particular poem than that one be a murderer in order to enjoy Macbeth. Furthermore, in my own case, various subsidiary themes facilitate my entrance into the dominant theme: the theme of twentieth century scepticism, of doubt of immortality, the vision of the world as an infinitesimal island floating in infinite space. These themes, however, might merely increase the difficulty for Dante; but allowing Dante the same opportunity for the historical study of our period that we enjoy in the study of his, we may reasonably guess that he would be able to understand the poem fairly well.

My chief objection to a hedonistic philosophy is not that it contradicts my own view of human experience, but that it offers a very small portion of it in place of the whole, and that the error of mistaking that portion for the whole may prove very serious; that portion, however, may be truly described. On the other hand, Emerson, I believe, contradicts the most elementary and obvious facts of experience, and his poems may offer a problem of considerable difficulty. Emerson believes that all good comes from surrender to instinct and emotion; all evil from the functioning of the rational faculty.

Emerson's ideal man would be, it appears to me certain, an automaton, a madman; it is simply impossible to envisage human experience in these terms, for the terms are a negation of everything that we know. When Emerson, therefore, preaches his doctrine directly, in purely didactic terms, and with intentions purely to explain and convince, as in *The Problem*, he achieves a kind of incomprehensibility comparable to that in the passage from Keats. His language is very general, with the result that certain passages, if found in isolation, might be given a significance anything but Emersonian, as, for instance, could this passage about Michael Angelo:

> The hand that rounded Peter's dome,
> And groined the aisles of Christian Rome,
> Wrought in a sad sincerity;
> Himself from God he could not free.

Standing alone, these lines offer an impressive portrait of the devout Christian artist. But if we take them in the entire poem, we find that they mean something the reverse of Christian: we find that the God in question is the God of the Pantheist, and that the artist could not free himself from Him, simply because he wrought automatically as a determined and inseparable portion of the whole. If we could force ourselves to see what Emerson meant, and refuse to be misled by the traditional associations of the language when it is considered fragmentarily, then the poem, it seems to me, would be damaged past remedy. Of course we can never quite do this; the traditional associations are there, and they keep the poem alive in a marginal and unsatisfactory way, but nevertheless alive, and this is true of much similar poetry.

And one might find a poem stated throughout in terms so general that alternative interpretations might be possible. Consider, for example, Blake's *Introduction* to the *Songs of Experience*. Blake's philosophy resembles that of Emerson, except that it is not pantheistic; it contradicts the common observation of human nature in much the same fashion. The *Introduction* is, in fact, an invitation to humanity to throw off the shackles of intellect and law, and thus to free the true God, who was overthrown by Lucifer and bound in Hell: it rests on a precise inversion not only of Christian mythology, which perhaps does not matter, but of Christian morality as well. Yet we know this only by examining Blake as a whole; the poem as an isolated invocation might as well be Christian. What then are we to do with such a poem? Are we to read it with an attempt to accept for the moment Blake's full meaning, even if that meaning appears to be nonsense? If we do that, we shall have the same difficulty as in the poem by Emerson. Are we to read it with a resolute determination to give it as much of our own private meaning as the nature of the statement permits, even while realizing that Blake's meaning was the reverse of this? Such a procedure would be justified, so far as it might be possible, I believe, if it were necessary. In this poem, however, the abstract statement is very general: the poem is an invocation to humanity to free itself from evil and to enter the good life; the feeling of the poem is a feeling proper to that very general statement, and we may reasonably take the poem in that condition of generality and not trouble ourselves about the difficulties of Blake's philosophy until we actually trip on them.

These speculations, however, all derive from the conviction that the thought of a poem must be in some sense acceptable; that the thought is of the greatest importance as a part of the poem itself. Eliot, in the last passage quoted, would like, it appears, to make some such admission, but is hampered by the contrary trend of his general theory; and he once more takes refuge in mystery. But the believer in pure poetry will probably demand to know what there will be in pre-romantic poetry for the reader who believes with Emerson. The question in one form or another is constantly raised, and is mildly interesting. One may reply at the outset that the romantic theorist is by his nature either an untalented or an untrained theorist, and is therefore, like Emerson, practically certain to be inconsistent. His inconsistencies will probably rescue a good deal of the poetry in question for him. However, his understanding of such poetry, like Emerson's, is likely to be a very imperfect affair. If we could find a truly consistent Emersonian, it is certain that he would understand nothing of pre-romantic poetry or of anything else; furthermore he would have no particular rights in the matter. One might as well demand poetic rights for those who cannot read or speak, or poetic rights for idiots. Poetry is for the intelligent.

V. *Tradition*

Much of what has been thus far discussed verges on the question of tradition. The question is one that has fascinated Eliot from the beginning, and on which he has made some of his most interesting comments. In the early essay, *Tradition and the Individual Talent*, he writes: [22]

"We dwell with satisfaction upon the poet's difference from his predecessors, especially his immediate predecessors; we endeavor to find something that can be isolated in order to be enjoyed. Whereas if we approach a poet without this prejudice we shall often find that not only the best but the most individual parts of his work may be those in which the dead poets, his ancestors, assert their immortality most vigorously. And I do not mean the impressionable period of adolescence, but the period of full maturity."

This seems to me admirable as far as it goes, but the relation of the individual contribution to the traditional procedure

[22] Ibid., p. 4.

is not made very clear. One may depart from it in almost any direction, and Eliot in regarding Pound as the greatest modern poet in English, seems to depart somewhat curiously: what, precisely, is Pound's relationship to tradition, and why is it superior to that of Bridges, Hardy, or Robinson? And in what does it resemble the relationship of Valéry, whom Eliot apparently judges, as do I, to be the greatest modern in French? On the face of it Pound and Valéry appear to have almost nothing in common save native talent: Pound's relationship to tradition is that of one who has abandoned its method and pillaged its details—he is merely a barbarian on the loose in a museum; Valéry's relationship to tradition is that of a poet who has mastered and used the best of traditional method, and has used that method to deal with original and intelligent matter. Valéry is a living and beautifully functioning mind; Pound is a rich but disordered memory.

Eliot continues in the same essay:

"Yet if the only form of tradition, of handing down, consisted in following the ways of the immediate generation before us in a blind or timid adherence to its successes, 'tradition' should positively be discouraged. We have seen many such simple currents soon lost in the sand; and novelty is better than repetition. Tradition is a matter of much wider significance. It cannot be inherited, and if you want it you must obtain it by great labor. It involves in the first place, the historical sense, which we may call nearly indispensable to anyone who would continue to be a poet beyond his twenty-fifth year; and the historical sense involves a perception not only of the pastness of the past, but of its presence; the historical sense compels a man to write not merely with his own generation in his bones, but with a feeling that the whole of the literature of Europe from Homer and within it the whole of the literature of his own country has a simultaneous existence and composes a simultaneous order. This historical sense, which is a sense of the timeless as well as of the temporal, and of the timeless and of the temporal together, is what makes a writer traditional."

This passage raises much the same questions as the last, and even more emphatically: and these questions become central to the whole question of Eliot's influence when we arrive, as we shall arrive later, at the question of the determining effect upon a writer of his own time. Is Pound, for example, a man who possesses this historical sense, when he writes a formless revery loaded with quotations and literary reminiscences, but having no other discernible relationship to past literature? And is Eliot another such man, when he does almost the same thing with less skill? Or is Valéry such a man, when he brings to bear upon problems of the modern mind and of the modern sensibility a mode of thinking and of writing, an entire moral, literary, and philosophical apparatus descended from Greek antiquity but heavily influenced by the tradition of his own country from the time of its greatest literary period, that of Racine, to the present? Eliot has praised both men in equally high terms, but, though he has pillaged a few lines from Valéry, he has followed the method of Pound. If the view of tradition offered gives no reason for choice between two men so diverse, it is worthless, and if it leads us to choose Pound, it is vicious.

And finally it is interesting to note that Eliot informs us in this essay that tradition can be obtained only by hard labor, whereas in his later and Christian period he offers a less Christian view: [23]

"I hold . . . that a *tradition* is rather a way of feeling and acting which characterizes a group throughout generations; and that it must largely be, or that many of the elements in it must be, unconscious; whereas the maintenance of *orthodoxy* is a matter which calls for the exercise of all our conscious intelligence. . . . Tradition may be conceived as a by-product of right living, not to be aimed at directly. It is of the blood, so to speak, rather than of the brain."

[23] *After Strange Gods*, Harcourt, Brace, and Co., 1933. Pp. 31-2.

From which we may deduce that tradition is a way of feeling and orthodoxy the corpus of ideas by which we may criticize it. But in the paragraph preceding, the paragraph in which Eliot justifies his own poetry against the criticism of Paul Elmer More, a paragraph which I shall later have occasion to quote, Eliot informs us that tradition, so conceived, cannot be modified by orthodoxy, that the attempt to modify one's feeling as a result of self-criticism can lead to nothing save pious insincerity. Orthodoxy thus becomes a mere intellectual pastime, like chess, with no spiritual value, and one's feelings, from which poetry and character alike appear to be derived, are determined and beyond the power of self-modification.

Eliot's concept of the relation of the artist to tradition may be illustrated by one more characteristic passage: [24]

"I was dealing then with the artist, and the sense of tradition which, it seemed to me, the artist should have; but it was generally a problem of order; and the function of criticism seems to be essentially a problem of order too. I thought of literature then, as I think of it now, of the literature of the world, of the literature of Europe, of the literature of a single country, not as a collection of the writings of individuals, but as 'organic wholes,' as systems in relation to which, and only in relation to which, individual works of literary art, and the works of individual artists, have their significance. There is accordingly something outside of the artist to which he owes allegiance, a devotion to which he must surrender and sacrifice himself in order to earn and obtain his unique position. A common inheritance and a common cause unite artists consciously or unconsciously: it must be admitted that the union is mostly unconscious. Between the true artists of any time there is, I believe, an unconscious community. And as our instincts of tidiness imperatively command us not to leave to the haphazard of unconsciousness what we can attempt to do consciously, we are forced to conclude that what happens unconsciously we could

[24] *The Function of Criticism, Selected Essays,* Harcourt, Brace, p. 12.

bring about and form into a purpose, if we made a conscious attempt."

Such a phrase as 'organic whole' in this connection has a deterministic flavor almost as extreme as anything to be found in Taine. Further, if we are to indulge our privilege to be particular, what is the nature of the organic whole which includes and determines Pound and Valéry, Eliot and Robinson? And is it the function of the conscious intellect merely to accelerate and render efficient that which otherwise would happen unconsciously? If so, we have a determinism, which though perhaps not wholly pure, is surely pure enough.

The best possible comment on this kind of theorizing has been made by Eliot himself. In the *Introduction* to *The Use of Poetry and the Use of Criticism* [25] he has written:

"I hold indeed that in an age in which the use of poetry is something agreed upon you are more likely to get that minute and scrupulous examination of felicity and blemish, line by line, which is conspicuously absent from the criticism of our time, a criticism which seems to demand of poetry, not that it shall be well written, but that it shall be 'representative of its age.' "

But it is primarily Eliot and a small handful of his influential disciples, not the rest of us, who demand that our poetry shall be representative of its age; and they appear to have decided consciously that the unconscious tendency of the age is to produce poetry in the manner of Pound and Eliot, except when one of them by some unaccountable atavism occasionally happens to feel a liking for a poet of some other kind.

VI. *Determinism*

We have seen that the entire tendency of Eliot's thought is toward a deterministic view of literature. Yet Eliot is very severe

[25] *The Use of Poetry and the Use of Criticism,* by T. S. Eliot. Faber and Faber, London. P. 25.

in his comments upon deterministic views when he is able to recognize them. In the essay on John Bramhall, he writes as follows: [26]

"Hobbes' philosophy is not so much a philosophy as it is an adumbration of the universe of material atoms regulated by laws of motion which formed the scientific view of the world from Newton to Einstein. Hence there is quite naturally no place in Hobbes's universe for the human will; what he failed to see is that there was no place in it for consciousness either, or for human beings. So his only philosophical theory is a theory of sense perception, and his psychology leaves no place in the world for his theory of government. His theory of government has no philosophic basis: it is merely a collection of discrete opinions, prejudices, and genuine reflections upon experience which are given a spurious unity by a shadowy metaphysic.

"The attitude of Hobbes toward moral philosophy has by no means disappeared from human thought; nor has the confusion between moral philosophy and a mechanistic psychology."

In *Catholicism and International Order* [27] he writes:

"The non-Catholic, certainly the non-Christian philosopher, feeling no obligation to alter himself, and therefore no cogent need to understand himself, is apt to be under the sway of his prejudices, his social background, his individual tastes. So, I dare say, are we: but we at least, I hope, admit our duty to try to subdue them."

And on the next page of the same essay:

"Very few people, indeed, want to be better than they are; or, to put it in more consecrated terms, hunger and thirst after righteousness. And what we happen to like as individuals outside of the main current which is the Catholic tradition is apt to be what our own sort of people within a narrow limit of place and time have been

[26] *Selected Essays*, p. 303.
[27] *Catholicism and International Order*, in *Essays Ancient and Modern*, Harcourt, Brace and Co., N. Y., p. 118.

happening to like. We are likely to assume as eternal truths things that in fact have only been taken for granted by a small body of people or for a very short period of time."

And in *The Function of Criticism:* [28]

"The critic, one would suppose, if he is to justify his existence, should endeavor to discipline his personal prejudices and cranks— tares to which we are all subject—and compose his differences with as many of his fellows as possible, in the common pursuit of true judgment."

And three pages farther in the same essay:

"The question is, the first question, *not* what comes natural or what comes *easy* to us, but what is right?"

The general tendency of all of these passages is to affirm the power of man to criticize and improve himself, with reference to an absolute norm, and to affirm the necessity of his doing so. With this point of view I am in perfect agreement. It is with reference to this point of view, apparently, that Eliot objects to a passage from Herbert Read. At the end of his volume en- titled *After Strange Gods,* Eliot offers an appendix containing four specimens of modern heresy, of which Read's statement is the third:

"Character, in short, is an impersonal ideal which the individual selects and to which he sacrifices all other claims, especially those of the sentiments or emotions. It follows that character must be placed in opposition to personality, which is the general common denominator of our sentiments and emotions. That is, indeed, the opposition I wish to emphasize; and when I have said further that all poetry, in which I wish to include all lyrical impulses whatever, is the product of the personality, and therefore inhibited in a char- acter, I have stated the main theme of my essay."

[28] *Selected Essays,* p. 14.

Briefly, this passage means that poetry is the product of
what we are, and that any attempt to remake ourselves according to an ideal will damage the poetry, and Eliot objects to it,
I should judge, because it recommends the poet's doing what
is natural and easy to him instead of what is right. Yet Eliot, in
defending his own poetry, at the end of the first essay in the
same volume, uses Read's argument with no apparent realization of the fact: [29]

"From another aspect also I have a personal interest in the clear-
ing up of the use of the terms with which I have been concerned.
My friend Dr. Paul Elmer More is not the first critic to call attention to the apparent incoherence between my verse and my critical
prose—though he is the first whose perplexity on this account has
caused me any distress. It would appear that while I maintain the
most correct opinions in my criticism, I do nothing but violate
them in my verse; and thus appear in a double if not double-faced
role. I feel no shame in the matter. I am not of course interested
by those critics who praise my criticism in order to discredit my
verse, or those who praise my verse in order to discredit my opinion
in religious or social affairs; I am only interested in answering
those critics who, like Dr. More, have paid me the compliment—
deserved or not does not here matter—of expressing some approval
of both. I should say that in one's prose reflections one may be
legitimately occupied with ideals, whereas in the writing of verse
one can only deal with actuality. Why, I would ask, is most religious
verse so bad; and why does so little religious verse reach the highest levels of poetry? Largely, I think, because of a pious insincerity."

Now if we change Eliot's *ideals* to Read's *character* (an ideal
concept), and Eliot's *actuality* to Read's *personality*, and the
terms in these two passages are certainly interchangeable, we
have exactly the same statement in both men, and it is less
excusable in Eliot than in Read because Read has at least the

[29] *After Strange Gods*, p. 30.

virtue of being roughly consistent with himself. In both men the statement means about this: that our individual natures are determined for us, and our actual way of feeling cannot be changed, though it may be a pious and admirable practice to consider the theoretical characteristics of a better kind of nature—it may be a pious and admirable practice to do so, that is, so long as we do not indulge in the pious insincerity of attempting to conform our own nature to this ideal. The pious sincerity which Eliot has derived from his Christianity in the past thirteen or fourteen years would probably baffle the simpler sort of Christian.

And lest the reader think that I have misrepresented Eliot by taking a passage unfairly from its context, let me cite another and briefer passage from earlier in the same essay: [30]

"No sensible author, in the midst of something that he is trying to write, can stop to consider whether it is going to be romantic or the opposite. At the moment when one writes, one is what one is, and the damage of a lifetime, and of having been born into an unsettled society, cannot be repaired at the moment of composition."

At the moment when one writes, one is what one is: one has, in other words no power over that moment; one must surrender to one's feelings and one's habits at that moment if one is to achieve sincerity. Yet at what point in a poet's career does this become true? If it were true at the age of sixteen, the poet would develop but little beyond that age; and if the poet at the age of sixteen is to be encouraged to improve his literary habits, why should not the poet at the age of forty-six? Obviously one will not change one's literary habits between moments of composition; one will change them if at all in writing. And if one's conversion to Catholicism and to classicism is worth a flourish of the pen, it is worth risking a few years of

[30] Ibid., p. 27.

unsatisfactory composition in order to form new habits. I am reasonably certain that both Aquinas and Aristotle are on my side in this matter. Eliot's position is one of unmitigated determinism.

The point of view here indicated is, furthermore, related to the Marxist and Fascist view that the individual lacks the private and personal power to achieve goodness in a corrupt society; it is a utopian point of view, not a Christian one. Christianity rests upon the assumption that man can, with God's grace, save himself in a corrupt world; and if Eliot is convinced that the civilization of our period, bad as it may be, offers greater hazards, let us say than the Mediterranean civilization of the time of Augustine, or the British civilization of the time of Bede, he would do well to clarify his opinion.

Eliot appears to have adopted uncritically some such nostalgic historical lyricism as that of the later Henry Adams. Like Adams, he repeatedly contrasts the period of Dante and Aquinas with the twentieth century; and when he refers to the period of Dante and Aquinas, it is obvious that he refers especially to the minds of Dante and Aquinas, not to the vast underworld of sluggishly brutal paganism which surrounded them, as it is obvious that in his references to the twentieth century he has in mind his own confusion, as well as that of such men as John Dewey and Bertrand Russell, and not such minds as those of Gilson, Maillol, and Valéry. It is a difficult if not impossible thing to define the spirit of any age: the age of Pope, the mind of Pope himself, is a scene of complicated conflict; and nearly any other age is more complicated still. The inept deism of *The Essay on Man* was not forced upon Pope by the age: Pope himself, by virtue of his inability to think and his ability to write as if he thought perfectly, did at least as much as Shaftesbury to impose it on the age, and had he possessed as sharp a mind as Samuel Johnson the history of the age might easily have been greatly different from what it was.

The writer bent on finding the spirit of an age is certain to be the victim of impressions of a very limited kind; and seeking the spirit of his own age, in order that he may conform to it and thus be at once sincere and properly determined, he is likely to be the victim of impressions which merely flatter his weakness. In order to illustrate this difficulty, let me cite two passages from Eliot describing the age of Shakespeare. In the essay on John Ford we find the following statement: [31]

"In the work of Shakespeare as a whole, there is to be read the profoundest, and indeed one of the most sombre studies of humanity that has ever been made in poetry; though it is in fact so comprehensive that we cannot qualify it as a whole as either glad or sorry. We recognize the same assumption of permanence in his minor fellows. Dante held it also, and the great Greek dramatists. In periods of unsettlement and change we do not observe this: it was a changing world which met the eyes of Lucian or of Petronius."

And in *Shakespeare and the Stoicism of Seneca* [32] we meet this alternative impression:

"In Elizabethan England we have conditions apparently utterly different from those of Imperial Rome. But it was a period of dissolution and chaos; and in such a period any emotional attitude which seems to give a man something firm, even if it be only the attitude of 'I am myself alone,' is eagerly taken up."

If the second statement is a true one, then we cannot but cite the cases of Jonson and Shakespeare to prove that art need not be chaotic in a period of chaos; if the first statement is a true one, we must cope with Webster and Fletcher. The two statements taken together, along with the speculations which they inspire, may reasonably lead us to believe that most periods are varied and full of hazards, that the existence of Gilson and Valéry in our own period may be real and not an

[31] *Selected Essays*, p. 179.   [32] Ibid., p. 112.

illusion, and that any attempt to gauge the spirit of the age by a glance of the eye is likely to result in very casual impressionism.

VII. *The Dramatic Element in Lyric Poetry*

"It has been said by T. S. Eliot that the best lyric poetry of our time is dramatic, that it is good because it is dramatic." So writes Allen Tate,[33] and though I cannot put my finger on the passage in Eliot in which the statement occurs, there are many passages nearly as explicit.

F. O. Matthiessen writes: [34]

"Perhaps the most important thing that is revealed by applying Eliot's conception of the 'objective correlative' to his own work is the essentially dramatic nature of all his poetry. What is said by one of the speakers in his 'Dialogue on Dramatic Poetry' certainly seems expressive of one of his own most sustained beliefs:

'What great poetry is not dramatic? Even the minor writers of the Greek Anthology, even Martial, are dramatic. Who is more dramatic than Homer or Dante? We are human beings, and in what are we more interested than in human actions and human attitudes? Even when he assaults, and with supreme mastery, the divine mystery, does not Dante engage us in the question of the human attitude toward this mystery—which is dramatic?'

In the terms of such a description the dramatic element in poetry lies simply in its power to communicate a sense of real life, a sense of *the immediate present*—that is, of the full quality of a moment as it is actually felt to consist."

33 *Reactionary Essays on Poetry and Ideas,* by Allen Tate, Scribners, N. Y. P. 200.
34 *The Achievement of T. S. Eliot,* by F. O. Matthiessen, Houghton Mifflin, Boston and N. Y. P. 66.

What Eliot means by the dramatic in lyrical poetry, one can only deduce as best one is able: the combination of Homer and the minor writers of the Greek Anthology, for example, gives one ample opportunity to think at large. The notion, derived by most of his disciples, however, and one of the two upon which they most commonly act, is indicated by the phrase *the immediate present,* which is italicized in Matthiessen's commentary. Poetry is dramatic—and hence good—in so far as it produces the illusion that the experience described is taking place in the immediate present.

Now when Matthiessen suggests that there is any relationship between this concept and the concept of the objective correlative, he is merely indulging in incoherence. The idea of the objective correlative is this: that the poet starts with an emotion and after casting about finds objective data which he believes can be used to embody it; nothing more. Matthiessen's concept seems to place the main emphasis on the data themselves. Matthiessen does not attempt, as I remember, to reconcile this concept of the dramatic with the concept of autotelic art, but it would be well worth his trouble. The idea of an art which is about itself, yet which is successful in so far as it gives a sense of the immediate present in dealing with something other than itself, would provide a worthy foundation for a system of esthetics.

Matthiessen is by no means alone. Theodore Spencer [35] in an essay on Yeats, written more or less in answer to an essay by myself on T. Sturge Moore, has written as follows:

". . . Mr. Yvor Winters has recently compared the poetry of W. B. Yeats with the poetry of T. Sturge Moore . . . In his opinion, Moore is a greater poet than Yeats . . . To say that Moore is a

[35] *The Later Poetry of W. B. Yeats,* by Theodore Spencer, Hound and Horn, Vol. VII, p. 164, and *Literary Opinion in America,* ed. by M. D. Zabel, Harpers, N. Y. P. 263. My essay on Moore is in the Hound and Horn, Vol. VI, p. 534.

better poet than Yeats seems to me meaningless. . . . Compare, for
example, the opening lines of Moore's sonnet, 'Apuleius Medi-
tates,' which Mr. Winters praises very highly, with the opening of
Yeats's sonnet on Leda and the Swan.''

Spencer then quotes the passages, which the reader may examine if he desires, and proceeds:

"There is an important distinction illustrated here, a distinction
which applies to other poetry than that of Moore and Yeats. It is
the distinction between the poetry of revery and the poetry of immediacy."

He elaborates upon this distinction in terms which indicate
that his concept of immediacy is essentially similar to that of
Matthiessen.

Now I agree with Spencer that the lines from Yeats are better
than the lines from Moore: the poem by Yeats is one of his two
or three best, perhaps his best, and the lines from Moore, as I
pointed out in quoting them, are extremely faulty. Spencer in
failing to note my criticism of these lines adhered rigidly to a
convention of contemporary literary controversy against
which it would ill become a very young writer like myself to
protest. But whatever the faults of Moore's poem, it is not a
poem of revery; it is, like other and better poems by Moore
and other men, a poem of meditation. Pound's *Cantos* are
poems of revery and so likewise are most of Eliot's poems:
revery proceeds by the random association of daydream, and
possesses a minimum of rational coherence; in fact, in the form
it takes in the stream-of-consciousness novel, it is frequently
defended because of the sense of immediacy it produces, the
assumption being that this is the way people really think.
Spencer is very revealing when he fails to distinguish between
revery and meditation.

For what, after all, is a poem, if we approach it in my own
innocent state of mind? It is a statement about an experience,

real or imagined. The statement must follow the experience in time: Donne, for example, could not have written *The Ecstasy* while engaged in the experience described. The poem is a commentary upon something that has happened or that has been imagined as having happened; it is an act of meditation. The poem is more valuable than the event by virtue of its being an act of meditation: it is the event plus the understanding of the event. Why then should the poet be required to produce the illusion of the immediate experience without intervention of the understanding? Perhaps the understanding is supposed to occur surreptitiously, while the poet is pretending that something else is occurring. But what is the value of such deception? Is it assumed that understanding itself is not a "real" form of experience? The practical effect of the doctrine of dramatic immediacy is to encourage a more or less melodramatic emotionalism: such melodramatic emotionalism is perhaps the worst fault of Yeats, a poet whom Eliot admires, I should judge, little more than do I, but who is admired uncritically by Eliot's most eminent disciples.

Eliot has given rise, however, to another and in some respects different view of the way in which lyrical poetry may be dramatic. Many of his essays are attempts to define the stylistic qualities of one or another of the Elizabethan dramatists; they quote dramatic passages which he analyzes at length, the same passages being requoted and reanalyzed by many younger writers who appear to be more familiar with Eliot's views of the dramatists than with the dramatists themselves; and his own poetic style, even as early as Prufrock, has been heavily influenced by the style of these dramatists. *Gerontion,* for example, which I believe to be his best poem, is written in a more or less Websterian blank verse, has the texture of dramatic monologue, and seems to imply a dramatic context from which it has been excised. But this texture is the wrong texture for a lyric. Such poetry in a play is intended to exhibit the mannerisms of a character, so that Eliot runs the risk of imitating Bosola rather than Webster, which is a serious risk indeed; and such a passage in a play is likely to be full of allusions to matter within the play but without the passage, so that imitation of the style in a short poem is likely to result in incomprehensible irrelevancies. In the second and third essays in my volume called *Primitivism and Decadence* I endeavored to analyze some of these particular effects in *Gerontion* itself.

It is worth noting that Shakespeare and Jonson, for example, the two greatest dramatists in English and two of the half dozen or so greatest masters of the English lyric, employed dramatic blank verse only when writing drama, and employed the conventions of the lyric in writing the lyric; and further that one will be hard put to find a passage in any of their plays which, as a passage, and clean of its context, will stand serious comparison with any of a dozen short poems by either man.

No matter how the doctrine of dramatic immediacy is understood, it is a doctrine which leads to illegitimate emotionalism; and understood as it appears in Eliot's practice, it leads to irrelevance and to incoherence as well.

VIII. *Eliot's Poetic Practice*

Before attempting to relate Eliot's poetry to the body of opinion which I have been endeavoring to elucidate, I must summarize very briefly the career of Ezra Pound, who is beyond question the chief influence on Eliot's style. I shall describe the poetry of these men in the most general terms, for I have already dealt with it, and with similar poetry, in greater detail in a volume of criticism called *Primitivism and Decadence*. In that book I dealt with the types of poetic structure employed by these and allied poets, and sought to show the necessary effect of such structures upon the ultimate value of their work. I am concerned now, not with a detailed description of these structures, which I feel that I may reasonably take for granted, but with some of the principal concepts which generated them.

Ezra Pound, Eliot's master in poetry, began his poetic career as a student of the troubadours and of other early Romance poets, and as a disciple of Swinburne, the pre-Raphaelites, and the early Yeats. If we examine such a poem as his *Canzon: Of Incense,* for example, we see a poem written in a difficult Provençal form, but showing a quality of feeling which appears to derive from the late romantics. It is part of an attempt, extending over some years, by a belated disciple of the nineties, to recreate early Romance poetry in the modern world, and with very little explicit reference to the modern world. The attempt was doomed at the outset: the late romantic influences were unsound, and the early Romance models, though admirable in their kind, represented an elaborate development of a very limited state of mind, the elaboration and the limitation equally being the product of a very special social system and philosophy now dead these many hundred years. One might imitate Dante more successfully than Arnaut Daniel, I imagine, as one might imitate Jonson more successfully than Spenser: Dante and Jonson are timeless stylists; Spenser, and I should judge from what little I know of him, Daniel, display—with great beauty, no doubt—the eccentricities of their times, in spite of the fact that there are apparently important differences between the respective eccentricities. The curious thing about it, however, is this: that it came much closer to succeeding than one would have expected. The Pound of this period is not as good as the best Swinburne, but he is better than Dante Rossetti or the early Yeats, and by a comfortable margin.

About 1912 or a little later, however, Pound appears to have turned from his Provençal models except as he continued at

times to translate them; he became a modern. Pound's aim
appears now to have been no longer the recreation of a past
period, but the exploration of the life of his own time as he
might be able to understand it. We have as a result the tentative beginnings to be found in his collection called *Lustra:*
satirical thumb-nail sketches of people seen in London, and
simple but real fragments of life seen more seriously, though
very impressionistically, such as *Fish and the Shadow.* This
poetry, whether satirical or not, is notable mainly for the effect
it gives of charming fragments, as of something valuable shat-
tered, a quality which I have elsewhere described as essentially
primitive: aside from differences of subject matter, it greatly
resembles the slight but startling observations to be found in
much of the poetry of the American Indian. We have a trained
and refined sensibility unsupported by a unifying intellect,
and employing the brief and annotative method apparently
proper to it.

It was at about this stage in Pound's development that the
widow of Ernest Fenollosa appears to have been struck with
the idea that Pound was the man to put into final literary form
the many literal translations left by her husband. According
to the story current, she was impressed by the similarity of
Pound's poetry to the Chinese, in spirit if not in form. She
may well have been impressed by the translations which Pound
had already made from other languages: his version of the
Anglo-Saxon *Sea-Farer,* and of a certain Provençal alba, alone,
are enough to place him among the very few great translators
in English. In any event, Pound got the manuscripts and set
to work on them. They apparently provided him with material exactly suited to his talents at that stage of his development: the Chinese poets, like Pound, were primitive in their
outlook, and dealt with the more obvious and uncomplicated
aspects of experience; but their outlook, though primitive,
like Pound's, differed from Pound's in a richness and security

of feeling within its limits—their subjects, though simple, were nevertheless more rich than any with which Pound had thus far dealt, and, though this may not seem important at first glance, they lent themselves to the composition of poems longer than most which Pound had thus far attempted, so that he had an opportunity to explore the possibilities of the free verse which he had previously begun to employ.

Whether or not the first *Cantos* were begun before the work on the Fenollosa manuscripts I cannot say; but the first three *Cantos* as they originally appeared in *Poetry: A Magazine of Verse* were awkwardly Browningesque affairs which bear little resemblance to the later *Cantos* or to their own later forms. The *Cantos* in general come after the Chinese translations: in length they quite surpass the Chinese translations, and in meter they show a greater development as well, for whereas the Chinese translations are written in what is really a heavily cadenced prose that continually verges on verse without achieving it, the *Cantos* are written in a slow and heavily accentual verse, which at its best displays an extraordinary suavity and grace of movement.

But in the *Cantos* Pound is thrown back on his own subject matter, and although his style has developed enormously since the poems which preceded the Chinese versions, his general intelligence has remained about where it was. He is no longer at liberty to borrow the technical and more or less intellectual framework of the troubadours, and he has none of his own to offer, yet he is bent on fusing his impressions into some kind of whole, and he seems to desire a whole which shall not falsify them or violate their essential quality: only one convention is plausible, the convention of remembered impressions, or revery. Thus we get the *Cantos*, poems in which a poet remembers his past experience of all kinds, literary, personal, and imaginative, and moves from recollection to recollection purely and simply by means of suggestion. We may observe as a brief and fairly obvious example of the method the passage in the fourth *Canto* which begins in the second paragraph and extends to the passage beginning "Thus the light rains." This section takes us through references to a number of stories, some historical and some mythological, of cannibalism and of transformation, and the two kinds of stories appear solely because both elements appear in a few of them, so that the transition from allusion to allusion is easy. The other transitions in this *Canto* may appear more arbitrary if one merely decribes them, but the feeling inherent in the revery is so constant that one is not troubled so long as one resigns oneself to the form of revery and asks for no more.

Pound at maturity, then, sees life primarily as a matter of remembered impressions, and his art is an art of revery: he is a sensibility without a mind, or with as little mind as is well possible. It is this Pound who provides the foundation for the more ambitious work of Eliot.

Eliot's earliest poems display various influences if one regard the detail. The influence of Elizabethan dramatic verse is already evident in *Prufrock,* and the influence of Pound's satirical sketches is to be found in some of the short early poems. The principal influence is probably that of Laforgue, whose poetry Pound had begun to champion at least as early as 1917: the influence is seen not only in translated passages, but in the whole attitude of romantic irony in an urban setting, of which Laforgue is perhaps the most interesting exemplar among the French poets of the late nineteenth century. The longer poems in this book already display the structure of revery which is carried farther in Pound's *Cantos* and in the later Eliot. There follow a few poems in rimed quatrains, which display a trace of the influence of Corbière, a strong influence of Gautier, and very little of Pound, except in so far as Corbière and Gautier are two of Pound's favorite poets. In the same original collection with these appeared *Gerontion*, the first example of Eliot's later manner and matter, and in my own opinion the most considerable of his poems.

Gerontion is the portrait of an individual from whom grace has been withdrawn, and who is dying of spiritual starvation while remembering his past; it is thus a prelude to *The Waste Land*, a portrait of a society from which grace has been withdrawn and which is dying of its own triviality and ugliness. I should like to deal primarily with *The Waste Land*, for its method is that of all the later work and it illustrates very clearly the problems to which I have been leading, and the faults which seriously weaken even a poem of so much strength as *Gerontion*.

The matter of *The Waste Land* is Baudelairian. It is no accident that the last line of the introductory poem of *The Waste Land* is also the last line of the preface of *Les Fleurs du Mal*. That preface details the sins of the modern world as they appeared to Baudelaire, and it names as the most horrible of them all the sin of Ennui. Now Ennui, as it appears in much romantic literature is very much the same sin as the Christian sin of acedia, or spiritual torpor, and it might well be regarded as the most deadly of sins because it leads to all the others and interferes with one's struggling against them: it would be above all other sins the one most likely to appear, if we accept Christian postulates, in a man or a society deprived of grace.

Both poets deal with such a society, and both endeavor to judge it from a more or less Christian position. But there is this difference between them, if no other: that Eliot surrenders his form to his subject, whereas Baudelaire does not do so. Henry Adams, whose influence on Eliot's entire poetic theory is probably greater than has been guessed, worked out in his *Education*, in *Mont Saint Michel and Chartres*, and in certain minor essays the entire theory of modern society and its relationship to the society of the Middle Ages, upon which Eliot's critical theory rests; and near the end of *Mont Saint Michel and Chartres* he offered the now commonplace theory that modern art must be chaotic in order to express chaos [36]—a variant, I suppose, of the earlier romantic doctrine of organic form sponsored by Coleridge; and Eliot was sufficiently moved by him to construct one of the better lines of *Gerontion*—"In depraved May, dogwood and chestnut, flowering judas"—from the first paragraph of the eighteenth chapter of the *Education*.

Now if the modern world is demonstrably chaotic in relationship to the world of past periods, and if we accept the postulate that the poet is formed by the society into which he is born, that this age must give him not merely his subject matter but his entire spiritual shape, as it were, so that the form of his art will be determined by the quality of his age, then the formlessness of Pound's *Cantos* is something determined by forces more important than any in Pound's character: the *Cantos* offer the only form available to the poet who would write honestly and sensitively; this in spite, as I have already suggested, of the awkward presence of such writers as Valéry, Robinson, Bridges, and Hardy. Eliot, in dealing with the chaos of this graceless world, found his form ready to use, and he produced *The Waste Land*.

Baudelaire, however, did something very different. Eliot writes of him as follows: [37]

"To say this is only to say that Baudelaire belongs to a definite place in time. Inevitably the offspring of romanticism, and by his nature the first counter-romantic in poetry, he could, like anyone else, only work with the materials which were there. It must not be forgotten that a poet in a romantic age cannot be a 'classical' poet except in tendency. If he is sincere, he must express with

[36] *Mont Saint Michel and Chartres,* by Henry Adams. Houghton Mifflin Co., Boston and N. Y., p. 375: "Art had to be confused in order to express confusion; but perhaps it was truest, so."
[37] *Selected Essays,* p. 340.

individual differences the general state of mind—not as a *duty,*
but simply because he cannot help participating in it."

This passage should sound remarkably familiar to the reader
who has been so patient as to reach it; it contains an element
of truth and a larger element of error. What Baudelaire actually accomplished in his best work was a vision and evaluation
of evil as it appeared to him in his own time, that is, in the
guise of romantic excess. He was not a rigorous thinker, though
his thought was often profound, and his judgment was sometimes beguiled by the romanticism which at other times he
judged with appalling lucidity. A poet is conditioned by his
time to this extent, that it offers him most of his subject matter; but what he does with that subject matter—let me insist
at the risk of excommunication—is very largely the result of
his own intelligence and talent. A minor talent, or an imperfect
talent, may be grievously damaged through the influence of a
bad tradition, such as the tradition represented by Pound and
Eliot; but a greater talent need not be. To assume that Shakespeare and Jonson possessed no great intellectual power may
occasionally be comforting to us, but a study of either man
will not support the assumption. As H. B. Parkes has said
in another connection, there is nothing inevitable about
stupidity.

The subject matter of *The Waste Land* is in general similar
to that of *Les Fleurs du Mal.* Yet if one will compare let us
say *Le Jeu* with *A Game of Chess,* one may perhaps note what
Eliot overlooked. Eliot, in dealing with debased and stupid
material, felt himself obliged to seek his form in his matter:
the result is confusion and journalistic reproduction of detail.
Baudelaire, in dealing with similar matter, sought to evaluate
it in terms of eternal verity: he sought his form and his point
of view in tradition, and from that point of view and in that
form he judged his material, and the result is a profound

evaluation of evil. The difference is the difference between triviality and greatness.

The difference is in part, however, merely the difference between a poet with a great native gift for poetic style and a poet with very little gift. Eliot has written in his essay on Massinger: [38]

"One of the surest of tests is the way in which a poet borrows. Immature poets imitate; mature poets steal; bad poets deface what they take, and good poets make it into something better, or at least something different. The good poet welds his theft into a whole of feeling which is unique, utterly different from that from which it was torn; the bad poet throws it into something which has no cohesion."

Such a statement might easily be used in defence of Pound, who, except for Eliot, borrows more extensively than any other poet of our time: Pound's revery has a discernible consistency at its best, and the borrowed material is either selected or re-worked so judiciously that it seems in place. And such a statement might be cited in defense of *Gerontion* and even of some of Eliot's earlier work, frail as it is. But the meter of *The Waste Land* is not the suave meter of *The Cantos* or of *Gerontion:* it is a broken blank verse interspersed with bad free verse and rimed doggerel. And what is one to say of the last eight lines of *The Waste Land,* which are composed, as nearly as I can determine with the aid of the notes, of unaltered passages from seven sources? A sequence of such quotations cannot by any stretch of the imagination achieve unity, and its disunity can be justified on no grounds except the Adams-Eliot doctrine of modern art, of which the less said by this time the better. The method is that of a man who is unable to deal with his subject, and resorts to the rough approximation of quotation; it is the method of the New England farmer who meets every situa-

[38] Ibid., p. 182.

tion in life with a saw from *Poor Richard;* it betokens the death of the mind and of the sensibility alike. The last line, in fact, is a classic of its kind. It reads: "Shantih shantih shantih," and in the note at the end of the poem Eliot tells us that " 'The Peace which passeth understanding' is a feeble translation of the content of this word." Surely there was never another great sentiment expressed with such charming simplicity!

Eliot, in brief, has surrendered to the acedia which Baudelaire was able to judge; Eliot suffers from the delusion that he is judging it when he is merely exhibiting it. He has loosely thrown together a collection of disparate and fragmentary principles which fall roughly into two contradictory groups, the romantic on the one hand and on the other the classical and Christian; and being unaware of his own contradictions, he is able to make a virtue of what appears to be private spiritual laziness; he is able to enjoy at one and the same time the pleasures of indulgence and the dignity of disapproval. He is right in confessing that his later work has not appreciably changed, and Mario Praz is right in finding in it more of the nature of dream than of vision. And he is right again in regarding as heretical, that is, as anti-Christian, the ideas which he has used to justify his failure to change when he meets those ideas expressed by another writer; though it is strange that he should fail to recognize the heresy when he employs it himself. When Eliot announced his conversion to Catholicism and to Classicism in 1927, his modernist followers were astonished, and they have never really forgiven him; but they might well have spared themselves so much devout feeling, for the conversion appears to have been merely nominal; at least, so far as one can judge from what Eliot has written, it really meant nothing at all.

There are scattered essays, especially early essays analyzing qualities of style, which are valuable even when one does not agree with them, and his poems display charming or excellent passages here and there as well, and *Gerontion* in fact deserves much higher praise than this. To this side of Eliot I may appear unfair. The fact of the matter is, however, that it has received far more than its due praise from other hands than mine; and the theory and influence of Eliot, with which I am at present dealing, seem to me the most dangerous and nearly the least defensible of our time. They have grown upon our time with all the benumbing energy of a bad habit, till any attempt to analyze the defects of modern poetry in the light of civilized standards is accepted merely as evidence that the critic is not of the elect, is not a recipient of the grace of the Zeitgeist; till the good poetry written in our time is more commonly than not excluded from consideration and even from publication, because it is regarded as insensitive to the realities of the twentieth century. And when one seeks closely to find the features of the divinity, the primal spirit of the age to whose will surrender is required, one may well be appalled; for behind the shadows thrown by veil after veil of indeterminate prose one will find, if one is patient, the face of Ezra Pound in apotheosis.

JOHN
CROWE
RANSOM

OR THUNDER WITHOUT GOD

I. *Ransom's Concept of Morality in Poetry*

IN DISCUSSING RANSOM'S THEORIES of poetry, I shall concentrate on those theories; I shall not examine his estimates of other critics. But in this respect I shall be forced to make one exception: I must consider in some detail the matter of his objections to my own position, for I am endeavoring to clarify and defend that position, and it is only with respect to that position that I can write intelligibly of Ransom. However, I shall not take the trouble to defend myself against Ransom's objections to incidental details in my criticism, but shall defend merely my essential concepts, the concepts to which he takes the most extreme exception.

Ransom objects primarily to my concept of the morality of poetry, and in order to make myself clear I shall have to restate that concept briefly and then indicate briefly the way in which Ransom misapprehends it. My theory rests on the observation that language, if one disregard for the present its phonetic values, is dual in nature; that each word is both conceptual and evocative, denotative and connotative, and that the feeling, evocation, or connotation is directly the result of the concept and dependent upon the concept for its existence. The word *tree* is conceptual: it refers to a class of objects. The word, or rather the concept, suggests a loose body of perception and feeling, the result of our experience with large numbers of individual trees. What the genetic relationship may be between percept and concept, I am not sufficiently philosophical to say, but when we come to use the language, it is the concept which evokes the feeling. Deprive the sound of its conceptual content, and the sound will evoke nothing in particular. In words which represent qualities, ideas, or states of mind, such as *justice* or *malice,* the content of sensory perception is for most persons negligible; but these words are at least vaguely evocative of emotion, and can be made precisely evocative if properly employed.

Now a poem is composed of words; that is, it is conceptual in its origin, and it cannot escape from its origin. A poem about. a tree is composed primarily of abstractions, and secondarily of the feelings aroused by those abstractions: the tree, its leaves, its bark, its greenness, its brownness, its roughness, its smoothness, its strength, its motion, and all its other qualities must be indicated in terms which are primarily conceptual. These terms, however, all suggest certain loose possibilities in the way of perception and feeling; and the poet's business is so to relate them, or others similar to them, that a single and definite idea emerges, in company with a mental image of some aspect of a tree, and in such a way that the feeling is communicated which is appropriate to the total idea-image both as a whole and with respect to each detail as one comes to it in reading.

The poet, then, understands his subject in rational terms,

and he so employs language that he communicates simultaneously that understanding and the feeling which it properly motivates. The poet differs in this respect from the writer of theoretical prose, who endeavors as far as may be to use language cleared of all save its rational content. The act of the poet I have described in a number of essays, and I have repeatedly called it an act of moral judgment. The act of moral judgment so considered is far more difficult, is a much fuller experience, than an act of classification; it is a full and definitive account of a human experience.

Ransom's difficulty is that he can understand the idea of morality or of moral judgment only with reference to an act of simple classification, or with reference to an overt action deriving from an act of simple classification. He reads this meaning into my every use of the terms, in spite of all my precautions against such misunderstanding, with the result that most of my criticism, even when he believes that he approves it, is incomprehensible to him. He writes: [1]

. . . for moralism conducts itself very well in prose, and conducts itself all the better in pure or perfect prose. And the good critics who try to regard the poem as a moral discourse do not persuade themselves, and discuss the poem really on quite other grounds.

And again: [2]

It is like according a moral dimension to poetry because there are some poems which not only present their own content but in addition moralize about this content.

From both of these statements we may see that Ransom cannot understand that poetry can have moral content except in the form of didacticism; that is, in the form of purely

[1] *The New Criticism*, by John Crowe Ransom, New Directions, Norfolk, Conn., 1941, page 279.   [2] Ibid., p. 283.

theoretical statement. The same notion appears in an earlier volume: [3]

And all the poets famous in our tradition, or very nearly all, have been poets of a powerful moral cast.

So I shall try a preliminary definition of the poet's traditional function on behalf of society: he proposed to make virtue delicious. He compounded a moral effect with an aesthetic effect. The total effect was not a pure one, but it was rich, and relished highly. The name of the moral effect was goodness; the name of the aesthetic effect was beauty. Perhaps these did not have to co-exist, but the planners of society saw to it that they should; they called upon the artists to reinforce morality with charm.

This passage rests on the notion that the moral content of poetry can be only didactic; that the content which is not didactic must be aesthetic. My own idea is that the term *æsthetic* has been used primarily to conceal a great deal of inaccurate thinking. This passage is essentially Horatian, and Ransom reverts to the same ideas later, with reference both to Horace and myself: [4]

Horace decreed that the aim of poetry was *aut prodesse aut delectare,* either to be morally instructive or to be delightful; and presently he decided that it was both; at any rate he kept the rider along with the moral formula. . . . There has risen increasingly in modern times a concern about Horace's rider; a concern as to how a moral discourse which goes to all the trouble of being technical poetry distinguishes itself from a moral discourse in prose. That is the critical problem.

But if that is the critical problem, it is a very simple one, for the poet is more explicitly concerned with communicating the feeling which ought properly to be motivated by the idea than is the writer of prose; and that is the sole distinction. But

[3] *The World's Body,* by John Crowe Ransom, Charles Scribners Sons, New York, 1938, page 57.   [4] *The New Criticism,* pp. 213-14.

Ransom continues without break to discuss my own theories, in a passage of remarkable innocence:

> Winters believes that ethical interest is the only poetic interest. (If there is a poem without visible ethical content, as a merely descriptive poem for example, I believe he thinks it negligible and off the real line of poetry.)

At this point I must interrupt again to comment. I believe, to be sure, that ethical interest is the only poetic interest, for the reason that all poetry deals with one kind or another of human experience and is valuable in proportion to the justice with which it evaluates that experience; but I do not believe that a descriptive poem is negligible or off the real line of poetry. A descriptive poem deals with a certain kind of experience, an extremely simple kind, but one of real value; namely, the contemplation of some fragment of the sensible universe. This is a moral experience, like any other, and the task of the poet is to evaluate it for what it is worth.

Ransom continues, still writing of myself:

> Now I suppose he would not disparage the integrity of a science like mathematics, or physics, by saying that it offers discourse whose intention is some sort of moral perfectionism. It is motivated by an interest in mathematics, or in physics. But if mathematics is for mathematical interest, why is not poetry for poetical interest? A true-blue critic like Eliot would certainly say that it is, though he would be unwilling to explain what he meant. I think I know why all critics do not answer as Eliot would: because criticism, a dilettante and ambiguous study, has not produced the terms in which poetic interest can be stated. Consequently Winters is obliged to think that mathematics is for mathematical interest—or so I suppose he thinks—but that poetry, in order that there may be an interest, must be for ethical interest. And why ethical? Looking around among the stereotyped sorts of interest, he discovers, very likely, that ethical interest is as frequent in poetry as any other one.

This is a curious statement, for Ransom appears to speculate upon my inner psychological life with the same bland impartiality with which he examines that of the lower animals; but it is offered seriously, and I suppose one must reply to it seriously. As I have already said, any scientific or philosophical statement endeavors to employ as far as may be the conceptual content of language and no other. The scientist is interested in ideas, not in the feelings they motivate; his interest is purely conceptual and amoral. Mathematics, I take it, is the one kind of scientific statement which is able to realize this ideal perfectly, for it subsists wholly in a language of its own. I offer this suggestion with some hesitancy, for I really know very little about mathematics, and I have not the ability, which Ransom possesses in an eminent degree, to write algebraic equations for the purpose of illustrating my critical theories. The subject matter of poetry, on the other hand, is human experience; it can therefore be understood only in moral terms. The language of poetry is normal human speech, which was devised for dealing with normal human experience, and I have already indicated the nature of that speech. When Ransom refers to my finding "that ethical interest is as frequent in poetry as any other one," he is again confusing the terms *ethical* and *didactic* and misunderstanding me in his own private fashion.

This misunderstanding accounts for his objections to my remarks upon Baudelaire. Of Baudelaire I wrote: [5]

He was determined by his period only to this extent: that he dealt with the problem of evil in the terms in which he had met it, the terms of the romantic view of life; and it was because of these terms that he was able to embody the universal principles of evil in the experience of his own age and evaluate that experience.

[5] *Primitivism and Decadence,* by Yvor Winters, Arrow Editions, New York, 1937, p. 90.

Ransom quotes this passage and writes of it as follows: [6]

I have no doubt that Baudelaire evaluated his experience of evil. I honor Winters for not being so tender-minded as to shy off from Baudelaire's poetry because its flowers are "flowers of evil." I wish he could say that the logical materials are evil, but that poetic flowers grow out of them; and drop the business of the "moral evaluation" and the "spiritual control." Aesthetic experience is beyond good and evil in a plain temporal sense . . .

I have no wish to be honored for not "shying off" from Baudelaire; and one reason for my not saying what Ransom wishes me to say is that I do not understand it. The "logical materials" of most of Baudelaire are no more evil than the materials of Shakespeare. The topics of both men are bad enough, for both explore human nature rather far; both depict evil as evil and make us know it as evil. Ransom might conceivably understand what I mean if he would compare *Une Martyre*, a poem which deals with a sadistic murder and which treats it fully and richly and for what it is worth, with *Porphyria's Lover*, a poem on a similar topic by Browning, which endeavors to make the topic cosy and domestic.

I should like to mention two secondary objections made by Ransom in passing. He writes: [7]

I am struck by the fact that the moral evaluations Winters obtains from the poems are so negative in their effect; the poems seem to evaluate experiences by just imagining them, by having them vicariously, so that it becomes unnecessary for the poets and the readers to have them actually. Poetry becomes the survey of experience, reporting it in such a way as to indispose us to it. . . . It is a kind of moral decadence.

I do not know how a poem can evaluate an experience or do anything else with it except by "just imagining" it; for the poem exists on paper. One cannot commit a murder and

[6] *The New Criticism,* page 228.   [7] *The New Criticism,* page 233.

write about it at the same time; the two acts are distinct. I can imagine further that both *Une Martyre* and *Macbeth* might indispose us to murder, but I can see neither harm nor decadence in that; I can imagine no good reason why most love poems should indispose us to fall in love or why most descriptive poems should indispose us to take walks in the country.

Ransom appears in this passage, however, in an unfamiliar role, that of a defender of overt action. He himself is on record, as I assuredly am not, as believing the work of art to be valuable as a check to action. The work of art, for Ransom, as we shall presently see, is an act of sensibility, or, as he sometimes puts it, of cognition; it is an objective apprehension of something outside ourselves, with the sole purpose of apprehending the unique object as nearly as possible in its unique and whole form, and with no ulterior, or practical, end in view. In *God without Thunder* Ransom first develops his thesis that overt action is degrading because it is motivated by ideas, that is by incomplete apprehension of the objective world, and because it aims at the satisfaction of practical, or generalized, appetites, such as lust or hunger. Even as late as *The New Criticism* [8] he identifies morality as belonging to the same class of motives:

Morality is for the practical rather than the aesthetic stage; coördinate with greed, or envy, or lust, or whatever appetites and affections it sets itself up in opposition to.

And in *God without Thunder*,[9] he praises the sensibility as follows:

In order to be human, we have to have something which will stop action, and this something cannot possibly be reason in the narrow sense. I would call it sensibility.

[8] *The New Criticism*, p. 226.
[9] *God without Thunder*, by John Crowe Ransom, Harcourt, Brace and Co., 1930, p. 190.

Sensibility is offered as a substitute for Babbitt's Inner Check, but, unlike Babbitt's safeguard, functions as a check to all actions instead of to some.

The other objection by Ransom with which I wish to conclude this section is better founded, for it rests on a careless statement of my own, though if Ransom had read me more carefully and above all if he had read my second volume of essays as well as my first, I believe that he might have understood my intention. In the first essay of *Primitivism and Decadence*[10] I wrote of the poem:

It is composed of an almost fluid complex, if the adjective and the noun are not too nearly contradictory, of relationships between words . . . a relationship involving rational content, cadences, rhymes, juxtapositions, literary and other connotations, inversions, and so on, almost indefinitely. These relationships, it should be obvious, extend the poet's vocabulary incalculably. They partake of the fluidity and unpredictability of experience and so provide a means of treating experience with precision and freedom.

Of this Ransom writes:[11]

The freedom does very well; the freedom is unpredictability, and the unpredictable or free detail cannot be precise in the sense that it was intended, that it unfolds logically according to a plan. To have an unpredictable experience seems quite different from treating experience with precision.

Ransom reverts a number of times to this objection in treating other passages in my criticism. He reads the passage with his own theory of poetic structure in mind. This theory I shall later examine in detail; it will suffice at present to say that Ransom sees the poem as composed of a logical core and a tissue of irrelevancies: I borrow his language, because I do not understand it quite well enough to paraphrase it. He

---

[10] *Primitivism and Decadence*, p. 3.   [11] *The New Criticism*, p. 221.

therefore assumes that I see fluidity and unpredictability in the finished poem, whereas I see them rather in the medium of expression.

What I meant to indicate, or should have indicated, is that the poetic medium has a more finely detailed vocabulary than has the medium of prose, and that one never knows exactly how finely detailed the vocabulary may prove in a given poem until one has done one's best to write the poem. Perhaps the main reason for this subtlety of poetic vocabulary is meter, and I shall try to explain it at least in part when I arrive at the discussion of meter. The poem will treat matters that would be lost in the gaps of the relatively rough vocabulary of prose; but the statement, once it is made, is precise. The poet is like a musician who plays an instrument which does not operate on fixed intervals: the musician can play notes not on the keyboard of the piano, but the notes when played are definite notes. That the poet will scarcely envisage every detail of his poem before he has written it seems likely enough, and that his first rough judgment preceding composition will be improved by revision in the course of composition is devoutly to be hoped; in such ways, the writing of a poem involves a good many unpredictable experiences. But if the poet allows himself irrelevancies in any true sense of the word, his poem will be damaged, and if he allows many it will be spoiled. A good many unpredictable experiences will have to be pruned away, and those which are kept should be kept for their accuracy.

II. *The Unique Experience*

Ransom is a nominalist, at least in intention, and as far as may be by persuasion, although the entire business gives him a good deal of embarrassment. It would be only with hesita-

tion and regret that he would admit that he and I both are
men and that the concept *man* is of the first importance if
we are to be understood; this in spite of the fact that he and
I are able to conduct an argument on what we take to be the
same subject, and, when all things are considered, to understand each other fairly well; in spite of the fact that neither
one of us, I imagine, would offer occasion for much astonishment either to an anatomist or to a psychologist. It seems
fruitless to revive a question that was thoroughly exhausted
in the middle ages; it seems especially foolish for a pair of
wholly unscholarly amateurs to revive it. The conflict between
realism and nominalism, from the standpoint of pure logic,
is sufficiently obscure; the empirical fact that the unique and
the general both have reality but that neither can be known
in and for itself alone is obvious and incontrovertible, and
every act of our lives is testimony to it. This is, I suppose, one
of the elemental mysteries of theology and of philosophy
equally; it can be neither understood nor ignored: it is like
the creation or the difference between prescience and predestination. The best way to deal with such questions is that of
Aquinas: to accept the solution which provides the best beginning for an understanding of the rest of our experience;
to judge the proposition in terms of the relationship between
its consequences and the whole of what we know. The Thomistic distinction between prescience and predestination may
be hard for the imagination to seize, but it saves one from
greater difficulties which follow upon the refusal to make the
distinction.

Ransom has written: [12]

Nevertheless, the life of Jesus was remarkable, and so were all
the other events I have named—and how can the "short-hand of
routine experience" ever explain satisfactorily what is remarkable?

[12] *God without Thunder,* p. 63.

It will never cease to be difficult for science, with its naturalistic principles, to account for any remarkable event. Such a particular tends too obviously to exceed its type, too spectacularly to strain against the confinement of its law. *It tends always to exhibit more particularity than type.* It tends, that is, to be *unique,* and to escape from science altogether.

Yet a Christian realist, of an extreme variety, might reply very simply that Ransom does not know the exact limits of the type from which he assumes Jesus to be a variation; that from the realist's standpoint, every man varies from the type, not by overflowing its limits but by failing to fill them, that variation is deficiency or deprivation; that Ransom is drawing conclusions about the true nature of the concept *man* from his own imperfect observation of imperfect individuals; and that precisely the remarkable thing about Jesus as man is this, that he is a perfect realization of the type. And a scientific realist might conceivably make a similar answer, except that he would add that he too does not know the exact limits of the type, and is constantly forced to alter his definition in the hope of improving it. A few pages later[13] Ransom states the same view in more poetic terms:

The myth of an object is its proper name, private, unique, untranslatable, overflowing, of a demonic energy that cannot be reduced to the poverty of the class concept—

a statement which renders the problem more dramatic and perhaps less mysterious than I am inclined to imagine it to be.

I should like to lay the reader's fears at rest, and say that I am prepared to offer no solution to the problem, unless the reader is satisfied with that of Aquinas, which, though not wholly armed against logical attack, is probably more satisfactory than any other. I am willing to grant without argument

[13] Ibid., p. 65.

that as far as common observation goes the particular appears to exist; but I feel sure that we are aware of it only in so far as we are aware of the universal. The *Socratitas* of Socrates will scarcely be evident to the mind wholly unfamiliar with the idea of man.

And I should like to recall another proposition to which I have already alluded and which I shall have to mention again: that one can say nothing about any object, be it unique or not, except in words, that is through the subdivision and inter-relation of abstractions; and that any feelings one may try to express about the object will be expressed through the connotations of those words, that is will be motivated by abstractions—not by the object but by our understanding of the object. And it is perhaps fair to add that the extreme Christian realist already mentioned, with the expenditure of only a little ingenuity, could make much of this fact in the defense of his position.

The difficulty with Ransom's position is this: that he knows, finally, that he cannot get rid of abstractions, yet he has an abhorrence of the rational processes which is less related to that of Ockham than to that of the romantics; it is a traditional feeling—I refer to romantic tradition—which makes him abhor words such as *moral, ideal,* or *rational* without troubling really to understand what they mean. As a result, he tries always to theorize about poetry as if he had actually got rid of the general as a vicious delusion, and sometimes he actually does so theorize. But he has not got rid of it, and it makes him a great deal of trouble.

III. *Hedonism*

It is natural that a nominalist should be a hedonist, provided he is not, like Ockham, a voluntaristic Christian; and it is

natural that he should endeavor to justify a hedonistic philosophy; and it is natural that he should fail in this attempt
at justification. For if one cannot understand, one can at least
hope to enjoy; it is in human nature to offer a rational defense
of one's way of life, real or imagined, even if that way of life
is anti-rational, as we can discover to our weariness and confusion by reading almost anywhere in the critical literature
of the last three hundred years; and it is impossible to devise
a philosophy which will show us how we can enjoy a universe
from which all distinctions have been eliminated.

Of the inner life of cattle, we have, I presume, an imperfect
knowledge, but Ransom is more or less plausible in assuming
that they see greenery, for example, generically and vaguely,
as something to be consumed. And yet *generically* would
hardly seem to be the word if the cow lacks reason. Ransom
writes on this subject: [14]

As an animal merely, man would simply partake of the banquet
of nature as he required. As an animal with reason, he would only
gorge himself the more greedily upon it and have more of it to
gorge upon. But as an animal with sensibility, he becomes fastidious, and makes of his meal a rich, free and delicate aesthetic experience.

And in his second book: [15]

An intelligent individual attachment is, therefore, a great luxury,
permitted to human animals almost exclusively, because they are
the only animals who can afford it with safety. Our trained scientists, marvelously advanced in technique beyond the lower animals,
are valuable to us because their labors improve the production and
distribution of necessary commodities and also, incidentally, enable us to indulge sentiment without having suicidal mania. But
to the extent that they have to stick to their profession and devote
themselves only to commodities, they are scapegoats. They are not

[14] *God without Thunder,* p. 189.   [15] *The World's Body,* pp. 224-5.

infants or lower animals, but it is their fixed rule to pursue the general rather than the particular, and that is exactly the animal or infantile practice. To use an adult and human analogy, under this restriction they are like the sailor in port who pursues generic rather than individual woman.

Persons who are idealists by conviction, or on general principles, are simply monsters. (I mean the Platonic ones, the kind of idealists who worship universals, laws, Platonic ideas, reason, the "immaterial.")

From these passages we may observe that man's reason, a gift which the animals lack, makes him more an animal than they, more like them than they are like themselves, or would do so were he not saved from this fate by his sensibility. Now a common, less ingenious, and less contradictory view of the matter would be this: that the animals are guided by a relatively vague and primitive sensibility and may or may not have some rudiments of reason; but that man's sensibility is refined by the intervention of reason, so that he can scarcely dispense with reason or with any part of it without a corresponding loss of sensibility. Ransom appears at times to suspect some such truth as this, as when he writes: [16]

Croce, for example, does not seem to suspect that the pre-logical experience of the child differs from the mature and sometimes desperate adventures of the artist . . .

These adventures must seem to us desperate indeed if they consist in blasting from beneath himself the foundations of the very structure in which he stands.

And as a matter of fact, Ransom is not able invariably to get along without some kind of idealism: [17]

The formal tradition, as I have said, lays upon the poet evidently a double requirement. One is metrical or mechanical; but the measured speech is part of the logical identity of the poem; it goes

[16] *The World's Body*, p. 256.   [17] *The World's Body*, pp. 40-41.

into that "character" which it possesses as an ideal creation, out of the order of the actual. The other requirement is the basic one of the make-believe, the drama, the specific anonymity or pseudonymity, which defines the poem as poem . . .

This anonymity is also a kind of idealization, a merging of the individual in the type as represented by the tradition, and the essay on *Lycidas* in the same volume deals primarily with the function of the poet as a kind of ideal and highly generalized spokesman. And in the essay on Edna St. Vincent Millay, he objects to female poets in general because he finds them insufficiently intellectual and too exclusively and sentimentally devoted to objects of sense.

Ransom's hedonistic attitude interests me little in itself, however; little even for the extraordinary social and religious doctrines which he deduces from it, although these last have their own fascination. What interests me is the influence of the hedonism on his theory of poetry. As we shall see presently, Ransom regards, or tries to regard, the work of art as an imitation, purely and simply, of some aspect of objective nature, an imitation made for love of the original object; and he takes elaborate pains to eliminate from the entire process all emotions on the part of the artist except love of the object. Some of the citations bearing in part on this theory will have to be reserved for subsequent sections of this essay, but in *God without Thunder* he writes: [18]

The esthetic attitude is the most objective and the most innocent attitude in which we can look upon the world, and it is possible only when we neither desire the world nor pretend to control it. Our pleasure in this attitude probably lies in a feeling of communion or *rapport* with environment which is fundamental in our human requirements—but which is sternly discouraged in the mind that has the scientific habit.

[18] *God without Thunder,* p. 173.

I should say the esthetic attitude is definable with fair accuracy in the simple and almost sentimental terms: the love of nature.

This statement, if taken in the narrowest possible sense, would appear to limit poetry to the description of landscape; but we discover as we read farther in the three books, that this is intended as a formula for the treatment of almost any subject. But how applicable is it to the subject of *Macbeth* or of *Othello*? Were these plays written because of the love which Shakespeare felt, either for their actions as wholes or for any major part of their actions? Did Shakespeare love the spectacle of ambition culminating in murder, or of jealousy culminating in murder? Did he write of Iago because he loved him so sentimentally that he wished to render him in all his aspects? To ask the questions is to render the theory ridiculous.

Shakespeare wrote the plays in order to evaluate the actions truly; and our admiration is for the truth of the evaluations, not for the beauty of the original objects as we see them imitated. And how, one may wonder, can Shakespeare evaluate these actions truly except from the position of a moralist? To evaluate a particular sin, one must understand the nature of sin; and to fix in language the feeling, detailed and total, appropriate to the action portrayed, one must have a profound understanding not only of language, for language cannot be understood without reference to that which it represents, not only of the characters depicted, but of one's own feelings as well; and such understanding will not be cultivated very far without a real grasp of theoretic morality.

The following passage shows how completely Ransom identifies the poem with its subject and our feeling for the poem with our feeling for its subject. He offers a brief definition of the poem, and then comments on his own definition: [19]

[19] *The New Criticism*, p. 54.

A beautiful poem is an objective discourse which we approve, containing objective detail which we like.

This version mixes objective and subjective terms, but goes much further than simply to say that poetry is a form of discourse which enlists our favorable emotions. It tells where the favorable emotions come: in the pleasure of handling the specific detail while we are attending effectively to the whole. It talks about what we like, and I see no overwhelming necessity to do that, for we shall not have poems nor things in poems, unless we like them; liking is interest, and ultimately I suppose it is part of our unarguable biological constitution.

There is a little more of this commentary, but the remainder does not clarify the issues that interest me. The passage refers more or less implicitly to Ransom's favorite structural theory, the theory of the logical core and the texture of irrelevancy, but that matter will have to wait. We see identified explicitly our liking for the poem and our liking for its subject, an identification deriving from Ransom's doctrine of imitation; but the impossibility of such identification I have already shown.

If we like the poem without liking its subject, however, in what sense do we like it? The word *like* requires more explanation than Ransom is willing to give. To identify liking with interest is preposterous. We may be interested in communism, cancer, the European war, or Ransom's theories of poetry without liking any of them. According to Ransom's theories, the scientist does not like, in this sense, the objective universe, but that he is desperately interested in the objective universe there cannot be the slightest doubt. If we like the poem, we like it because of the truth with which it judges its subject, and the judgment is a moral judgment of the kind which I have already described.

Ransom's devout cultivation of sensibility leads him at times to curiously insensitive remarks. In comparing the subject of a poem by Stevens with that of a poem by Tate, he writes: [20]

The deaths of little boys are more exciting than the sea-sur-faces—

a remark which seems worthy of a perfumed and elderly can-nibal. And in a poem of his own, entitled *Bells for John White-side's Daughter,* a poem which deals with the death of a little girl, the dead child herself is treated whimsically, as if she were merely a charming bit of bric-a-brac, and the life of the poem resides in a memory of the little girl driving geese. The memory, as a matter of fact, is very fine, but if the little corpse is merely an occasion for it, the little corpse were better omitted, for once in the poem it demands more serious treat-ment: the dead child becomes a playful joke, and the geese walk off with the poem.

IV. *Art as Imitation of the Unique Experience and Art as Unique Experience*

Ransom believes that the arts are essentially one, and that principles true of painting, for example, should be equally true of literature. In the last paragraph of *The World's Body,* [21] he writes:

Similar considerations hold, I think, for the critique of fiction, or of the non-literary arts. I remark this for the benefit of philosophers who believe, with propriety, that the arts are fundamentally one.

Such an assumption strikes me as extremely uncritical. If one can show the arts to be fundamentally one by analyzing each of the arts separately and arriving at similar conclusions

[20] *The World's Body,* p. 61.   [21] *The World's Body,* p. 349.

for all, one can make such a statement with some show of reason; but thus far the demonstration has not been made. That all the arts have certain principles in common is perhaps possible; that any two of them will have certain principles in common seems much more likely; but that these principles play the same part in any two or more of the arts appears to me very doubtful. The arts employ different media and enter the consciousness by different routes, and there may well be fundamental differences between them. I should be inclined to inquire, for example, just how Ransom finds a Bach fugue to be an imitation of an unique object in nature.

Ransom definitely regards the work of art as the imitation of an unique object, however, and he employs the word *imitation* in a simple and literal sense, to understand which one need know nothing of the history of criticism; and at the same time he regards the work of art as an unique object in itself; a curious theory, for if the work of art is a true replica, the two are scarcely unique, and if the imitation is not a replica, it is either an imperfect imitation or something other than an imitation. In *God without Thunder* [22] he writes:

If M. Bergson had defended the freedom of inorganic as well as of organic objects, he might readily have become the great champion of the arts, for the freedom of their objects is precisely what they are devoted to. The artistic representation of a particular is itself particular—infinite in its wealth of quality, though doubtless an abridgment of the infinity of the original. Art celebrates the concrete, the richly sensible, and M. Bergson as the exponent of the free will was in a position to expound also the freedom of the artistic object.

Such a position, however, leaves him with some need to justify the existence of art in a world which without its help is already teeming with natural uniqueness; especially as the

[22] *God without Thunder*, p. 222.

work of art appears in this passage to be merely an abridgment of the original object. In *The World's Body* [23] he writes:

And as for the painting: it perhaps does not occur to naïve persons that some painter from his window will command permanently his view of the city roofs, and yet be impelled to paint the imitation of it on a canvas beside the window, and to return again and again to the canvas in preference to the window as the occasion of his aesthetic experience. The studied aesthetician will admit to this fact, but will contend perhaps that the painting is better for the purpose than the view from the window, because the painting has suppressed something, or added something, or distorted something; being quite unable to conceive that its superiority may lie in the simple fact that it is the imitation of something rather than the original. An imitation is better than its original in one thing only: not being actual, it cannot be used, it can only be known. Art exists for knowledge, but nature is an object both to knowledge and to use; the latter disposition of nature includes that knowledge of it which is peculiarly scientific, and sometimes it is so imperious as to pre-empt all possibility of the former.

The imitation is here justified because it is a check to action, because it eliminates the useful, which in Ransom's terminology is coördinate with the scientific and rational; so that here as throughout Ransom, we see the constant straining to define an art which shall subsist as nearly as possible without rational content, which shall realize as nearly as possible the primary principle in the system of Poe. Ransom employs the analogy of painting still further: [24]

We are sensible of the love behind all the labor that the patient artist has put into his work, and we respond with ours.

I use the term love not too fearfully. The motive for engaging upon the other kind of transcript is glory, according to the metaphysical idealists; duty, according to the moralists; power, accord-

[23] *The World's Body*, pp. 196-7.　　[24] *The World's Body*, pp. 208-9.

ing to the practical scientists; and, for the appetites, greed. It is a single series, and as opposite to love at one place as another.

One of the trick questions in aesthetic suggests itself here, with its proper answer in terms of Greek mimesis. Why would not a photograph of the landscape be superior to the painting? The idea is that the photograph would be both fuller and more accurate as a presentation. But it is not fuller, strictly speaking; to be particular at all is to be infinitely full of detail, and one infinite is as full as another. And it does not matter about the meticulous accuracy of the representation; the painter's free version may be for the eye the more probable version and the more convincing, by the same reasoning by which Aristotle prefers poetry as an imitation to history. The great difference between the two versions lies elsewhere. The photograph is a mechanical imitation, perhaps, but not a psychological one. It was obtained by the adjustment of the camera and the pressing of the button, actions so characterless that they indicate no attitude necessarily, no love; but the painting reveals the arduous pains of the artist. . . . The pains measure the love.

We have seen previously that the painting is preferable to the object painted, because it separates knowledge from usefulness; here we see that the painting is superior to the photograph and the object equally because it is produced with labor which is a proof of love. But is this second difference symbolic or real? That is, if we merely met the finished products with no knowledge of the techniques in question, would we feel this difference? Or is there actually a difference in the finished product, the result in the painting of a living mind having made every detail as a commentary on something else? And if there is any truth in this last possibility, what is the nature of the commentary? Is it merely an assertion of the artist's love for the object? We have seen the difficulties into which this notion leads us in connection with Shakespeare and Iago, and we might well meditate upon the difficulties into which we should wander if we tried so to consider the work of Goya, or even much of the world's great portraiture, for example scores of surviving portrait busts of the Romans, in which we see an interest on the part of the artist which is far other and far more interesting than mere liking or love. Here as elsewhere, Ransom is confused by the difficulty that his imitation is not really an imitation but is something else.

In *The New Criticism*,[25] Ransom develops this theory, or something very like it, in a somewhat new direction. He states that our emotion for the artistic object cannot be the same as our emotion for the original object. "The original emotion blinded us to the texture of the object, but now there is leisure for the texture." In other words, our imitation in retrospect is more complete than was the object imitated, at least as we saw the object, and is no longer an abridgment. This curious variant comes of an attempt to reconcile in some manner Ransom's doctrines with Eliot's doctrine of autotelic art, that is with Eliot's theory that artistic emotion is generically different from the emotion of human life. In this connection, I should like to reiterate the distinction which I made in discussing this theory of Eliot: namely that the emotion created by the original experience is immediate, provisional, and confused; in so far as we succeed in clarifying our understanding of the situation and in modifying our feelings accordingly, we approach the judgment possible in the poem; but it is only in the poetic form that something close to a final and defensible judgment is possible, for in poetry we have a finer and more flexible language than we can find elsewhere, and in writing the poem we have an opportunity to fix the judgment in preliminary stages, examine it, and revise it.

I discuss the matter in terms of poetry not out of prejudice against the other arts but because I understand their princi-

25 *The New Criticism*, pp. 158-9.

ples insufficiently well. For reasons already given, I refuse
to discuss questions of painting or music in any serious fashion,
and I refuse to be bound by any apparent analogies between
these arts and poetry. But Ransom is bound by his own analogies, and what he has said of painting we may fairly assume
that he means of poetry. And when we come to poetry, his
doctrine of imitation unmistakably collapses, for poetry is
composed of words, which are primarily abstractions. No combination of abstractions, however fine their subdivision or
ingenious their arrangement, will reproduce an unique experience, and if we endeavor to violate their nature in using
them we shall merely use them badly.

The poem cannot then be an imitation of an unique experience, but it may conceivably be an unique experience in itself,
and in a way which Ransom has not taken into consideration.
If we can imagine two poets of talents equally sound and essentially similar in scope, and imagine them describing the
same tree, or writing of the experience of love, it is very unlikely that we can imagine them writing the same poem. Their
past lives will be different; the relevant circumstances of their
present lives will be different; with the result that the definition of each will not be a definition of the thing in itself, which
is an impossibility, but a definition by each poet of his own
relationship to the thing, and the definitions, though different,
may be equally valid, and without our having recourse to any
relativistic doctrine to justify them; and the feelings motivated
will likewise differ accordingly. The whole procedure, however, is fed on ideas and dies without them.

V. *Art as Cognition*

Ransom's doctrine of cognition, as nearly as I can understand
it, is merely an aspect of his doctrine of imitation. The work

of art is an imitation of an object, undertaken for love of the object and in the effort to understand the object; to understand it, not rationally, but in its uniqueness. The term *cognition* is employed by Ransom also in connection with the rational activities of scientists and philosophers, and when so used is a term of disparagement; as employed in connection with art, its meaning is different and to myself is very obscure.

Ransom says that the work of art is objective: it deals with the object itself, not with the artist's feelings or emotions, except, I suppose, the one emotion of love for the object, yet Ransom repeatedly speaks of the emotions communicated by the poem, and when he endeavors to deal with his theory of cognition he is forced in some manner to account for them. In *The New Criticism*,[26] he reproves I. A. Richards for dealing with poetry as if it consisted of emotion more or less independent of a motivating object:

> He employs a locution which is very modern, and almost fashionable, but nevertheless lazy and thoughtless. He refers to the distinctive emotion of a poem instead of to its distinctive cognitive object.

And a few pages farther he develops this theory at length in terms that seem for a moment closely to resemble my own: [27]

> The specific quality of any emotion is all but indefinable in pure emotive terms, and that seems to be because the distinctness that we think of as attaching to an emotion belongs really to the object toward which we have it. For example, there is hardly an instance of terror-in-general, or of terror-on-principle, but only terror toward a particular object or situation; like a father, or men armed with machine guns, or the day of doom. That is obvious enough. But I have seen too many instances where literary critics, like Mr. Richards above, find the cognitive object of the poem intellectually obscure, yet claim to discover in the poem an emo-

[26] *The New Criticism*, p. 17.   [27] *The New Criticism*, pp. 20-21.

tion which is brilliantly distinct. I should think there is generally and ideally, no emotion at all until an object has furnished the occasion for one, and that the critic is faking his discovery of the emotion when he cannot make out its object; and that if he should try to describe to us the emotion he would find himself describing it as whatever kind of emotion would be appropriate toward a certain object, and therefore presently, before he realized it, beginning to describe the very object which he had meant to avoid. That seems to me the case history of Richards' commentary on Eliot's poem above. Once I had a friendly critical passage with a good student who insisted that there were cores of value in poetry which were emotional, and not accessible to logic, or were "metalogical," as he liked to phrase it. When I pressed him he wrote a paper in which he chose a poem and showed how from time to time in it the reader grasped perfectly an emotion which did not receive in the text any adequate logical communication. But it seemed to me that in every instance the emotion realized by the reader was simply the one that was perfectly appropriate to the situation objectively established by the text; though it may have been a highly particularized situation, not easy to put in a few words. It was true that the emotion remained mysterious and ineffable in its own terms, and the poet never bothered about that, but it was not without statement in terms of the object. From this incident I concluded again that emotions are correlatives of the cognitive objects, and all but unintelligible for us in their supposed independent purity.

This passage, which exactly reverses Eliot's doctrine of the objective correlative, states that the emotion is motivated by some cause (the object) and that the emotion is appropriate. It implies, however, that if the cognition of the object is sound, the emotion is automatically appropriate; and states further that a sharp emotion cannot be communicated without adequate cognition as a motive. This I doubt profoundly. The second essay in my volume, *Primitivism and Decadence,* lists many kinds of inaccurate motivation; the false motivation in

Crane's poem *The Dance,* and the false motivation in many of the poems of H. D. may be taken as examples, if the reader will have the patience to examine what I wrote about them. In these poems an emotion is asserted and in a large degree communicated which is far in excess of any discernible motive.

In actual life, unsound motivation is the commonest thing one meets, but Ransom, I suppose, would say that this results from unsound cognitions, and that it is the business of the poet to make his cognitions, or imitations, genuinely accurate; the impossibility of doing this, however, I have already endeavored to show. What I have already written ought to show further, that it is impossible for the poet to leave the emotions to shift for themselves, for the emotions like the ideas are communicated by the words, and the poet chooses every word. If his choice is based on only one aspect of the language, the emotions are much more likely to go wrong automatically than to go right; and if he does this—that is, bases his choice on purely conceptual content—he is unlikely to please Ransom any more than myself.

Before leaving this topic, I wish to cite further passages which will show more plainly that Ransom holds the doctrine of the automatic accuracy of the emotion. In *The World's Body* he writes:[28]

The primary business of theorists is to direct their analyses of poetry to what is objective in it, or cognitive, and they will always be safe in assuming if they like that behind any external body of knowledge there will have been feeling enough, possibly amounting to passion, to have attended the subject through his whole exercise. Indeed the feeling must have been entirely appropriate to the exercise.

And in *The New Criticism:*[29]

[28] *The World's Body,* p. 289.   [29] *The New Criticism,* p. 50.

But we must remark once more, no feeling is identified by a metaphor until an objective situation has been identified by it. In short, the one automatic and sure method of identifying a feeling is to furnish an objective situation and say: Now imagine your feeling in this situation. Under these circumstances I do not see why the critic needs to do more than talk about the objective situations. The feelings will be their strict correlatives, and the pursuit of the feelings will be gratuitous.

And a few pages farther: [30]

The affections are involved by a poem, but the important thing for theory to see is that they attach spontaneously to the items of context. And since they attach spontaneously, they scarcely need to enter into critical discussion. We need only to say that the poem develops its local particularities while it progresses toward its functional completion.

And not only does Ransom believe that the emotions may be neglected by critic and poet alike, because they attach themselves with spontaneous accuracy, but he believes that it is unhealthy to consider them critically: [31]

Nor, under that procedure, do we feel the ignominy of concerning ourselves about our mental "health," when we are occupied healthily and naturally with our external concerns.

Self-knowledge and self-judgment are morbid as well as unnecessary; if we will merely love the objective universe and endeavor to "know" it objectively and fully, our emotions will take care of themselves automatically.

The emotions, however, are not alone in being able to take care of themselves. In a footnote of considerable length Ransom writes: [32]

The artist resorts to the imitation because it is inviolable, and it is inviolable because it is not real. In strict theory it might be

[30] Ibid., p. 58.   [31] Ibid., p. 26.   [32] The World's Body, p. 198.

said that his purpose is to exhibit the typical along with the characteristic, but in view of his actual occasion it may be said much more simply to be: to exhibit the characteristic. He has no fear that the typical at this late date will be obscured.

Thus we see that the typical, or the rational, will take care of itself, exactly as does the emotion; it is the poet's business to concentrate on the cognition. But what is the cognition, and precisely through what virtue or aspect of language does it materialize? It is neither abstraction nor emotion nor any relationship of these two. If we were to accept seriously the occasional hints in Ransom's criticism that what he wants is a purely descriptive poetry, we might suppose that he desired the poet to use only words denoting classes of concrete objects and to use them with reference primarily to their connotations and more especially with reference to their connotations of remembered sensory impression. If we could write such poetry, it would be an extreme form of imagism; but we could never write it, and there is a preponderance of evidence in Ransom's books to show that he does not really want us to write it. But what does he want? If we are to believe in the existence of his cognition, I fear we shall have to take it on faith. And if the poet is to realize it, or fool himself into thinking that he can realize it, he will have to work out a method of deliberately violating the nature of language; and this is exactly what Ransom recommends.

VI. *Deliberate Obscurity*

Ransom's great embarrassment as a theorist is that he knows that the poet cannot dispense with rational statement; that at times he even seems to admire poetry for having a measure of rational content; yet that he does not know what to do with the rational content, how to account for it or evaluate it. In the preface to *The World's Body* he writes: [33]

I had the difficulty of finding a poetry which would not deny what we in our strange generation actually are: men who have aged in these pure intellectual disciplines, and cannot play innocent without feeling very foolish. The expense of poetry is greater than we will pay if it is something to engage in without our faculties. I could not discover that this mortification was required.

And the same general notion is stated at many other points in his criticism.

In the same volume [34] he discusses two poems, one by Wallace Stevens and the other by Allen Tate, in one of the most revealing passages he has ever written:

A good "pure" poem is Wallace Stevens' *Sea Surface Full of Clouds*—famous, perhaps, but certainly not well known . . . The subject matter is trifling . . . Poetry of this sort, as it was practiced by some French poets of the nineteenth century, and as it is practiced by many British and American poets now, has been called pure poetry, and the name is accurate. It is nothing but poetry; it is poetry for poetry's sake, and you cannot get a moral out of it. But it was to be expected that it would never win the public at large. The impulse which led readers to the old poetry was at least as much moral as it was aesthetic, while the new poetry cannot count on any customers except those specializing in strict aesthetic effects. But the modern poets intend to rate only as poets, and would probably think it meretricious to solicit patronage by making moral overtures.

Now although this is a little aside from my principal interest, it is perhaps fair to say that the subject of Stevens' poem is not quite trifling; the subject is a sequence of half-apprehended glimpses of the supernatural in a seascape and in its observer. And the subject on the whole is fairly well executed,

[33] *The World's Body*, Preface, p. viii.   [34] Ibid., pp. 58-61.

though most of the valuable elements in the poem had been employed by the poet previously in better works; the chief defect in the poem itself is a fairly large amount of playful and essentially weak repetition. If the poem were as nearly pure description as Ransom appears to believe, however, one would still think Ransom committed to admire it for that reason at least, for it would approximate, if anything were capable of approximating, Ransom's formula of disinterested imitation of the objective universe. And I again should be forced, as a plausible moralist, to defend it, if the description were rendered justly and without the importation of foreign emotions, for the reason that the contemplation of the objective universe is a possible human experience and may be justly evaluated.

Ransom's comments are curious. "You cannot get a moral out of it," he writes; a statement which indicates once more that he sees no possibility of there being any morality in poetry except in the form of a moral. And although he dislikes a moral in his poetry, he appears to be displeased with this poem because he finds it so wholly free from one. He confuses the moral with the conceptual, and though he dislikes the conceptual, he wants his poem to have conceptual content. The following passage continues without break from the last:

As an example of "obscure" poetry, though not the most extreme one, I cite Allen Tate's *Death of Little Boys*. Here are some of the verses:

Then you will touch at the bedside, torn in two,
Gold curls now deftly intricate with gray
As the windowpane extends a fear to you
From one peeled aster drenched with the wind all day . . .

Till all the guests, come in to look, turn down
Their palms; and delirium assails the cliff

Of Norway where you ponder, and your little town
Reels like a sailor drunk in his rotten skiff.

There is evidently a wide difference between Stevens and Tate,
as poets. Tate has an important subject, and his poem is a human
document, with a contagious fury about it: Stevens, pursuing
purity, does not care to risk such a subject. But Tate, as if conscious
that he is close to moralizing and sententiousness, builds up deliberately, I imagine, an effect of obscurity; for example, he does
not care to explain the private meaning of his windowpane and
his Norwegian cliff; or else, by some feat, he permits these bright
features to belong to his total image without permitting them to
reveal any precise meaning, either for himself or for his reader.
Stevens, however, is objective from beginning to end; he completes
all his meanings, knowing these will have little or no moral importance.

Before commenting on Ransom's comment, I should like
to say a few things about the two stanzas, which seem to me as
bad as poetry can often be found and thoroughly characteristic
of the bulk, though not of the best, of Tate's work and of all
of the work which I have seen by his and Ransom's younger
disciples in the Southern School. The phrase "torn in two" is
merely a crudely stereotyped assertion of violent emotion.
The word *deftly,* a characteristic word among these writers,
introduces an element of false precision; deftness is irrelevant
to the situation, and the word has the effect of a cheap trick.
The fear in the next two lines is not in the least obscure; it is
the fear of death and bereavement. But Tate, in motivating it
by a peeled aster, whatever that may be, and projecting it
through a windowpane, endeavors apparently to achieve a
concrete image where a concrete image is improper; the whole
effort is made with a very heavy hand. The turning down of
the palms in the next stanza is meaningless and slightly ridiculous; it seems again an effort to achieve the concrete at
any cost. The Norwegian cliff is far less mysterious than Ran-

som assumes: it is an image representing the sense of remote isolation in the face of death and in the experience of grief. The reeling, the drunken sailor, and the rotten skiff, are all trite and over-violent; and they are not realized in themselves, any more than is the cliff. These images represent one of the commonest weaknesses of Tate, Ransom, and their school: a fear of the abstract statement in itself, a fear so acute that they will invariably substitute for it a trite, vague, or even badly mixed figure if they can think of one. Thus in Tate's *Ode to the Confederate Dead*, there occur the fine lines:

> And in between the ends of distraction
> Waits mute speculation, the patient curse.

But instead of putting a period at the end, Tate does not punctuate and adds two more lines:

> That stones the eyes, or like the jaguar leaps
> For his own image in a jungle pool, his victim.

Now if anything so immaterial as speculation or a curse is to be represented by a concrete image, there will have to be an exact allegorical propriety in the representation, and the concrete image will have to be good in itself. But the image of a stoner of *eyes* is fantastic in itself, and could be justified only by some close relationship to the idea; the necessity of speculation or a curse *stoning* anything is not clear; and violent action on the part of that which is *patient* is still more perplexing. Nor does one see why a stoner of eyes should leap, like a jaguar, into a pool, nor why the owner of the eyes should not thereby be benefitted. Further, jaguars do not hunt jaguars; a jaguar would not be misled by a reflection in a pool; and cats do not like water. And all of this nonsense appears to have arisen from a doctrinaire conviction that a mere abstract statement cannot be poetry: the statement must trail its clouds of glory.

One could illustrate the blunders resulting from this idea and others similar at great length. The lines quoted by Ransom are not obscure, although the poet seems to have tried to make them so; they are trite, pretentious, and clumsy. It is only fair to add that Tate occasionally forgets himself and writes a good poem. *Shadow and Shade* and *The Cross* are two of the great lyrics of our time, though something short of perfection, and there are other poems containing beautiful passages.

But let us turn to Ransom's remarks. Tate "has an important subject, and his poem is a human document," statements which appear to me to derive from some notion of moral importance. His poem has a "contagious fury," but we have been told elsewhere to neglect the emotion which the poem communicates. The windowpane has a meaning, but Tate is praised for keeping it private; from which we can deduce only that the poem is more satisfactory to the reader than to Tate, and this by virtue of a deliberate act of trickery on Tate's part; but a few lines further we are reassured by learning that it may possibly have no meaning for Tate either. Stevens is "objective from beginning to end," thereby fulfilling one of the requirements upon which Ransom commonly insists very strongly, yet on this occasion Stevens is blamed for it. Tate's poem is superior because of its greater moral content, yet this content must be strangled, and a virtue made, somehow, of the unavoidable presence of the corpus delicti.

There follows a paragraph which merely repeats the main ideas which we have seen, and then come two short paragraphs of summary:

To be more technical: it is as if the pure poet presented a subject and declined to make any predication about it or even to start predication; and as if the obscure poet presented a subject in order to play with a great deal of important predication without ever completing any.

Personally, I prefer the rich obscure poetry to the thin pure poetry. The deaths of little boys are more exciting than sea-surfaces.

I do not understand how a subject can be presented in language without predication, although I am familiar with many ways of confusing the predication, It is impossible to present a subject in language without saying something about it, either well or badly. But to make a clear rational statement about a serious subject would be to "moralize"; and Ransom, as I have already pointed out, has an irrational and habitual fear of that word and of all its relatives. Ransom prefers the subject which is humanly more important, that is morally more important; but he cannot justify his preference on moral grounds and finds himself driven to justify it on hedonistic: he finds the death of a little boy more exciting than sea-surfaces. It is my own feeling that the death of a little boy in actual fact is likely to be a very sad affair and to merit honest and serious treatment. I do not believe for a moment that Ransom is personally as unpleasant as he appears in this unfortunate statement—in fact, I have excellent reasons to believe the contrary—but as a scholar and a philosopher, he should have been wiser and more wary than to let himself be forced by his own reasoning into a position where such a statement was inevitable. If we are to take Ransom at face value, he loves the deaths of little boys more than he loves sea-surfaces, but he believes that the poet should only play with predication about them. This is a view from which all principles of rightness of evaluation have been eliminated; it implies that the poet is in search of meaningless excitement.

Yet Ransom complains[35] of Miss Millay's "overwriting," a term which implies a standard of rightness of some kind or other, and he says on the subject:

[35] *The World's Body*, p. 82.

To wish to make a thing look pretty or look smart is to think poorly of it in itself, and to want it more conventional, and to try to improve it is to weaken and perhaps destroy it.

But he has shown that Tate thinks poorly of his subject and has tried to conceal and confuse it. Tate's writing is as bad as Miss Millay's, and for much the same reason.

VII. *The Structure of Poetry:*
The Logical Core and the Texture of Irrelevance

We have seen Ransom defending a procedure of deliberate obscurantism in general terms; it remains to examine his theories of the mechanics of poetic structure by which he endeavors to explain this obscurantism. In *The World's Body* he writes: [36]

A poet is said to be distinguishable in terms of his style. It is a comprehensive word, and probably means: the general character of his irrelevances, or tissues. All his technical devices contribute to it, elaborating or individualizing the universal, the core-object; likewise all his material detail. For each poem even, ideally, there is distinguishable a logical object or universal, but at the same time a tissue of irrelevance from which it does not really emerge.

We may observe here again the characteristic elements of Ransom's critical theory: the concept, inescapable and necessary, but regrettable, and having no definable function, hopelessly entangled in detail which is admirable largely in proportion to its being irrelevant to the concept. As usual, Ransom fails through failing to note the double function of language, the simultaneous communication of connotation and denotation. The rational content of a poem is not a *core* to which irrelevancies are attached in a kind of nimbus; it is something

[36] *The World's Body*, p. 348.

which exists from moment to moment, in every word of the poem, just as does the feeling; and the value of the poem resides precisely in the relationship between these two elements, and not in qualities supposedly attaching to one of the partners in the relationship.

Ransom restates this theory many times, and in *The New Criticism* especially, with an emphasis which makes it impossible that one should overlook its implications. The following passage will serve as an example: [37]

What is the value of a structure which (a) is not so tight and precise on its logical side as a scientific or technical prose structure generally is; and (b) imports and carries along a great deal of irrelevant or foreign matter which is clearly not structural but even obstructive? This a- and b-formulation is what we inevitably come to if we take the analysis our best critics offer. We sum it up by saying that the poem is a loose logical structure with an irrelevant local texture.

And earlier in the same book [38] he makes a statement which may be fairly regarded as completing this:

And an almost quantitative rule might be formulated, as one that is suggestive if not binding: the more difficult the final structure, the less rich should be the distraction of the texture; and the richer the texture as we proceed toward the structure, the more generalized and simple may be the structure in the end.

From these passages it is evident that Ransom wants as little rational content as possible, and that he sees texture, or what I should call feeling or emotion, as existing independently of structure and yet in some obscure manner not wholly escaping from its presence. If he were able to see the manner in which denotation and connotation exist simultaneously throughout the poem, and the manner in which connotation is momently

37 *The New Criticism*, p. 280.   38 Ibid., p. 274.

dependent upon denotation for its very existence, he would not regard the poem as a constant effort on the part of connotation to escape from denotation in ways wholly inexplicable in terms of the nature of language.

The anti-intellectual tendency of this doctrine is clear enough in the following passage from *The World's Body*: [39]

The poetic impulse is not free [he means free from entanglement with ideas] yet it holds out stubbornly against science for the enjoyment of its images. It means to reconstitute the world of perceptions. Finally there is suggested some such formula as the following:

Science gratifies a rational or practical impulse and exhibits the minimum of perception. Art gratifies a perceptual impulse and exhibits the minimum of reason.

This is a close approximation of the doctrine held by Poe and Mallarmé to the effect that since plain prose deals with truth, or reason, and poetry is different from plain prose, poetry should, if possible, contain no truth or reason. The difference between plain prose and poetry is real, as I have endeavored to show, and it is closer at hand than these ingenious theorists have imagined: poetry is merely a more complete statement of experience than prose, and is not a form of nominalistic delirium.

The italics in the above passage are Ransom's. The seriousness with which he means them may be seen in a recent commentary on *Finnegans Wake*. He writes: [40]

I do not know to what lengths the race will react, keeping company with its artists; nor whether for a total action such as is implied in our "age of science" there must be an equal and opposite reaction. But I believe that *Finnegans Wake* is the most comprehensive individual reaction we have yet seen to all that we have accomplished with our perverted ideal of perfect action. . . .

[39] *The World's Body*, p. 130.   [40] The Kenyon Review, I-4, pp. 425-8.

Joyce exploits at least two prime devices for obfuscating discourse. One is stream-of-consciousness, which is prepared to excrete irrelevances in any situation. The other is the verbal device of going from the relevant meaning of the word to the irrelevant meaning, or from the word to the like-sounding words, and then to the words like the like-words. . . . His book is the most allusive in literature, except for the dictionaries and encyclopedias, and the allusions are rarely used as structural elements, and never kept to their logical and historical identities. . . . I should judge that Joyce's book is not a unit of design, because the sections do not obey it, but have their own disorderly energies; nor are the sections because they have pages; nor the pages because of the sentences; and as for the sentences, the little fragments of discourse dissipate themselves as readily as the great ones, and apparently for the same reason, in order to obtain a "maximum connotation." The sentences have the words. . . . To the literary critic Joyce suggests some extreme exponent of surrealist or "abstractionist" painting. The painting seems to intend to render genuine fragments of finished objects, but assembles them in confusion as if to say that these pieces of life will never add up to a whole. . . . Long ago Mr. Richards laid down a canon of relevance: Anything is relevant to the total meaning which belongs to the psychological situation. The canon might as well read: Anything is relevant . . . Yet Joyce's book is on the side of the angels, and I do not like to abuse it. For the poets it is sure to become an inexhaustible source of courage. It shows at most places how to escape from conceptual prose, and into the contingent world; a difficulty that most poets seem unable to surmount.

Ransom apparently has faint doubts about the propriety of the method which he is describing, but they are faint indeed; he would prefer the risk of having no conceptual content to the risk of having too much: and quite rightly from his own point of view. If the method here described, however, represents the infinity toward which true poetry should draw as near as possible without ever quite reaching it, and if his concept of poetry rests, as Ransom frequently assures us, upon a study of traditional English poetry and a deep sympathy for it, one cannot but feel that something has gone wrong in the study. I am reminded of Robert Bridges, who, after devoting years to the study of Milton's meter, formulated what he supposed to be the principles of that meter and then wrote *The Testament of Beauty* to demonstrate the proper application of the principles.[41] And one is inclined to wonder at this point what has become of the unique object, of love for the unique object, and imitation of the unique object. The only object left to us now is the universe, and the universe is so chaotic that it can scarcely be called unique with any real sense of security; and the work of art, which in spite of Ransom's having expressed dislike for the theory is a perfect illustration of the doctrine of expressive form, is merely a shapeless conglomeration of supposedly unique fragments. This, however, is what one would expect of a work of art of which the essential characteristic is described as a tissue of irrelevancies, and of which the function is pure imitation in a nominalistic universe.

So far as traditional poetry is concerned, Ransom discloses two major concepts of the nature of irrelevancy. One of these is very simple, and I think may be simply refuted. He sees the texture of irrelevancies as that which is left over when one has made a formal outline of the theme of the poem. That is, if one should take a narrative poem with a descriptive background, such as *Peter Grimes*, by George Crabbe, a summary of the plot would exclude most of the descriptive detail, along with other material; and it would no doubt be possible to rewrite the poem from the summary, even with the use of the same general setting, in such a way as to fill in with other

---

[41] This curious subject is discussed in the last essay in my volume, *Primitivism and Decadence.*

details. But the details are none the less relevant: they show where and how the action takes place and each contributes in its own particular way to the whole narrative. Another set of details might do as well, but then they would be relevant. On the other hand, it is not quite foolish to assume that there is a basis of selection among all the possible details of the original situation, and that the poem is good at least in part in proportion as the poet approximates the perfect selection.

The other form of irrelevance enters the poem by way of metaphor and simile. This constitutes a considerable subject in itself, and I therefore reserve it for separate discussion.

VIII. *Metaphor and Simile:*
The Importation of Irrelevance

Ransom regards metaphor and simile as a direct means of introducing irrelevance into the poem: that is, if the poet compares Time to the driver of a winged chariot, then a winged chariot, which is essentially irrelevant to the subject under discussion but pleasant to contemplate for itself, is introduced to dissipate the interest. He speaks of metaphor as "a device for bringing in new and, I think, surely irrelevant content."[42] He says further,[43] employing Richards' term, *vehicle,* to indicate that to which the original subject is compared:

I am not prepared to lay down principles for effectiveness in metaphor. I should feel disposed at the moment to argue for a logical propriety, a specific "point of the analogy," as the occasion for any given metaphor; and then for brilliance and importance in the body of the vehicle in its own right. But it seems scarcely open to question that the vehicle must realize itself independently and go beyond its occasion. (And I think nowhere does Richards

[42] *The New Criticism,* p. 67.   [43] Ibid., p. 85.

say the contrary.) In doing this the vehicle becomes irrelevant to the structure of the argument, and asserts the poetic undertaking to incorporate local texture.

The logical propriety which Ransom demands, however, is little more than a conventional occasion; as we have seen in the preceding section of this essay, he desires as little logical propriety as possible and as much irrelevance as possible. Now metaphor can unquestionably be used in some such fashion as that here indicated, and the technique, if the poet is bent on it, can be carried very far. One of the supreme examples of the technique in the older English poetry is *The Weeper,* by Crashaw.

Crashaw uses the tears of the Magdalen as the occasion of metaphorical excursions in all directions; the poem is constrained only by the necessity of praising the Magdalen's piety, but the constraint is slight enough, I should think, to satisfy even Ransom. The first five stanzas illustrate the method to perfection. The first stanza compares the weeper's eyes to various kinds of springs; the second stanza translates the springs to heaven, the tears being compared to falling stars, the stars to seeds which will raise a harvest of piety on earth. But the third stanza states that this comparison to seeds was an error, that the tears are too precious for us on earth and merely seem to fall but do not fall in reality; and the fourth stanza continues this argument by saying that the eyes weep upward, and the tears, being stars, form the cream of the milky way. This is a sufficiently bold comparison, but one can still trace by somewhat whimsical and devious routes the "logical propriety" of this figure from the initial notion of the weeper's piety. The fifth stanza, however, though its starting point is the idea of the cream, and though it contains the faint flavor of the original piety, is one of the most remarkable triumphs of irrelevance with which I am acquainted:

Every morn from hence
A brisk cherub something sippes
Whose sacred influence
Adds sweetnes to his sweetest Lippes.
Then to his musick. And his song
Tasts of this Breakfast all day long.

The cherub, intrinsically, is charming; he is nearly as diverting as the elves of Herrick's *Nightpiece*—

And the elves also
Whose little eyes glow—

elves which, however, are in comparison almost scandalously relevant to the subject of Herrick's poem. But if we can reach the cherub by this route, we can surely reach any point by others similar; and Crashaw before he is done reaches a number quite as remote.

Of Crashaw's poem as a whole, one can scarcely avoid the conclusion that it is foolish and displays in an extreme form an error of method. Much of the detail is bad, and some of it is good, though perhaps none is as fine as the cherub; but even if the detail were all perfect, the poem could be nothing but a chaos of irrelevancies not much better organized than a section of *Finnegans Wake*. The theory of the morality of poetry does not break down in the face of such a poem, for if any detail is successful it will communicate the feeling proper to its individual subject. The trouble is that one does not have a poem: one has a conventional occasion for irresponsible excursions, the result being an agglomeration of minor poems very loosely related to each other. This is what is called baroque, or decorative, poetry; and although a man of genius may sometimes engage in it with brilliant if fragmentary results, it is fundamentally frivolous. It realizes Ransom's formula to perfection.

But let us examine another figure, this from a speech of Wolsey in Act III, Scene 2, of Henry VIII:

> I have touched the highest point of all my greatness;
> And from that full meridian of my glory,
> I haste now to my setting: I shall fall
> Like a bright exhalation in the evening,
> And no man see me more.

The question here, as I see it, is this: to what extent do we have the fall of a star which is irrelevant to the fall of Wolsey? Wolsey's fall is human and therefore spiritual; but it is not visible as a literal fall. The fall of the star is visible. The visibility of the fall derives from the star; the grandeur from Wolsey. A mere falling star could not be described in such a way as to move us as this passage moves us, for we have here the tragedy of a man, the end of a great career; yet the star gives a great sweep of visibility to the image, at the same time that it is kept closely related not merely to the human, but to human grief and helplessness, by being named, in the language of the time, not a star, but an exhalation. That there is an element of Ransom's irrelevance in such a figure is possible, and that the star should be, as it is, as well realized in itself as possible is certain, for the star will accomplish nothing toward reinforcing the tragedy of Wolsey unless it lives in its own right; but the star is introduced for its relevance, and the strength of the figure lies in the similarity between the matters compared. The best poets do not seek such occasions as ends in themselves; they use them when they need them and only when they need them, and they keep them pared as close to the point of relevance as the occasion permits. The occasional margin of decoration that may result from such practice may well be afforded by a strong poem; but to seek to transform the whole poem into decoration is mere aimless debauchery.

Marvell's chariot occupies a position somewhat between

these two extremes, I imagine, but closer to Shakespeare's star than to Crashaw's cherub:

> But at my back I always hear
> Time's winged chariot hurrying near.

The logical propriety is real, and not merely conventional: the image suggests pursuit by an immediate, persistent, and supernatural enemy; the physical embodiment of the enemy is perhaps arbitrary, the chariot being chosen as much for its picturesque qualities as a chariot as for anything else. It seems to me very doubtful, however, that the chariot has any great vigor in itself and distinct from the idea of Time: if we change the phrase to "A winged chariot," we shall find that the irrelevancies are vaguely realized indeed; and if we examine the third and final section of the poem, we shall find that the images are much vaguer, both as irrelevancies and as functioning parts of the poem—this in spite of the fact that the blurred writing of this section appears to receive the greatest share of Ransom's approval or at least the smallest share of his explicit disapproval. The poem has been overestimated, I believe, largely as a result of Eliot's admiration; Herrick's *Gather ye rosebuds*, on the same subject and with no irrelevancies worth naming, is clearly superior.

Before leaving the subject of Time, however, I should like to cite four lines which are among the greatest in English poetry. They will be found in number CIV of Shakespeare's sonnets:

> Ah! yet doth beauty, like a dial hand,
> Steal from his figure, and no pace perceived:
> So your sweet hue, which methinks still doth stand,
> Hath motion, and mine eye may be deceived.

Here the subject is the change by which we perceive and measure Time, but especially as that change occurs in a human face: the change on the dial is employed to make us realize more strongly that change is occurring momently in the face as well; and the mind is fixed on the change at the moment when it is occurring and when it therefore cannot be perceived. There is a minimum of irrelevance here; it would be hard to say that there is any. The comparison is used to make the fearful judgment absolutely certain and inescapable. It seems to me fairly sure that poetry of this kind is greater than poetry resembling *The Weeper* or *Finnegans Wake;* in addition that poetry in general is great precisely as it approaches this kind of concentration, and not, as Ransom endeavors to convince us, as it departs towards general dispersion.

IX. *Meter and the Theory of Irrelevance*

I should begin this section by remarking that Ransom possesses a talent sufficiently rare among living critics and poets: he is able, as far as the evidence appears, to mark the scansion of a line of poetry correctly.

But the theory of meter which he erects upon this ability is less admirable than the ability itself. The theory contains two main propositions: the first, that meter is not a means of expressing any part of the meaning or feeling of the poem, but that it offers an independent phonetic pleasure of its own; the second, that such independent activity must interfere with the statement of the meaning as the meaning must interfere with the meter, with the result that irrelevancies are forced upon both in the course of this conflict.

I shall have to quote Ransom's own statements with regard to these doctrines, before discussing the doctrines. He writes: [44]

And finally we must take account of a belief that is all but universal among unphilosophical critics, and flourishes at its rankest

[44] *The New Criticism*, p. 326.

with the least philosophical. It is: that the phonetic effect in a poem not only is (a) metrical and (b) euphonious, but preferably, and very often is (c) "expressive;" that is, offers a sort of sound which "resembles" or partly "is" or at least "suggests" the object that it means. It is necessary to say rather flatly that the belief is almost completely fallacious; both theoretically, or on the whole, and specifically, or in detail for most of the cases that are cited to prove it.

And in regard to the other part of the theory, he writes: [45]

At once a question or two should present themselves very vexingly to the nebulous aesthetician: What sort of liberties does the poet take with a discourse when he sets it to meter? And what sort of discourse is prepared to permit those liberties?

An argument which admits of alteration in order that it may receive a meter must be partly indeterminate. The argument cannot be maintained exactly as determined by its own laws, for it is going to be undetermined by the meter.

Conversely, a metrical form must be partly indeterminate if it proposes to embody an argument.

There is no relationship, then, between meter and meaning; the meter, like the meaning, goes its own way, gathering irrelevancies to itself; but the two coöperate to this extent, that in interfering with each other they increase the irrelevancies of the total poem. Ransom at no point explains why we take pleasure in the irrelevancies of meter; he merely states it as axiomatic that we do so. He nowhere suggests the romantic theory that meter is a form of music, arousing the feelings by pure sound: indeed, his theory precludes the possibility of such an idea, for if meter can do this it is expressive of something. Ransom apparently assumes that we take pleasure in metrical irregularities for their own sake, as we might take pleasure (if we were so constituted) in the bumps and holes

[45] Ibid., p. 298.

in a concrete sidewalk. Since the meter has no relationship to any other aspect of the poem, it is easy to see that the writing of regular meter will be merely a mechanical task and beneath the dignity of a true poet, who will take pains to introduce roughness for the mere sake of roughness: [46]

It is not merely easy for a technician to write in smooth meters: it is perhaps easier than to write in rough ones, after he has once started; but when he has written smoothly, and contemplates his work, he is capable, actually, if he is a modern poet, of going over it laboriously and roughening it.

And a few years later: [47]

It is not telling the whole truth to say that Shakespeare and other accomplished poets resort to their variations, which are metrical imperfections, because a determinate meaning has forced them into it. The poet likes the variations regardless of the meanings, finding them essential in the capacity of a sound texture to go with the sound structure. It is in no very late stage of a poet's advancement that his taste rejects a sustained phonetic regularity as something restricted and barren, perhaps ontologically defective. Accordingly he is capable of writing smooth meters and then roughening them on purpose. And it must be added, while we are about it, that he is capable of writing a clean logical argument, and then of roughening that too, by introducing logical violence into it, and perhaps willful obscurity.

Strictly speaking, however, it is impossible to write with perfect metrical regularity, for no two syllables, as far as I can determine, are of exactly the same length or degree of accent, and length and accent do not very often wholly coincide; so that one might write scores of lines which technically would not vary from the iambic norm, no two of which would be alike. The norm is wholly ideal, and one recognizes every line as a particular variant from the norm; it is the idea of the

[46] *The World's Body*, p. 12.   [47] *The New Criticism*, p. 324.

norm that gives the variant precision, but the poet with his wits about him knows that he cannot cleave to the norm and certainly does not regard the variant as an imperfection, even as a desirable imperfection. The constant variation from an ideal norm provides a situation from which the skillful writer can create rhythm, and the importance of rhythm I shall discuss a little later. For the present I should like to call attention to the following line:

> Where thy pale form was laid with many tears.

The line is perfectly iambic:[48] yet the unaccented syllable of the second foot is more heavily accented than the accented syllable of the first; the first syllable of *many*, which is accented in its foot, is one of the four most lightly accented syllables in the line, and two others of the four, *was* and *with* (both of which are unaccented in their respective feet) are longer than the accented syllable of *many* and are nearly as long as any other syllables in the line. There is great rhythmic strength even in this isolated line.

It is possible, of course, to write meter that sounds monotonous, but the defect is a defect of rhythm and not of roughness: the rough meters of Ransom and of Tate are frequently very monotonous indeed; and a poem which is rhythmically monotonous will be faulty beyond the limits of the meter, for reasons which will presently appear. To assume that the irregularities in Shakespeare's sonnets are of the same kind as the irregularities in the poems of Ransom and of Tate, and that they differ only in degree and because Ransom and Tate find it too easy to write like Shakespeare—and this is precisely Ransom's claim—is a very rash assumption. There is something wrong somewhere.

---

[48] It is possible to read the first foot as reversed, but, taken in its context, it seems to me iambic.

There are various inconsistencies in Ransom's theory. Ransom objects to relatively regular meter because it is mechanically easy; yet he recommends a mechanical roughening, a roughening which is purely an end in itself. He believes that metrical difficulties force irrelevancies into the logical argument, yet we have seen him admit that Joyce, writing without the aid or obstacle of meter, has achieved greater irrelevancy than any poet he can name. And we are bound to observe in this theory an additional inconsistency with his doctrine of imitation, for a poem which contains a meter which is independent, an end in itself, cannot in any comprehensible sense be called a true imitation of some "object" devoid of meter.

To clear up this whole matter, I think we shall have to start with the assumption that meter, or rather the total phonetic quality of metrical language, is in some way or degree expressive, in spite of the fact that a great deal of illiterate foolishness has been written to defend or illustrate this idea, as Ransom at various times has abundantly demonstrated.

In the first place, music is expressive of emotion. I do not understand the relationship between sound and emotion, but it is unquestionably very real: the devotional feeling of Byrd or of Bach, the wit and gaiety of much of Mozart and Haydn, the disillusioned romantic nostalgia of Franck, these are perfectly real, and it is not profitable to argue the point. The correlation between sound and feeling may have its origin in some historical relationship between music and language, or it may, like the capacity to form ideas, have its origin simply in human nature as that is given us.

Metrical language, as pure sound, is no substitute for music; a poem read aloud in a foreign language will never equal a Mozart concerto. But metrical language has one of the properties of music; namely, rhythm. And it has in the phonetic forms of the original and unmetered language certain minor but usable qualities which music lacks. And metrical language, if we understand the language, is not pure sound; the sound is merely one quality of the total meaning, but it contributes, or can be made to contribute, to the meaning.

If we consider the matter merely in its broad and obvious aspects, this will become reasonably clear. Had Milton chosen the meter of *The Ancient Mariner* as the medium for *Paradise Lost,* he would obviously have written a bad poem. The meter of *Paradise Lost* contributes largely to what I have defined in *Primitivism and Decadence* as the convention of the poem; that is, to the initial and general state of feeling within which the poem shall occur. And it is not merely the blank verse which does this; it is the Miltonic blank verse. The blank verse of the early Fletcher, for example, is almost song-like in comparison, and could never have sustained the gravity of the Miltonic theme. It is a common-place to assert that Miltonic blank verse is one of the greatest metrical inventions in the history of poetry; and no one except Ransom, I imagine, or some one of his disciples, would assert that Milton invented Miltonic blank verse for the sake of Miltonic blank verse. He invented it for the sake of *Paradise Lost;* the poem could not have been written without it, and we may fairly assume that it functions as an instrument for the expression of something essential to the poem. Different metrical forms establish different kinds of feeling; and certain metrical forms, as I have shown in detail in my essay on meter in *Primitivism and Decadence,* are such that they can be used to suggest within a single poem the effects of a variety of other forms, and thus achieve great complexity of feeling.

If the total rhythmic structure can affect the total feeling of the poem, it is only reasonable to suppose that there is a similar relationship within the details. When the contribution of meter to the detail is primarily musical, in the imperfect sense in which this term can be applied to poetry, it is necessarily elusive, and elaborate attempts to describe it will always be clumsy. Within the detail, however, the contribution of the meter is not always purely musical, but at times is in some measure imitative or suggestive. When Herrick writes of

> . . . the elves also
> Whose little eyes glow

the quick movement of the second line is actually amusing: perhaps in part because of some intrinsic quality of sound, however slight it may be in language; perhaps in part because there is a suggestion of the quick movement of the little creatures who are being described.

I should like to run the risk of quoting a passage from my own poetry. I have the advantage of knowing my intention, and with all due respect to the reader, even if the reader should be Mr. Ransom, I am reasonably sure of my effect. The passage is from a poem called *The Fall of Leaves*:

> So was the instant blurred;
> But as we waited there,
> The slow cry of a bird
> Built up a scheme of air.

The meter is iambic trimeter, and the first, second, and fourth lines are similar in general structure, the first foot of each being reversed, but not heavily, the second and third feet being normal. The third line departs strongly from this norm, however, and for a purpose. The accented syllables of this line are all heavy and long, the unaccented light and short, so that the feet are clearly marked. The first foot, however, differs from the first foot of each of the other lines in being iambic, and the second foot differs in being reversed, so that two long and heavy syllables instead of two short and light are brought into juxtaposition, and in such a way as to slow the line so strongly that the inexpert metrist would probably scan *cry* as a monosyllabic foot, and the words following as a trisyllabic foot. Now the words *slow cry* in this context do not imitate any bird-call known to me, but they suggest the slowness of the cry and the emergence of a definite sound from a surrounding context. The sound apart from the meaning would not have this effect; nor would the sound and meaning of these words alone and apart from the total passage or poem; but I am fairly certain that here they have it.

Effects such as those I have just described have little or nothing, I believe, to do with the suggestion of emotional or dramatic speech; yet in dramatic or narrative poetry, this kind of suggestion is sometimes important:

> *O lente, lente curite noctis equi*:
> The starres moove stil, time runs, the clocke will strike,
> The divel wil come, and Faustus must be damned.
> O Ile leap up to my God: who pulls me downe?
> See see where Christs blood streames in the firmament.
> One drop would save my soule, half a drop, ah my Christ.

The slow smooth movement of the Latin line, especially as it appears in the context of the English language and a different meter, accentuates the nervous rapidity, suggesting terror, of the next two lines. The extra syllable in the fourth foot of the fifth line prepares the way for the violent aberration of the sixth: in the sixth line there are six feet instead of five, the fourth of these being inverted, and the fifth, although normally accented, having a rhetorical cesura between the unaccented syllable and the accented, so that the latter part of the line is divided into two rhetorical units of a foot and a half apiece. The rhythm of this line is so curious that it quite eludes description; but that it contributes to the expression of agony and terror I should assert without hesitation. In fact, the main power of this entire passage is derived from its sound.

These lines and others in the same speech are extremely violent and obvious as compared to the expressive variations possible within lyric poetry; I have chosen them because they are too obvious to be overlooked. Within the shorter and subtler form of the rhymed lyric, aberrations so extreme would destroy the total form if they occurred; and further, within a short and strongly defined form, finer effects may be obtained by subtler variations. The whole topic, along with others here mentioned, as well as the general laws of metrical effectiveness, I have discussed at length in the last essay of *Primitivism and Decadence*. It is perhaps worth adding, however, that the abuse of the effect of dramatic speech is one of the commonest defects of recent poetry: it is very easy, apparently, to write in meters which simulate the looseness of conversation in the belief that they simulate the effect of dramatic speech; in fact, it is hard sometimes to determine whether the poet is working on this theory or on the theory of arbitrary roughening, for the effect is about the same in either case. Much of Frost and of Yeats displays this looseness, and much also of the work of the Southern School.

The reader familiar with my writing may wonder whether I am not here defending the doctrine which I have called the doctrine of expressive or imitative form, and which I have elsewhere attacked. I can state categorically that I am not. The doctrine of expressive form states that the poet is "expressing" his subject matter, and that the form of expression is determined by the subject matter. My belief, on the contrary, is this: that the poet is expressing his own understanding of his subject matter and the feelings properly motivated by that understanding; that the value of the poem depends upon the quality of the understanding and the justness of the motivation; that the phonetic form of the poem is an important part of the instrument of expression; that any surrender of the poet to his subject, any attempt to imitate the subject with the form, as Joyce attempts to imitate chaos in *Finnegans Wake*, will result in a more or less serious impairment of the poet's own understanding and control; and that writing in all its aspects is governed by principles, which I have endeavored to elucidate in *Primitivism and Decadence,* and which cannot be seriously violated without a total loss of ability to express anything whatever. Herrick succeeds, perhaps, in suggesting the motion of his elves in a single line, not because he has been trying to imitate their movements or Julia's throughout a poem, but because he has established a metrical form with its own musical values, both general and detailed, and is able for an instant to make a slight movement which suggests the movement of a physical being: the movement would not be perceptible except in the frame, and it is so slight as not to disturb the frame.

As to the notion that meter interferes with meaning, and meaning with meter, whether to the advantage or to the disadvantage of the poem, I should like again to object. If the phonetic value of metrical language is expressive of emotion, or better is capable of qualifying the expression of emotion, even though most of the time very slightly, then the value of any word in metrical language will differ from its value in unmetered language; and the value of the same word will never be quite the same in any two metrical passages, for the precise nature of its sound and its relationship to the context of sound will vary with each passage. To this extent, the poet may be said to create his language as he proceeds, though he is far from being a wholly free agent in creating. He is not endeavoring to invent a logical argument, then meter it, then confuse argument and meter in the interests of excitement. He is seeking to state a true moral judgment; he is endeavoring to bring each word as close to a true judgment as possible; and he has it in his power to modify the values of words within certain limits.

But the medium is incalculably difficult, and for that reason there are very few first rate lyrical poems. The language is crowded with poems which in whole or in part give evidence

that the poet proceeded hastily or in ignorance. Ransom examines some of these passages in *The New Criticism* and adduces them as evidence in support of his theory of meter; I
should cite them as evidence that good poetry is hard to
achieve. If one is indifferent to the distinctions between good
and bad, one can approach the whole subject of poetry with a
kind of scientific impartiality and deduce laws which will have
nothing to do with excellence. Ransom is scientific, in this
connection, without knowing it, and though I am a moralist,
I find myself forced to protest.

It is for this reason that I have spoken of meter as having
moral significance. Meter has certain phonetic values of its
own, and it clarifies, identifies, and even modifies the phonetic
values of unmetered language. And the total phonetic value
of metrical language has the power to qualify the expression
of feeling through language. Since the expression of feeling is
a part of the moral judgment as I have defined it, the meter has
moral significance, for it renders possible a refinement in the
adjustment of feeling to motive which would not otherwise be
possible. This being true, the poet is not likely to find it em-
barrassingly easy to write in the "smooth" meters of Shakespeare and Jonson: those meters are difficult in proportion to
their smoothness, for they achieve a maximum of effect with a
minimum of variation. Every movement in such meter is perceptible, and, in the hands of the good poet, makes its contribution to the total poem. In the lurching meter employed for
the most part by Tate, Ransom, and their group, the effectiveness of meter is at a minimum; the meter staggers for the sake
of staggering. It is quite as difficult to be Shakespeare today as
it was in the year 1600.

In *Primitivism and Decadence,* where the whole problem of
meter is discussed more fully than I can hope to discuss it here,
I wrote: [49]

49 *Primitivism and Decadence,* p. 120.

. . . in traditional verse, each variation, no matter how slight, is exactly perceptible, and as a result can be given exact meaning as an act of moral perception . . .

and Ransom, in quoting this passage,[50] adds the parenthetical comment, "though he means merely exact phonetic value." The fact of the matter is, that I meant what I said.

X. *The Triviality of Poetry*

Scattered through Ransom's prose one finds a few brief passages which indicate that his faith in the value of poetry is not all that he would like it to be. In *The World's Body* he writes:[51]

Our arts, certainly our poems, should fill us with pride because they furnish our perfect experiences. But they fill us also with mortification because they are not actual experiences. If we regard them in a certain mood, say when the heat of action is upon us, they look like the exercises of children, showing what might have been. Participating in the show which is poetry, we expel the taint of original sin and restore to our minds freedom and integrity. Very good. But we are forced to note presently, when we go out of the theater, that it was only make-believe, and as we go down the same street by which we came, that we are again the heirs of history, and fallen men.

So we see that Ransom's qualification of the doctrine of imitation, to wit that the imitation expresses the disinterested love of the artist for the object and hence is preferable to the object, does not at all times convince him. Like the Crispin of Wallace Stevens' poem, Ransom prefers the plum to its poem, for the plum is more than the poem, and the poem adds nothing, really, to the plum. The poem was the result of a delusion.

And it is characteristic of Ransom, that in his essay on

[50] *The New Criticism*, p. 267.   [51] *The World's Body*, p. 249.

Aristotle's cathartic principle,[52] he should insist that Aristotle intended us to understand that tragedy is merely a dose for getting rid of our emotions. He adduces in support of this view the fact that Aristotle was a physician; he fails to add that Aristotle, as a disciple of Plato, is comprehensible only within the Platonic context. I myself am incompetent to discuss the question of what Aristotle really meant, but if his meaning was the one that Ransom attributes to him, one can only regret it, for so great a man should have done better; the fact that Ransom can see no possibility of a better interpretation is characteristic of his awkwardness in writing of the function of poetry and of the manner in which his theories render poetry contemptible. There are, it is true, certain remarks about music in the *Politics,* which support Ransom's view very strongly, but the discussion of music, like Aristotle's other discussions of the arts, is brief, incomplete, and extremely contradictory.

And poetry, according to Ransom's theories, is precisely contemptible. Aside from the doctrine of imitation, which is so confused that it will not stand criticism even within the terminology of Ransom's own thought, Ransom offers no principle of rightness in poetry. Poetry is an obscure form of self-indulgence, a search for excitement by ways that Ransom cannot define, in which we proceed from a limited and unsatisfactory rational understanding of our subject to as complete a confusion as we are able to achieve; it is a technique, not of completing rational understanding, but of destroying it and getting nothing in return. The poem is composed of rational understanding, which is there because we cannot quite get rid of it, but of as little as possible; of a conglomeration of irrelevancies of meaning; and of what Eliot would call, I suppose, an autotelic meter, which goes on its secret way, accumulating irrelevancies of its own and helping to force additional irrelevancies into the meaning.

[52] Ibid., p. 173.

We can see the fruits of these theories in most of the poetry of Tate, of which the lines already quoted are an average sample; and although Ransom's poetry is in general less confused than Tate's, largely, I think, as a result of its being less ambitious, it is quite clearly modeled on its author's doctrines. Ransom is at his best in a few poems on small themes, which, or parts of which, he has handled with real ability: the best of these, as far as my knowledge extends, are *Bells for John Whiteside's Daughter*, in which the memory of the little girl driving the geese is very lovely, and *Piazza Piece*, which, though slight, seems to me wholly successful. *Captain Carpenter*, however, represents what appears to be his aim, or at any rate it is a fair specimen of the quality of most of his work. I quote its final stanzas:

> God's mercy rest on Captain Carpenter now
> I thought him Sirs an honest gentleman
> Citizen husband soldier and scholar enow
> Let jangling kites eat of him if they can.

> But God's deep curses follow after those
> That shore him of his goodly nose and ears
> His legs and strong arms at the two elbows
> And eyes that had not watered seventy years.

> The curse of hell upon the sleek upstart
> Who got the Captain finally on his back
> And took the red red vitals of his heart
> And made the kites to whet their beaks clack clack.

The poem illustrates the doctrine of irrelevancy much better than the doctrine of imitation, as one can discern upon examining either the kites or the curses; but that is only what one might expect. It displays a kind of ponderous whimsicality, which endeavors to engage in the labor of wit, and an effort to spin out small themes as far as possible in the absence of any better way of dealing with them. It is a marvel of lucidity, however, as compared to many poems by Allen Tate and the younger Southerners.

XI. *Determinism*

Ransom is not really impelled, as Eliot is impelled, to devise an historical justification of modern poetry, for he does not believe that the poetry needs that kind of justification. His entire philosophy is aimed at showing, not that the more confused moderns are helpless on the current of history, but that they are wisely and deliberately working toward a better kind of poetry.

Nevertheless there are a few passages in his work which indicate a deterministic doctrine very much like that of Eliot:[53]

Apostate, illaureate, and doomed to outlawry the modern poets may be. I have the feeling that modernism is an unfortunate road for them to have taken. But it was an inevitable one. It is not hard to defend them from imputations against their honor and their logic. It is probably a question of whether we really know them, and understand their unusual purpose, and the powerful inhibitions they impose upon themselves.

But let us approach the matter from a slightly different angle. Poets have had to become modern because the age is modern. Its modernism envelops them like a sea, or an air. Nothing in their thought can escape it.

And a few pages later: [54]

I suggest that critics and philosophers fix their most loving attention upon certain natural compounds in human experience. But I say so diffidently, and not too hopefully. It will take a long

[53] *The World's Body,* p. 62. [54] Ibid., p. 75.

time to change the philosophical set which has come over the practice of the poets. The intellectual climate in which they live will
have to be altered first.

These passages are not important in themselves or in connection with the general plan of Ransom's thought; but they
indicate the manner in which it is possible for the systems of
Ransom and Eliot to support each other in the minds of
younger men, such as Blackmur, Tate, and the young Southerners. On the one hand, Ransom defends the sort of poetry
these men most admire; and on the other hand, Eliot proves
that no other kind of poetry is possible among honest men in
a degenerate age. The two systems are not strictly consistent
with each other, but, as Eliot would no doubt remind us, consistency is not one of the virtues of our age.

POST SCRIPTA

I.

I HAVE TRIED in this book, in addition to pursuing my examination of the mere history of American literary theory, to indicate a theory of my own, to complete the discussion undertaken in my first book, *Primitivism and Decadence,* which was mainly a discussion of style, and which had little reference to the ideas generating styles.

I have tried also to select for examination the minds which represent the most influential tendencies in the literary practice of our time, and as far as may be the most influential minds themselves. The influence of Adams and Eliot has been great for years; that of Ransom has more recently become great. The influence of Stevens as a theorist is probably negligible, for I doubt whether many of his admirers understand his theories; but he represents a common attitude, and since he is a man of genius and of unlimited audacity as a writer, he represents the effects of that attitude more perfectly than anyone else I can

find. I had thought originally to write of Allen Tate and of
R. P. Blackmur, but my book has grown too long and I must
refrain. I am convinced, besides, that there is nearly nothing
in their thought which is not to be found in Eliot and Ransom: a study of their criticism would be valuable largely in
connection with the effect of their borrowed ideas upon their
critical taste and upon their poetic style. But that will have to
wait for another time.

The writers whom I have discussed are all men of some
native ability. Adams wrote a great historical work; Stevens has
written great poetry; Eliot and Ransom display sufficient poetic talent to be interesting. But they think as badly as possible,
and it is curious that men of so much talent should think so
badly, as it is likewise curious that they should so often impose
their thought on other men of talent. On the other hand, although there are many literary scholars who have done important work and a few who have done great work, I have yet to
discover a professor of English, except for a few relatively
young men who are also poets, who could judge a new poem
accurately.

The antagonism between the poet and the scholar, I suppose, is in part the result of temperamental differences between extreme types in both groups; it is mainly, however,
something left us by the romantic movement, and it is still sufficiently strong so that the older literary men who are in the
academic profession frequently show but little trace of academic influence. Yet it is only, I believe, in a combination of the
talents of the poet with the discipline of scholarship that one
can hope to produce a really finished critic. And the literary
life of our time, like the academic life, stands in dire need of a
handful of critics who not only are sensitive but know more
or less what they are talking about. Unless the critics are forth-
coming, literature runs the risk of falling into the hands of
the barbarians.

I have showed but little respect, I fear, for the four subjects of the long essays in this book. I should like to indicate very briefly the types of mind to which they seem to me to be surrendering literature.

II.

I suppose that many scholars recognize the weakness of Parrington, yet Parrington's [1] history is apparently the text most widely used in the teaching of American literature, so that the number of scholars unaware of the exceptional badness of the text must be appallingly large; it is likewise more influential than any other book in its field, I should judge, upon the Marxist critics of the past ten or fifteen years. The text is wholly dependent upon two very serious errors: namely, that one can write the history of a culture with reference only to one intellectual tradition, in this case a tradition of very small influence in the first hundred and fifty years, that is, during the formative period; and that one can determine the ideas governing a work of art without making any attempt to understand the art as art. I should like to enlarge upon these points.

Parrington writes as follows in his first chapter: [2]

Unless one keeps in mind the social forces that found it convenient to array themselves in Puritan garb, the clear meaning of it all will be lost in the fogs of biblical disputation, and some of the ablest men the English race has ever bred will be reduced to crabbed theologians involved in tenuous subtleties and disputing endlessly over absurd dogmas. But tenacious disputants though they certainly were, pursuing their subtleties into the last refuge and cranny of logic, these Puritan dogmatists were very far from being vain practitioners of eccentricity. It is the manner and dress

[1] *Main Currents in American Thought*, by V. L. Parrington, Harcourt, Brace and Co. 3 vols.   [2] Ibid., Vol. 1, page 6.

and not the matter of their arguments that is strange; and if we will resolutely translate the old phrases into modern equivalents, if we will put aside the theology and fasten attention on the politics and economics of the struggle, we shall have less difficulty in discovering that the new principle for which those old Puritans were groping was the later familiar doctrine of natural rights; and the final end and outcome of their concern for a more equitable relation of the individual to society, was the principle of a democratic commonwealth, established in the conception of political equalitarianism. Here are liberalisms in plenty to reward the search for the inner core of Puritanism."

In other words, if we will resolutely neglect ninety-nine hundredths of what the Puritans wrote during their first century and a half, we shall arrive at a true understanding of what they were trying to say, and we shall have made a clear and undeceptive beginning to a history of American literature. This is a view of history to which I am unable to subscribe; but it is the view of Parrington, and, whether they realize it or not, of his disciples and admirers. To those who believe with Parrington that we may safely put aside the theology, let me recommend the latest work of Perry Miller; [3] and to those who believe that the Puritans were greatly concerned with the later familiar doctrine of natural rights, the latest work of Professor Andrews.[4] A consideration of these two works alone should make it evident that Parrington and his point of view should be discarded.[5]

[3] The New England Mind, by Perry Miller. Macmillan, 1939. See also Miller's paper, *Jonathan Edwards to Emerson,* New England Quarterly, XIII-4.

[4] *The Colonial Period of American History,* by Charles M. Andrews. Yale U. Press., 4 vols., 1934-38.

[5] It would be a pity to stop here, however: The two essays by H. B. Parkes, Hound and Horn. Vol. V, and *The Puritan Mind,* by H. W. Schneider, though less rich in detail, are probably more incisive in defining essentials than is Miller; they deal with other matter than that of Andrews.

Of Parrington's two initial fallacies, however, the one which I have just considered is the less serious. The more serious is to be found clearly stated in the first two sentences of his introduction: [6]

I have undertaken to give some account of the genesis and development in American letters of certain germinal ideas that have come to be reckoned traditionally American—how they came into being here, how they were opposed, and what influence they have exerted in determining the form and scope of our characteristic ideals and institutions. In pursuing such a task, I have chosen to follow the broad path of our political, economic, and social development, rather than the narrower belletristic; and the main divisions of the study have been fixed by forces that are anterior to schools and movements, creating the body of ideas from which literary culture eventually springs.

The term *belletristic,* here as elsewhere in Parrington, is a term of contempt for any interest in art as art. Parrington assumes that the best way to understand a work of art is to neglect entirely its nature as a work of art, and to deal with its ideas. He believes that we can know what an artist thinks, without knowing what he does. This is almost brutally crude thinking. At an obviously ridiculous level it leads to identifying the theories of Ahab with the theme of *Moby Dick,* or the morality of Iago with the morality of Shakespeare. I suppose that serious scholars no longer do this sort of thing. But it also leads to identifying the paraphrasable content of the poem with the meaning of the poem; to neglecting the quality of feeling with which the paraphrasable content is stated, to neglecting, that is, the final and irreducible act of judgment which gives the poem its essentially poetic identity. It leads in general to fastening on the idea lying detached before the eye and to neglecting its function in the unified work, to neglecting,

[6] Op. cit. Vol I, p. iii.

that is, what the artist does with the idea; it thus eliminates carefully the possibility of understanding what a writer means when he states a given idea. Parrington's method offers what appears to be a short-cut to history, though unfortunately it is a short-cut which avoids nearly all of the proper subject-matter of the history in question.

Parrington, then, deals with literature only in so far as literature is a matter of fragmentary ideas clearly visible to the innocent eye; furthermore, he deals only with a limited range of ideas, and relegates the rest to the region of illusion. Had Parrington written, as he seems to imply that he meant to write, a history of Jeffersonian liberalism, and neglected all matter irrelevant to his subject, he might have been more or less successful. But he unquestionably did not do so: he wrote what purports to be a history of American literature, but treated wholly in terms of what he conceives to be the development of Jeffersonian liberalism.

The result could easily have been forecast. His frame-work of ideas has no serious relationship to most of the great writers, and, since he thus has no way of understanding them, his treatment of them is almost purely impressionistic. His treatment of Cotton Mather, I should judge, is notorious among specialists in colonial history, and it ought to be equally notorious among men of letters, for Mather was in his way and in his best passages one of the great masters of English prose; his treatment of Poe, or rather his confession that he has no way of treating Poe, that he is literally rendered helpless by his method, is also notorious. But the handling of Melville, Henry James, and Henry Adams, to name only a few of the more obvious failures is almost as bad. The essay on Melville, for example, is merely a pseudo-poetic summary of the sensational and uncritical book by Mr. Raymond Weaver. One coming upon it, with no knowledge of Melville, would receive no clue whatever to the subject-matter or to the form of any of Melville's books, to Melville's own intellectual history, or to the intellectual history of which Melville is in some part the product. The value of the essay, if it has any, lies wholly in the soundness of Parrington's unguided personal impressions (not to mention Weaver's), and in the beauty of his prose; the virtues are purely belletristic. I prefer to leave the praise of this aspect of Parrington to an admirer. William T. Utter has written as follows of Parrington's artistry: [7]

It must have been apparent to all who knew him that Parrington was essentially an artist. To all classes it was shown in the care, almost meticulous, with which he polished his phrases, the search in his interpretation for harmonious balance and proportion, as if it were a structure of stone, rather than of ideas, which he was erecting. Those who knew him intimately were aware of his interest in architecture and painting; that he had studied in these fields during his first European residence; that he had even considered entering them professionally. He had more than ordinary ability as a poet, according to his friends, although his own judgment did not permit of publication. In his writing, this artistic temperament was to be demonstrated not only in his constant effort to attain unity but also in the care with which each phrase was turned—care which brings to mind the artistry of the eighteenth century conversationalist.

We have already observed the methods by which Parrington obtained unity; it is perhaps worth a moment to examine one of the carefully turned sentences, a more or less representative sentence, on the subject of Herman Melville: [8]

The golden dreams of transcendental faith, that buoyed up Emerson and gave hope to Thoreau, turned to ashes in his mouth; the white gleams of mysticism that now and then lighted up his path died out and left him in darkness.

[7] *Vernon Louis Parrington,* by William T. Utter; the Marcus W. Jernegan Essays in American Historiography, U. of Chicago Press, p. 306.
[8] Op. Cit., Vol. II, p. 258.

The style has a vulgar floridity throughout which is quite revolting; the mixed metaphor is one of the most ridiculous specimens that have ever come in my way; the sentence purports to discuss Melville and tells us nothing about him. Except for the metaphor, which is a remarkable thing of its kind, the sentence is characteristic and can be matched on many pages; in fact, many essays, that on Melville among others, are composed solidly in this style.

Such are the short-cuts to history and to criticism about equally. One could gather an interesting garland of comments upon Parrington, with very little labor, by specialists in various fields upon which he touched. Michael Kraus, whose estimate of Parrington is far higher than my own, makes this interesting comment: [9]

Historians complain that Parrington did not know enough history, while students of literature often disagree with his estimates of literary figures.

Even within either field, however, the comment is often somewhat as follows: [10]

Parrington's work is noble and in the main admirable, but he is unfortunately very ignorant of my particular subject.

Yet such a comment is unfair and imperceptive. No historian of a literature—or of anything else—can fairly be expected to be a specialist in every subject upon which he touches; Par-

[9] *A History of American History,* by Michael Kraus, Farrar and Rinehart, 1937. P. 480.

[10] Plagiarized, as regards the form of the statement, from a bibliographical note in *The Puritans,* by Perry Miller and T. H. Johnson, American Book Co., p. 805. Of Vol. I these gentlemen write: "A noble work that is still the best comprehensive history of American thought; inspired by a militant liberalism, consequently hostile and unsympathetic to Puritanism; based upon lamentably insufficient familiarity with the sources, and therefore to be read for stimulation, not for fact or accuracy."

rington's defect was a defect not in specialized knowledge but in common sense—it was a defect which made it impossible for him to use the work of specialists intelligently. His work is really as obsolete as the work of George Bancroft; in fact, it was so before it was written.

III.

The most ambitious piece of more or less recent Marxian criticism with which I am acquainted is Bernard Smith's *Forces in American Criticism*.[11] Its point of view as regards American literature derives from Parrington, although it would be hard to say how Smith reconciles Parrington's longing for a more Jeffersonian world, with Marx's economic determinism. The point of contact—a point of contact is usually sufficient for the modern critic—is of course the interest of both writers in the plight of the lower classes. This provides, however, a purely sentimental and irresponsible approach to literature. Of Parrington, Smith writes: [12]

Parrington's *Main Currents* arrived to supply the most needed things: an account of our literary history which squared with recent works on the history of our people and a realistic technique for analyzing the relationship of a writer to his time and place—in addition to a militantly progressive spirit. Professorial and literary circles had consciously been waiting for such a work, and if the one that did come forth was far more radical than some people cared for, it simply could not be rejected. The author was a professor too; his scholarship defied scrutiny; and his ideas were couched in terms that were native American, most of them having come over shortly after the *Mayflower*.

Smith, like Parrington, sees reality only in ideas which have what is known today as social significance; religion and moral-

[11] Harcourt, Brace and Co., 1939. [12] Ibid., p. 331.

ity are mere delusions—not only is there no truth in them, but they never really influenced anybody. Of tradition he writes: [13]

> Tradition was the accumulation of manners and beliefs which gentlemen had evolved and handed down to their sons and pupils; it was the symbol of order, the promise of social supremacy to those who were its guardians.

We have learned from Parrington that the first Puritans came to Massachusetts to found a democracy, and that their theological language was merely a blind; we learn from Smith that the Unitarian heirs of their spirit were concerned only with retaining their wealth, and that their morality was a shallow pretence.

Smith writes at length on Emerson, and with some perspicuity points out many of his worst errors; he then turns about and praises Whitman without reservation. The only real difference between Whitman's doctrines and Emerson's, however, resides in the fact that Whitman expresses a boundless sympathy with the masses, whereas Emerson is pretty sceptical about them. Smith derives his moral doctrines from his Marxist position and excoriates pre-Marxist morality,[14] and it is his moral doctrines which guide him in judging literature—he has great contempt for all impressionism or relativism. He does not say how he justifies Marxism, yet he appears to accept it because he believes it promises greater justice to men than other social doctrines. Yet justice is a moral concept, and one is perplexed to know whether he derives his concept of justice from Marxism or his Marxism from his concept of justice. After insisting that judgments of literature must be based upon the soundness of the author's social views, he yet defends Shakespeare against one of his more enthusiastic colleagues because of "the values in Shakespeare that are perma-

---

[13] Ibid., p. 233.   [14] Ibid., p. 287.

nent for all classes"; yet blames this writer for treating Shakespeare in terms that are ethical instead of materialistic.[15]

IV.

In the Autumn of 1940 The Southern Review and the Kenyon
Review published a joint symposium attacking the methods
commonly in use of teaching English. The chief complaint of
the contributors was this: that the departments of English in
the main teach history instead of criticism, whereas they should
teach criticism instead of history. This represents a fallacy, I
think, almost as serious as that of Parrington: I do not believe,
as I have said, that the history of literature can be grasped
unless one has a critical understanding of it; but it seems to
me equally obvious that a critical understanding is frequently
quite impossible unless one knows a good deal of history. The
critical and the historical understanding are merely aspects
of a single process. As to the quarrel which these gentlemen
picked with the philologists and the textual critics, it is quite
aside from my present concerns, although I believe it to be
foolish. There is far more need even yet for good textual criticism even of many standard writers than these critics seemed
to realize, and philology has always been and will always remain a subject of fundamental importance for the student of
literature. If more poets had studied philology, the quality of
our poetry would probably improve.

If we exclude from consideration, however, the philologists
and textual critics, and merely think of the scholars who teach
what is known as the history of literature, there is, I think, just
ground for objection to a very large part of what is being done,
especially, perhaps, in the field of American literature. I
should like to preface these remarks, however, with the state-

[15] Ibid., p. 291.

ment that I can feel little moral indignation at the errors of the unfortunate professors. The number of people capable of doing valuable work in literary criticism in any period is very small. A great critic, indeed, is the rarest of all literary geniuses: perhaps the only critic in English who deserves the epithet is Samuel Johnson. And the number of persons required to teach English is remarkably large: further explanation seems unnecessary. So long as the gentlemen of undeniable literary talent insist on indulging themselves in the strange adventures which we have been examining in this book, we can hardly blame the simple and honest professor if he occasionally becomes confused or even sinks into a kind of antiquarian melancholia.

We must not judge him too harshly as moralists; but as critics we are bound to see his work for what it is worth. I should like to indicate briefly some of the commoner types of blunders which might be classified under the heading of unenlightened specialization. And I should like to repeat that much of the moral responsibility for this kind of thing rests on a few of our more brilliant literary critics.

I have talked with a well-known specialist in Emerson, a man who knows in detail, I believe, the whole Emersonian text and very nearly everything that has been written about Emerson, but who at the time of my conversation with him had not read Cooper since childhood, knew only a small part of Hawthorne, and had a vague conviction that Melville was a transcendentalist in oilskins and Miss Dickinson a transcendentalist in dimity. This authority was almost wholly ignorant of Emerson's contemporaries and also of later American literature. I have talked with a well-known specialist in Poe, who shared all of the ignorance listed above and who was wholly unfamiliar with the French symbolists as well: in fact, American specialists in Poe, as a class, exhibit a kind of bucolic innocence which at times simply paralyzes comment; they appear to have not the vaguest idea of the kind of devilment with which they are dealing.

Now I respectfully submit that only a minute portion of what has been written on Poe or Emerson or any other subject has any considerable value, and that a good deal of what has been written and very respectably published is unmitigated twaddle; and further that no man will ever understand either writer who has not read his major contemporaries thoroughly and with comprehension; and further still, that no man will have done his best to understand either writer who has not done his best to understand not only the writers who led up to the subject of study but the writers who developed from him or from the school of writing to which he belonged. To understand Emerson, it is more important to understand both Cotton Mather and Hart Crane than it is to have bibliographical notes on a multitude of monographs. I do not deny that many of the monographs have value, and that one ought to read as many of them as possible. I merely insist on a proper scale of values: it is with the history of literature that we are dealing, not with the history of monographs, and either one by itself is a tremendous subject. In dealing with such a field as the history of eighteenth century literature in England or in France, a field in which there is already available a good deal of reliable historical and critical guidance, the scholar is relatively safe in extreme specialization; but he can never be wholly so.

The antiquarian habit of mind, moreover, if one can judge from its products, is likely to grow dimmer and dimmer simply of its own inanition. I should like to cite merely a few of the curiosities which have come to my attention in the past few years, and which indicate a blindness to what one would think fairly massive objective data.

The late Ernest Fenollosa died in 1908, a date sufficiently remote to be fairly respectable, and his contribution to Japanese culture was regarded by the Japanese themselves as so great that the emperor had his ashes removed from London to Japan, and, according to the story, in a Japanese battleship; and he had received many extraordinary official honors during his life. These facts have nothing to do with American literature, but they are the sort of thing that might help the scholar to notice Fenollosa, who is in other respects important. Fenollosa is the author of a large two-volume work on Chinese and Japanese art, which was published posthumously, and it was Fenollosa's literal translations from the Chinese poetry and Japanese drama which gave Ezra Pound the original material for his great English versions, versions which about twenty-five years ago initiated a poetic movement of great importance. Yet the name of Fenollosa, to the best of my knowledge, appears nowhere in any history of American literature now available. During the year 1941, while these pages were in process of composition, there appeared a short paragraph on Fenollosa in the *Oxford Companion to American Literature,* compiled by James Hart, this being the only academic recognition of the writer with which I am acquainted.

The Indian bulletins of the Smithsonian Institution have been famous for years. I do not know exactly how many of them there are, but they constitute an imposing library; and they are the most valuable body of information available on the subject of the American Indian. Furthermore, a good many of the anthropologists contributing to this series have translated admirably from the Indian languages; three of them, at least, Washington Matthews, Frances Densmore, and Frank Russell, are among the few really brilliant poetic translators in English. These and other translators of the same kind, moreover, have been famous for years: in 1918 George W. Cronyn published through Boni and Liveright a collection of Indian poems, drawn mainly from the bulletins, under the title of *The Path on The Rainbow;* the book was widely read and

widely discussed, resulted in the publication of other similar
collections, and probably left its mark on the poetry of the
time. Yet in all the histories of American literature which I
have by chance examined, I have noticed only one discussion
of Indian poetry, that by the late Mary Austin, in the *Cambridge History of American Literature:* the discussion is un-
informative, unintelligent, and in most respects worse than
useless. In 1933 the Oxford Press published a book by Albert
Keiser called *The Indian in American Literature,* which
makes no use of the anthropologists either as scientists or as
translators. And in 1938 there appeared in a series of text-
books published by the American Book Company and under
the general editorship of Professor Harry Hayden Clark a
critical text on Parkman; a text which disposes of the entire
subject of Parkman's understanding of the Indian (and Prescott's to boot, as a matter of fact) with no reference to the bulletins and apparently with no knowledge whatever of American anthropology or archaeology.

I happen to have on my shelves at the present writing two
fairly recent histories of American literature, of which the
authors are Percy Boynton and W. F. Taylor. I will not tire the
reader by citing the long list of their most obvious and least
discutable sins, but it seems to me interesting that neither
mentions the name of Adelaide Crapsey, who died in 1914,
who antedates many of the writers discussed, who is certainly
an immortal poet, and who has long been one of the most
famous poets of our century.

V.

When the argument over Irving Babbitt's New Humanism was
active, one of the objections made to the Humanists was this:
that even if their philosophy were sound, it would never prove

very effective, because it was represented by no social institution and so could never be brought to bear on more than a few scattered lives. Christianity had been represented by the Church, but what had the Humanists?

I do not consider myself one of the Humanists: I disagree with Babbitt on too many counts to do so, though I admire him and have learned a good deal from him; and Babbitt's colleagues have always appeared to me to be worth very little indeed. But the student of literature who takes his profession seriously, who wishes to quicken it and make it important, has an institution nevertheless. That institution, in spite of what I have been saying, is the university.

This statement, I dare say, will amuse the reviewers for the weekly journals. But notwithstanding all the sins of the literary scholars, the popular view of the academic world, as something cloistered and remote from reality, peopled by souls who have failed in the practical struggle, is a product largely of the Romantic Movement and of the colored funny papers. There have been great literary scholars and the race will continue; but questions of literature aside, most of the great minds in science, philosophy, and history will be found in the universities—these are not men who have taken flight from the modern world, but sometimes for better and sometimes for worse they are the men who are making it. The university is the intellectual and spiritual center of our world. It is likewise a national institution; in fact it was, until the New Order appeared in Europe, an international institution, and it will be again. It offers a concrete embodiment, an institutional representation, of the most important ideals of humanity; of the belief in absolute truth; of the importance, in spite of human fallibility, of the perpetual, though necessarily imperfect, effort to approximate truth; of intellectual freedom and integrity; of the dignity of man. Without the fairly explicit recognition of these ideals, the university would collapse. Even the

most irresponsible relativist or determinist—the Marxian romantics and their recurring problems of academic freedom
come immediately to mind—will invoke these ideals almost
automatically if he feels that they have been violated in his
particular case. In the entire history of civilization, only one
other institution, the Catholic Church, with its national off-
shoots, has played a comparable part. The university, within
its limits, is less self-conscious and less efficient than the
Church, but its limits are far more inclusive, and few of the
great men of our time are able to find their way into the
Church. I do not wish, as the reader may have suspected, to
flatter unduly the faculties of the universities, though I respect them for excellent reasons, even in the bulk. I am speaking of principles, not of persons. Great men are rare. The
academic ideals are frequently violated, but they remain as
ideals, as standards of judgment, and as the chief cohesive force
in our civilization; and the scholar is their professional guard-
ian.

One of the most curious facts about the poets of my own
generation and of the generation following—that is, about the
poets now, roughly, under fifty years of age—is this: that many
of the best of them are teaching in the universities. There has
been no comparable unity of profession among able poets
since the 17th century, when most of the best poets were members of the clergy.

I should like to list the poems that seem to me perhaps the
highest achievement of the writers in question: [16]

[16] The poems in this list may be found in the following collections: *Col-
lected Poems*, by Mark Van Doren (Henry Holt: 1939); *Chills and Fever*
(Knopf: 1924) and *Two Gentlemen in Bonds* (Knopf: 1927) by J. C.
Ransom; *The Keen Edge*, by Maurine Smith (Monroe Wheeler, Evanston,
Ill.: published in 1920, but undated); *Dark Summer* (Scribners: 1929)
and *The Sleeping Fury* (Scribners: 1937) by Louise Bogan; *The Collected
Poems of Hart Crane* (Liveright: 1933); *Selected Poems*, by Allen Tate

By Mark Van Doren: *Man, Report of Angels.*

By John Crowe Ransom: *Piazza Piece, Bells for John White-side's Daughter.*

By Maurine Smith: *Muted.*

By Louise Bogan: *The Mark, Simple Autumnal, The Al-chemist, Come break with Time, Henceforth from the Mind, Exhortation, Kept, Song for a Lyre.*

By Hart Crane: *Repose of Rivers, Voyages II.*

By Allen Tate: *The Cross, Shadow and Shade;* perhaps *The Subway* and *Ditty.*

By S. Foster Damon: *The Mad Hunstman.*

By Clayton Stafford: *The Swan and the Eagle, Cape Horn, Hyperborean.*

By Stanley J. Kunitz: *The Words of the Preacher, Ambergris.*

By Howard Baker: *Psyche, Pont Neuf,* perhaps *The Quiet Folk.*

By R. P. Blackmur: *Sea-Island Miscellany: V.*

By Lincoln Fitzell: *Gravestone, Erosion.*

By Barbara Gibbs: *For Her Who Wore This Shawl.*

(Scribners: 1937); Damon's poem, *The Mad Huntsman,* appears in Smoke, a small magazine published at Providence by Damon and his friends, in the issue for May 1931, and the issue for Dec. 1933 contains another remarkable but less perfect poem by Damon, called *Seelig's Confession; A Letter from the Country,* by Howard Baker (New Directions: 1941) and *Twelve Poets of the Pacific,* an anthology (New Directions: 1937); *Verse,* by Clayton Stafford (Alan Swallow, Albuquerque: 1941); *Intellectual Things,* by Stanley J. Kunitz (Doubleday Doran: 1930); *From Jordan's Delight,* by R. P. Blackmur (Arrow Editions: 1937); *In Plato's Garden,* by Lincoln Fitzell (Alan Swallow: 1941); *The Well,* by Barbara Gibbs (Alan Swallow: 1941); *The Helmsman,* by J. V. Cunningham (Colt Press, San Francisco: 1942); *New England Earth,* by Don Stanford (Colt Press: 1941); *Open House,* by Theodore Roethke (Knopf, 1941); a collection by Ann Stanford to be issued by the Colt Press in 1942.

By J. V. Cunningham: *Lector Aere Perennior, The Beacon, Bookplate, Fancy, Moral Poem, The Symposium.*

By Don Stanford: *The Grand Mesa, The Meadowlark, The Bee, The Seagull, Summer Scene, The Thrush.*

By Theodore Roethke: *The Adamant, Reply to Censure.*

By Ann Stanford: *The Book, Ash Wednesday, Bookplate* (*Time sets a term*).

The exact limits of any such selection as this are hard to define. I have deliberately excluded work that I like in certain respects. Elizabeth Madox Roberts falls within the chronological limits of the group by virtue at least of the period of her composition; but her best poems, the poems of childhood contained in *Under the Tree*, are of a highly specialized sort, and though they will remain, I believe, a classic of a kind, they represent perhaps a less serious effort than the work I have listed. There are a few poems by Pearl Andelson Sherry which I should not like to see forgotten, notably, *Cats* and *Polar Bear*,[17] but Mrs. Sherry has never been able to free herself from certain immature philosophical ideas and from a certain egocentric preciosity of style which obsessed the entire group to which she belonged as a very young writer, a group to which Miss Roberts, Glenway Wescott, Maurine Smith, and I myself belonged. Glenway Wescott [18] likewise displayed an interesting poetic gift as a young man, but diffused and lost it in a kind of obscurely ecstatic description. James Agee has written at least one poem, *A Chorale*,[19] which is remarkable. And there are at least two poems by Achilles Holt, *A Valley* and *To*

[17] These poems may be found in The Forge (Chicago) for Autumn of 1926, and reprinted in the Autumn number for 1927 on pages 43 and 44.

[18] Wescott published two books a good many years ago, *The Bitterns* (Monroe Wheeler: 1920), and *Natives of Rock* (Francesco Bianco: New York: 1925), but many of his better things will be found in Poetry and The Dial as late as 1927 or 1928.

[19] *Permit me Voyage*, by James Agee (Yale University Press: 1934).

Mélanie,[20] which momentarily seem to me more remarkable than a number of the poems on my list. I have omitted the name of Archibald MacLeish, who may conceivably fall within my limits, because his work, so far as I am concerned, wears thinner and thinner with time. I have omitted John Peale Bishop because his work seems derivative, with no real center of meaning, and extremely coarse in execution. And I have omitted some of the young Southerners whose reputation is at present rising, for more or less similar reasons, though the inclusion of these would strengthen my argument with reference to the academic profession.

The selection of poems is likewise difficult. Crane, Tate, Damon, Baker, and Blackmur, are almost as remarkable for certain passages in unsatisfactory poems as they are for the poems I have named. Baker, especially, may be at his best, in the conclusion of *The Passing Generation,* and in certain portions of his *Ode to the Sea* and *Destiny.*

Some of the poets whom I have listed are certainly very minor. I think one can say this of Van Doren, Ransom, Maurine Smith (who died at the age of 23, after a life of invalidism, and left a few poems comparable, perhaps, to those of Gladys Cromwell), Fitzell, Barbara Gibbs, and Blackmur; Miss Stanford might be added to this number, but is very young to be classified even tentatively.

On the other hand, a few of these poets seem to me among the major talents of our time: Miss Bogan, Tate, and Baker seem to me surely so; and I should not have to strain my convictions greatly to add Crane, Damon, Stafford and Cunningham, the main difficulty with Stafford and Damon being the scarcity of mature poems on which to form a judgment.[21]

[20] *Twelve Poets of the Pacific,* op. cit.

[21] I may as well go on record here that I believe my wife, Janet Lewis, to be one of the best poets of her generation, as well as one of the best fictionists; but I endeavor, on general principles, not to discuss her work.

There is always the danger that such a list as I have made may seem nervous and niggling, but if it has called attention to a few poems that might otherwise be overlooked, it is justified; and even if it contains a good many errors of judgment, it nevertheless indicates fairly enough certain general tendencies which I wish to be indicated. If these writers are compared to the outstanding talents of the preceding generation, that is, of the generation immediately subsequent to that of Frost and Robinson, their common characteristics begin to appear. The leading Experimentalists were Wallace Stevens, Adelaide Crapsey, W. C. Williams, Ezra Pound, Marianne Moore, T. S. Eliot, and H. D. If one looks for lesser talents in this tradition, one will have difficulty finding them, for small talents had difficulty surviving in modes so formless; and if one looks to the traditional poets in this generation, such as the Benets, Elinor Wylie, and Miss Millay, one will find them a very unsatisfactory lot of easy rimers. Stevens alone of his generation did great work in the traditional forms, but he did it early, and became more and more an experimenter. The poets whom I have listed, however, are all moving toward traditional practices and not away from them. Most of them display a certain intellectualism in their way of dealing with their subjects, even when the subjects are essentially anti-intellectualistic. Even those who, as critics, argue in favor of anti-intellectual doctrines, endeavor to argue more closely than did Pound, Williams, Miss Moore, and even Eliot: this is true to some extent of Tate; it is true, I think, as regards the intention, of Blackmur; and it is certainly true of Ransom; and the best poems of these men are straining obviously away from their critical theories. There is a great deal of confusion of intention in these poets, both individually and collectively, but in general they are trying to recover what the preceding generation had lost: and in some of them, mainly the younger ones, there is a good deal of maturity, not only of style but of mind.

Now out of this group, a large portion are professional scholars and teachers: Van Doren, Ransom, Tate, Damon, Baker,
Cunningham, Don Stanford, and Roethke. And the additional
number of serious young poets in the profession, whose talents
do not seem to me great, but who have, many of them, acquired reputations and who may conceivably prove in the end
to be better than I believe them, would if added about double
the academic group. The tendency which I have described
among all the poets mentioned is striking; the fact that the
tendency is most obvious among the younger poets makes it
more so. And the presence of eight of them, including some of
the very best, and the best of the youngest, on academic faculties, makes it obvious indeed.

It is in the younger poets that the meaning of this change of
emphasis is likely to be most evident eventually; it is most
evident already, perhaps, in the work of Cunningham, who
may prove to be the best of his generation, who is certainly, so
far as my personal knowledge extends, the best scholar and
critic among the younger Americans, and who of all, older and
younger alike, seems to show most clearly an understanding of
the implications of his adherence to the academic profession.

It is possible, of course, that the younger poets here named
may deteriorate, and that American poetry may start off in
another direction. But of this I feel sure: that this movement
offers more hope for the invigoration of American literature
than does anything else in sight; that it offers the only hope for
American criticism; and that it offers an opportunity for the
real improvement of the teaching of literature and the practice
of literary scholarship. A handful of brilliant poets, even if
congenitally minor, scattered judiciously throughout our best
universities, might easily begin to turn us a little in the direction of civilization.

INDEX